The Road to Socialism

"The money will go into channels which will carry it, not to the most productive, but to the most corrupt. By the standards of our time, the man who has the least to offer is the man who wins." *Atlas Shrugged, Ayn Rand*

Comments from some of Phil's friends:

Jan Blevins, Tea Party Group, Franklin, Louisiana. "Phil, my husband, Tad took your book away from me and won't give it back. What a great book."

"It reads like a novel not a history book, I am so glad you wrote it."

"Every high school student should read your book. You present information they will never get in a history class."

Julie Brady, a Great Patriot from Osprey, Florida and Cape Cod says, "Phil exudes an enthusiasm that makes him my favorite Red County Blogger. After much research, he presents facts and solutions on serious issues facing our country while communicating information through an engaging story usually based on his personal experience. I trust you will agree with me that Phil's writing educates, enlightens and entertains."

"Phil is a small business person and author whose patriotism shines through his writing as a guiding light to protect our freedom. His unique approach to studying Socialism is unparalleled and easy to read. "
Beth Colvin, Co-Founder of the Sarasota Patriots

"Phil is a true conservative leader and has the ability to organize, lead and bring people together for the cause. Here in Sarasota, Phil was one of the grassroots leaders that helped elect every Republican that was on running in the 2010 election cycle."
Joe Gruters, Chairman, Sarasota County Executive Committee

There is no one more passionate about life and what it has to offer than Phil Frommholz. Even better, he doesn't just "talk the talk", but he "walks the talk". *Casey Pilon, Retired and wife of Ray Pilon, Florida Representative, State House District 69,*

Pat Wayman, Founder of The Venice 912 Group and is active nationally said, "Phil is one of the first patriots I met in the Tea Party Movement. He is a true patriot and an asset to our Venice 912 Project…and an active member of the Tea Party Movement. "

Look for My Next Book Coming Out Soon

"You Can Count on Me," A 7 Step Program to Improve Early Education in America.

This project was selected as a Top 10 Finalist for an award from The National Be A Hero Day Foundation out of over 15,000 entries. The success of this new program has resulted in improving the FCAT Test scores for Third Graders at Suncoast School for Innovative Studies.

This simple book summarizes some of the problems facing our educators today and provides a hands-on solution to improve the level of education for our children starting in the early grades by developing teams of committed volunteers to teach arithmetic to children. This easy to read book and its revolutionary method will detail the tools and techniques to make this program a success for our children. It is based on volunteerism and will not increase the cost of our children's education by one dime.

The "You Can Count on Me Program" uses a system I have developed which I call "Conversational Math." It is based on a discussion with two students from China who both graduated with degrees in Mathematics from an Ivy League School. They explained to me the process used to teach math to young students in China, whose students are among the best in the world.

The goal of this program is to help to develop early self esteem in our young people and ensure that they never have to utter these defeatist words, "I don't do math."

"The volunteers under Phil's direction and guidance have made a true difference in the lives of many of our students. The time that they spend together is more than teaching math, they are changing lives. The students and staff both look forward to their arrival and are eager to spend time with the volunteers. I think that we are all a little better because of our time together." *Dr. Stephen Evans, Executive Director, Suncoast School for Innovative Studies, Sarasota, Florida*

THE ROAD TO SOCIALISM

Philip L. Frommholz, MBA

First Edition May 2011
Second Edition September 2011

ISBN-13: 978-0615482569

Published by Phil the Mover Publishing

Printed by Createspace.com, a Division of Amazon.com

**If you have questions or comments about this book
or would like to purchase additional copies Call 941-954-3838
or e-mail Philthemover1@yahoo.com**

DEDICATION

  This is dedicated first, to Rick Santelli whose CNBC rant started the Tea Party Movement by creating the first cause to unify an angry majority and Glenn Beck who started the 912 Project. His project influenced a National wave across the country to educate people about our loss of freedom and helped them take responsibility for their country.

  Also, there are my local leaders who started groups to help those of us who needed like minded ears to listen to our concerns: Karen Rodemaker started the first Sarasota 912 Group. Pat Wayman followed with her Venice 912 Group. Beth Colvin, Milton Thrasher, and Ted Malares started the Sarasota Patriots in their living rooms. Christine Prazeres with her 13 Patriots Group has weekly events to keep us informed and educated. Finally, to Janet and Dean Mixon who opened their Mixon Farms Orange Groves to be the home of the Manatee Tea Party.

  Finally, to the millions and millions of Tea Party Activists who should always remember the words of John Paul Jones, the Naval Commander who was asked to surrender during the American Revolutionary War. He responded with "I have not yet begun to fight." Our time to fight is now.

CONTRIBUTORS

Writing a book is a solitary process, but it doesn't happen without the support of many people. Firstly, I have to thank my wife, Judy Weber, for having the patience for putting up with me during this overwhelming project. Without her understanding and encouragement this project would have never been done. I also want to thank Judy and our daughter, Jackie Weber-Matos, for being my proof readers in the final stages of producing this book.

There were many others that have been highlighted in the Introduction: Tom Broderick, Ted Nutter, Herta Weiss, Dr. Doug Ross, and, there my many friends who encouraged me all along the way. But, most of all, I have to thank Russell J. Huff, my friend and editor, for convincing me to write this book and helping me by bringing his incredible talents to this project.

Russ is an extremely talented person and brought many of his extra talents to this book. He has published four books and many magazine articles, along with his long career as a Managing Editor for McGraw-Hill publications and as a public relations executive. Born in 1936 in Chicago, he went to the University of Notre Dame and earned a degree in Philosophy and then a Masters of Communications Arts. He also studied abroad and earned a Bachelor of Arts Degree in theology in Santiago, Chile. After working in the corporate world, he started an aviation memorabilia company, where he is considered an international authority. Russ has earned a number of awards for journalism and is listed in "Who's Who in America" and "Who's Who in the World." I am fortunate that Providence put us together for this special purpose, but more importantly, for the friendship and bond that we have forged together.

THE ROAD TO SOCIALISM

By: Philip L. Frommholz, MBA

Edited by: Russell J. Huff

Published by: Phil the Mover Publishing
4851 Oak Pointe Way
Sarasota, FL 34233
941-954-3838
E-Mail Philthemover1@Yahoo.com

Table of Contents

PREFACE

George P. Schultz was claimed to have once said, "Nothing gets undone until you have a real or perceived crisis." Today, we have a real crisis.

The chapters you are holding in your hands were not written by a college professor with a bunch of initials after his name, a school teacher or college professor. I am neither an economist nor an historian. I am just a small business person, who reached my period of self-enlightenment only recently and I wanted to do something to make a difference. The question I am often asked is, "What makes you think you can write a book about Socialism?" To be perfectly honest: I didn't think I was qualified to write this book. Fortunately, I am not the best judge of my own talents and many of my friends convinced me I could and should write this book.

This book not only provides the reader with a glimpse into Socialism in America, but the last Chapter "Become A Patriot" has been added with an Appendix outline the activities that are the Four Pillars to Become an Armchair Activist.

This is the second edition of the book. It has been updated to include more up to date information. It is envisioned that the basic material will never become out of date but the examples provided to highlight the abuses by our government will never cease to provide material requiring the updating of this book.

INTRODUCTION

After I settled into to my seat and buckled my seatbelt, I pulled out a book that I had been meaning to read for a couple of months. The three hour flight from Tampa, Florida to Plattsburgh, New York would give me a good chance to get a start on *The Road to Serfdom* written by Friedrich A. Hayek, an Austrian born economist, professor, and lecturer. The version I bought was The Definitive Edition, which included "Text and Documents." I did not realize how long the ride would be when I began flipping through the pages. Little did I know that struggling through this book in June 2010 would begin a trip that would change my life forever.

Before we pulled out of the gate for Take-Off I began reviewing the book. The full book is a study guide and includes 64 pages, about a quarter of the length of the entire book, of Forewards, Prefaces, and Introductions from previous editions of the book, first published in 1944. This should have been a tip-off of the difficulty level of the book for an amateur economist. The introductory pages chronicled Hayek's most popular work. I didn't actually begin reading the meat of the book until later than evening. The book was difficult to read due to the Austrian influence, the professorial style of writing, and long sentence structure often running over one hundred words in length. It took me several days to slog my way through this economic masterpiece.

During the next five days I spent all my free time studying the book. My ultimate weekend destination was to attend a High School Reunion in Lake Placid, New York where I attended Northwood School, a college prep school nestled in the Adirondack Mountains. In between cocktail parties, dinners, and various other school activities I picked my way through *The Road to Serfdom*. It didn't take long to realize that this was not a casual coffee table styled book, yet I was unusually intrigued by the contents of Hayek's message.

On Sunday morning nearing the end of the reunion, I was taking a self-guided tour of the Main school building prior to attending the traditional buffet breakfast that is the final goodbye venue for our periodic reunions. While wondering the halls, I met Tom Broderick, the Assistant Head Master. Tom is the head of the History Department. We casually chatted and I was curious about the history program and particularly about his approach to American History. Tom explained that it was a survey course not dependent upon a text book, but rather a series of independent books that provided a broader and more in-depth knowledge of our American History. We wandered back to Tom's classroom and he opened a cabinet full of student purchased books that had been abandoned by the current years graduating class. Tom pulled out over a dozen literary works and handed them to me until I couldn't hold any more. The books he gave me were the foundation of his American History classes. Several of the books he gave me provided the background knowledge to write the first two chapters of *The Road to Socialism,* which was never even a thought when I carried out a pile of books that filled half of my suitcase. Little did I know that soon I would write a book, much less a book about economics and American history, using Tom's special gifts that he bestowed upon me that day.

As I continued to wade through Hayek's work over the next couple of days, I strongly believed that more people should be aware of the threat of Socialism and the destruction Socialism causes in the free spirit of man. As a fellow free spirit, if a traditional conservative thinker can use that expression, I wanted to help more people realize the dangerous road we were on by following a European system of living. Hayek pointed out the dangers in his book, but I knew that the average reader would not go through a dry, difficult, and very wordy exhortation of early 20th century economic lectures. The fact that they were written by an Austrian professor made it even more difficult to immediately comprehend. After my first reading I picked up the book again with a highlighter and started marking up points of interest. I thought that if the concepts could be simplified and made relevant then more people would read the ideas presented by Hayek.

My first recollection of *The Road to Serfdom* began in January 2010 when Glenn Beck held up a copy on his television show and said, "Everyone should read this book." Mentally it went on my list, but I was on a crusade to read about the Founding Fathers, another series of Glenn Beck "Must Reads." In late May or early June Beck held up *The Road to Serfdom* again, and knowing I was going on trip I picked up the book. It is hard to read all of the recommendations of Glenn Beck. Between the books he writes and his recommendations it is a full-time job just to keep up. I have probably read over 50 books in the last 15 months plus hundreds of hours of on-line research which began as a quest to learn move about American History. I discovered that it was far more beneficial for me to adopt Tom Broderick' approach by studying various works rather than focus on ten pound text books. Reading about historical figures provides a sense of the person, their character and their motivations, and intentions, rather than dryly learning facts and dates.

Researching, reading, and running a small business left me very few hours for sleep. My life had become very crowded over the last few years and the thought of writing a book seemed impossible.

My best hope was to find a co-author who would be interested in researching and writing "a common American translation" of Hayek's ideas and putting it into everyday language for the non-economist. Hayek's book was very hard to read because of the assumption that everyone understood his references to early European economists, philosophers, and historians. Hayek was teaching economics to students who were studying to be economists: a far different type of reader than I wanted to address. The average American audience today has no knowledge of the European players that debated Socialism and Capitalism, nor are they familiar with early modern European history. Hayek based his book on a series of lectures that he presented over time, mostly to students at the London School of Economics, an extremely prestigious school at the time. It was my goal to find someone who would want to undertake the research of each chapter of *The Road to Serfdom* and help provide the needed background and relevant information required to emphasize the ideas Hayek presented. I had been writing articles on The Red County Blog Site for about 18 months and had developed a small local audience. I wrote a review of *The Road to Serfdom* with a plea for a co-writer to help with my project. Many people responded that they wanted to read the book, but none wanted to jump into anything as awesome as writing a book about Socialism. My best response was from Dr. Larry Southwick an economist and professor who lead me to the Readers Digest version of *The Road to Serfdom*. This version can be found on the *Taking Hayek Seriously* website at www.HayakCenter.org. Dr. Southwick later reviewed some of the early chapters of this book. Aside from Larry's help I was stuck. I talked to several people and none were ready to jump on board, but many offered to help. My greatest help came in the form of contributions of books on peoples, "Must Read List." When ever I mentioned that I was writing a book someone would say, "I have a book you should read."

In July a brief acquaintance called me and said that he sold his house and was moving to Texas. He wanted to know if I was interested in moving him to Austin. I told him that I did not do interstate moving anymore due to fact that I no longer had an Interstate ICC permit. I told Russ that I would be glad to consult with him and help him with the ins and outs of moving and would help him find a reliable mover. I met with Russ and his wife Diane in late June and we had long talks about moving and I agreed to provide him with packing materials to begin packing for his move. During the next couple of weeks we had a number of meetings and on one particular meeting he asked me to sit down so we could talk. Russ asked if I had any luck finding a co-writer for my project on Socialism. This caught me by surprise. I asked him how he knew about my plan to write a book. He said that he had read all my articles on RedCounty.com and that I should write the book. I pretty much denied that I had the ability to undertake a serious project like this on my own. I asked Russ why he thought I had the ability to write such a book. He then asked and answered a question that knocked me off his couch in the middle of his Living Room. "Do you know what I use to do for a living before I retired?" I sheepishly answered, "No," thinking that I should have had the answer to his question. Then he said, "I was one of the Senior Managing Editors at McGraw-Hill and I have edited for many people and you have the ability to write this book and you must write this book." I was astounded. Russ then followed up with, "If you write this book I will edit it for you. If it sells we will make an arrangement. Can you give me the first chapter before I leave in a couple of weeks?" I told him that I would go home and start working on it. Since Russ reviewed that first chapter in August he has been with me every step of the way.

I had often heard that I was a very good writer but I usually discounted the compliments thinking my friends were just being polite. I knew that I had a growing number of fans, but I never took my writing very seriously. It was more of a hobby to wake up with an idea and put it on paper. Just recently, I realized that I had written over 30 articles on www.RedCounty.com. I knew I had a certain ease about writing and felt that I could both write and sometimes entertain at the same time. Whenever I have an idea stuck in my head, I find it easy to write a 1,000 word article at one sitting. Many times I have been criticized for writing articles that were "too long." The recommended blog article is supposed to be 500 words. Yet, over a time span of about two years I have developed a modest following that seems to overlook my wordiness. My average article today gets over 700 hits. Several articles exceed 1,100 reads which is pretty amazing for a word of mouth blogger

My experience with Russ Huff has not been unique on this journey to write *The Road to Socialism*. Starting with Tom Broderick, who gave me a bag of books a few weeks before, and ending with Dr. Doug Ross who convinced me that I could Self-Publish this book, I have had miracle workers all along the way that appeared when I needed them the most. Many people have contributed to this book in various ways. Herta Weiss, a German born immigrant, fled Nazi Germany when she was a child. At a Tea Party Meeting one day she handed me a couple of history books that helped me write about European history and Nazism. Herta's personal fear is that we may turn into Europe someday. Edward "Ted" Nutter and his wife Ingrid, who I respect very much for their help over the years, have provided me with a sense of quiet inspiration. Ted and I went to Northwood School together and we have been close friends since we met in English class fifty years ago. Ted is a Patriot and was born on the 4th of July. I was born on Memorial Day, and we share a sense of mutual Americana together. He got the fireworks and I got the parade. Ted has provided me with the largest pile of books so far. His special interest is studying American Presidents and he has read one or more books on every American President. Hopefully he will get a chance to read about another new president in November of 2012. Much of the work I produced came from the books that used to sit on Ted's bookshelves before they covered my office floor.

The effort to write and produce *The Road to Socialism* has been a community effort based on the friendships I have developed through the Tea Party Movement. Over the last two years I have been asked to speak to groups on a variety of subjects and have never turned down an opportunity to try to help return this country to greatness. My inner motivation is based on trying to help steer the course of our country away from the storms of the greater and greater influences of Socialism: that all encompassing system that destroys ingenuity, takes away liberty, forestalls future greatness, and causes divisiveness that tears apart the fabric of the "All American Spirit" that many of us miss. It is difficult to find that sense of American Spirit today with riots and protests and a divided government.

I get a sense of the American Spirit during the National Anthem, the Pledge of a Allegiance, and at Veterans Day Parades, but never more than the experience when Judy and I spent a couple of days touring Virginia and Washington D.C. historical sites and when we stood at the feet of Abraham Lincoln at the Lincoln Memorial on November 27th. My special purpose that day was to see the Vietnam Memorial to visit friends I had lost from my hometown of Yorktown Heights, New York. I had collected all the names of the mere children we lost from my hometown before we left home. One of the most special was Steven "Teedie" Smith. I wrote an article on Redcounty.com, one of my proudest stories, about growing up with Teedie, my hometown, and what life was like living in small town America in the 1950s. That clear twilight and emotional evening at the Memorial was followed up the next day with the greatest collection of mankind I have ever witnessed at the *Restoring Honor Rally* presented by Glenn Beck. Nearly 500,000 peaceful, happy, joyous and free people gathered for a day of celebration. Had it not been for Rick Santelli and his CNBC rant that ignited the Tea Party Movement and Glenn Beck and his 912 Meetings across the country, I would have never embarked on the road I have travelled in the last two years. It has been an incredible ride. With that said, I am both pleased and proud to give you a little peek down *The Road to Socialism.*

It has always been my belief that when one invests their time in reading a book they should be able to walk away changed or bettered in some way. My purpose when writing is always "to educate, inform, and to help my readers to educate others." Hopefully this book will meet that criterion. The book was conceived to fill a small gap in understanding between history, economics, and politics in an easy to read format. It is based on the idea of sharing some of the greatest minds in history that have influenced our economic way of life, both the good and the bad. It is not a series of facts and dates, but attempts to show how certain events in history have changed our lives. It also provides some of the atrocities in history as a warning that governments with too much power are the greatest threat to mankind.

This book is a short summary of some of the high and low points in history. To provide a comprehensive analysis and presentation of 300 years of history would take volumes and would not meet the purpose of informing the greatest number of people. This book was designed to provide a basic understanding of the fear of unchecked Socialism which falsely asserts itself through its goals and ideals to solve mans greatest social ills. Following the progressivism of the Marxists, its ultimate goal is Communism. Unfortunately, you will see over and over again that Big Government, with its lofty goals, never seems to meet its intended purpose. Many accuse me of being biased and say that I hate Big Government. That is not exactly the truth. I hate the failures of Big Government that never meet their intended purpose and ruin the very lives of the millions they profess to care about. I hate the hypocrisy of dithering politicians pandering for votes. I hate the ignorance we are breeding into our children to manipulate their futures. I hate elected officials who violate the Constitution they have sworn to protect and believe reading it is meaningless. Let me explain how we have not learned from the history that we are repeating.

Today we have the highest level of unemployment since the Great Depression. We are following many of President Franklin Delano Roosevelt's failed expensive plans to cure unemployment. We have the greatest number of people living in poverty after fifty years of President Lyndon B. Johnson's Great Society which has increased the number of poor rather than eradicate poverty in America as promised. Our social programs and safety nets have not come close to solving the problems in everyday living for most Americans. We have successfully elevated poverty to a higher level of sustainability without ever addressing its root causes. Our Jobs Program does not create jobs. It creates workers for jobs that don't exist. Our Department of Justice denied selling thousands of guns to the Mexican Drug Cartels in a botched sting operation that resulted in those weapons being used to murder our Border Patrol agents. A House investigation discovered the government cover-up, but very little was reported in the media.

Washington spends over $90 billion per year on education yet, our children coming out of schools today can't read, write, or perform basic arithmetic and have educations far worse than their parents who didn't have Federal subsidized educations. Our children know all about sex and drugs, and are convinced that the Capitalists are destroying the environment, yet they can't find Washington D.C. on a map and do not know the name of the Vice

President. Less importantly, they all know who won last years American Idol Contest. We are told that are largest problem is solving the high cost of big healthcare. The "real problem" is Big Government which has poorly designed and administered socialized medicine to the poor and elderly for the last fifty years. If they really wanted to provide healthcare for the poor and elderly they would staff public health clinics with interns and physician assistants in the neighborhoods that have the highest incidence of free Emergency Room visits. Instead they want to nationalize the best healthcare system in the world. They are following the Cuban and Venezuelan approaches to government. How many people are escaping from America to flee to Communist countries for free healthcare? With free healthcare in those nations comes $20 a month salaries and government housing. No one ever came to America with the hopes of living in our government housing, yet that is where many end up. There is a move underfoot to eliminate public housing and give Vouchers to the poor. We have vouchers for everything except education. The Marxist loves poorly educated people because they are the easiest to control. Is there any parallel between our costly poor education system and our increase in government control?

The Road to Socialism is a partial tribute to Hayek's *The Road to Serfdom*. I say partial, because it does cover every idea and concept and theory proposed by Hayek. It is intended to highlight some of the ideas in his book. I use the same chapter names and often quote Hayek to relate his writings and warnings to our recent history and current events. His book was used as an outline to provide novice students of Socialism with the basic knowledge of Socialism, Communism, and Totalitarianism, which have become dirty words in society, but that alone does not change the direction of our society. There are no clear or consistent definitions of these three "isms." Every book, article, and pamphlet talks about them as growing, evolving organisms rather than static philosophies or economic theories.

Capitalism, the greatest enemy of the Marxists, is an economic system not tied to a particular style of government, but works best with minimal governmental interference, but with   responsible government controls. Our system is predicated on the private ownership of the means of production incorporating the various aspects of production and the distribution of products and services with the primary purpose to making a profit. Ironically, profit and its distribution is the lifeblood of the Socialist. Socialism requires somebody else's money to survive because the Socialist has never been very efficient at running anything.

What is Socialism? Ludwig von Mises, the mentor to Hayek devotes over 500 pages to the encyclopedic definition of Socialism in *Socialism, An Economic and Sociological Analysis.* There is not one single paragraph that says, "This is socialism." A simple but inadequate definition is that Socialism is the redistribution of wealth taking from those who have more and giving to those who have less. It does not care about the hows, the whys, or the equity of contribution when it determines its distribution. It is based on the premise that all should share their good fortune with those who are less fortunate. The often misstated reason is that those who have attained success did so to the disadvantage or the exploitation of those who have less. This is the belief of the Marxist.

For the ill, the downtrodden, and a great number in our society that are unable to legitimately contribute and provide for themselves, government has decided it is a right for those to be taken care of and provided for at the expense of those who are more fortunate. I do not dispute those in legitimate need. What I deplore is the constant creation of groups who become eligible for new forms of government assistance as a vehicle to pander for votes. Socialism is based on a system of economic distribution of money that provides a basis for providing for those less fortunate at the expense of those who have been determined to have too much. The successful are chastised publicly and the idea is promoted that far more is available to be shared by all but it is currently in the wrong wallets. It has already been determined that individual social responsibility will be ultimately regulated by the government and the United Nations wants to lead in that pursuit.

Socialism is not charity, and it is not voluntary. The donors have no control over the distribution, nor do they have any influence on who receives the benefits of their labor. The qualifying requirements to receive support, whether it is cash for food and utility bills, housing, tax credits, giveaway cell phones, or a free education is based on an ever expanding criteria that continually increases the number of citizens and illegal immigrants to qualify for unlimited amounts of our tax dollars. Our tax system is the conduit in the redistribution process. Unfortunately, we are unable to meet all the social goals and needs dictated by government, therefore our nation must borrow additional money, approximately 40% of our budget, to help meet the needs of the "underclass" and to operate an ever expanding government structure to develop, design and implement and provide on-going assistance to a particular category of people. Sir Winston Churchill summed up Socialism the best when he said, "Socialism is the philosophy of failure, the creed of ignorance, and the gospel of envy."

Communism is the ultimate goal of the Marxist, whose strategy includes destroying Capitalism and placing all means of production in the hands of the state. It eliminates the private ownership of property. It quietly begins with over-regulation and it can eventually and will quietly crush our individualism if it is not stopped. A much quicker means to that end is to resort to military control to take over the Nation through Totalitarian tactics like Nazi Germany or what we are seeing in the Middle East and North Korea. Communism destroys all materialism. Everything is owned by the state to provide the minimum basic level of subsistence. It is the national equalizer that has no history of success in the world. Cuba announced recently that they would allow the private ownership of small businesses. After fifty years of Communism they are tip toeing around the edges of Capitalism without admitting that Communism is failing as a mainstay of life in Cuba. At the same time, a Rasmussen Reports poll of March 3, 2011, reported "11% say Communism is better than the U.S system of Politics and Economics." This is a frightful statistic considering the failures in the world today. Much of the support comes from unions. The Communists and Socialists are in bed with our union leaders. Little do the union members know, that if a revolution takes place, then they will be standing in lines waiting for government handouts with the rest of us.

Our third "ism"- Totalitarianism is a style of leadership that also has no consistent definition. Our system of government, based on three branches of government, was designed to prevent individual abuse and the over reaching of authority through the restrictions and guidelines provided in the United States Constitution. Totalitarianism, even poorly defined, is a dictatorial style of government based on a sole individual leader and a single political party that overreaches its authority to arbitrarily rule for an individual purpose for the supposed good of the people in violation of the limits of its authority.

Some examples of Totalitarianism are partially nationalizing our car companies with funds provided by Congress to stimulate the economy and taking away private property. Another is taking over banks and investment companies like Venezuela or bombing Libya without any authorization from Congress. It is also controlling oil fields by not issuing permits to drill for oil while we rely on countries that hate us forcing us to send much needed money overseas which could be used to employ people in America. Totalitarianism is unconstitutionally taking over one sixth of the economy to socialize healthcare and relying on liberal judges to arbitrarily adjudicate that it is Constitutional based on ideology rather than law. Totalitarianism is using the military to control its citizens rather then to protect them. The ultimate form of Totalitarianism is when there is no higher authority for appeal to as we witnessed in Nazi Germany. Today we see Totalitarianism throughout the world. It ultimately results in death and violence. It never relies on or promotes humanitarian goals although that is often the stated purpose.

Dictators are not interim leaders as we witness the riots that are attempting to turn over regimes that have lasted 40 or 50 years. They are sometimes elected through sham elections that are put on for show.

Totalitarianism is the ultimate weapon used against the people to achieve "total control" through any unjust means.

It is my sincerest hope that as more people become knowledgeable about the truth of Socialism, Communism, and Totalitarianism and its gradual infiltration in our daily lives many will change their opinion on the role of government and seek elected officials to uphold the United States Constitution. The Rule of Law is our last salvation. As we move farther away from freedom and increase our dependence upon government we are progressively moving closer and closer to total government control of our daily lives.

For example, The San Francisco Bay Area eliminated Non-Sugar Free beverages in vending machines and the City of San Francisco requires a license to purchase a pet, but there are no prerequisites for unmarried teenagers having babies. New York City outlawed salt on restaurant tables to make us healthier, but they have the highest taxes on cigarettes in the country which helps to fill their coffers. The Federal government wants more calorie reporting on restaurant menus to discourage people from eating fattening foods. Food labeling hasn't worked in forty years and the government's solution to an obesity problem is larger print.

When we review our daily lives we become aware of the destructive nature of government when it is abused by our elected leaders and remains unchecked. *The Road to Socialism* is designed to be a series of lectures to help people understand the consequences of out of control governments based on history and actions taken today that are often overlooked. Our growing dependence upon government is by design rather than necessity. A review of our failing social programs beginning with the New Deal of President Franklin D. Roosevelt which were enhanced by President Lyndon B. Johnson in his Great Society have resulted in the destruction of our society. While aiding the poor we have increased poverty. By creating government housing we have built ghettos. By expanding home ownership we have created a financial collapse and increased foreclosures. By regulating medical care we have created the most expensive healthcare system in the world. Our emphasis on education has created more high school drop outs than any time in history and an education system that ranks in the bottom third of thirty industrialized nations. By adding more social programs we will not improve the quality of our failing social programs. No group has received more aid than the American Indian, yet they have the highest unemployment rates and lowest quality of life living in government owned housing. The government provides a dismal lifestyle with no effort or intention of creating self-respect, the key to building self esteem. When we compare our unemployment rate to other nations we appear to be more successful. Do not forget about those who were offered early retirement incentives to save money. They were bribed into unemployment. These people could have been working and living productive lives if we had a vibrant economy to provide them with more opportunities. We have a declining workforce that we falsely call progress, when in truth we are disguising our inability to be a productive nation. It is time for a change.

As you wander through the chapters of this book, I hope you may think of others who you may benefit from this information as we approach the edge of a great precipice. Share this information with your friends and family and encourage our young people to take an interest in the dramatic changes that may change our way of life for the next several generations. I have included a Bonus Chapter- Chapter 17 "Become a Patriot and the companion Appendix "The Four Pillars to Become an Armchair Activist" which includes information you can use to increase your knowledge and methodologies in your own home. This information will ultimately help you to become a Neighborhood Patriot.

It is my hope that each generation successively gains a greater quality of life with less government interference than the previous generation. When those who are lost along the road determine their error they must travel back to the intersection in their life where they turned in the wrong direction. Going back is often hard, but the road to Socialism is not a one way street. We have a choice today between Socialism and Capitalism.

Chapter 1   The Abandoned Road

"When the course of civilization takes an unexpected turn and instead of continuous progress which we have come to expect, we find ourselves threatened with evil associated by us with past ages of barbarism, we naturally blame anything but ourselves. Have we not all striven according to our best lights, and have not many of our finest minds incessantly worked to make this a better world? Have not all our efforts and hopes been directed toward greater freedom, justice, and prosperity? If the outcome is so different from our aims and if, instead of freedom and prosperity, bondage and misery stare us in the face, is it not clear that sinister forces must have foiled our intentions? We are the same victims of some evil power, which must be conquered before we can resume the road to better things?" F.A. Hayek, The Road to Serfdom.

This opening paragraph of *The Road to Serfdom* establishes the premise that we must awaken to the need to examine Socialism, one of the revolutionary "isms" that took hold in the 20th Century. Throughout history Socialism has been offered as a better alternative to our current economic system, Capitalism. This is our wake up call. Our system, the best system in the history of the world, is under serious attack and is being challenged from all sides.

We hear many who angrily condemn Capitalism because they think it has failed us, and they rail against the perceived lack of balance and "fairness" and injustices of our time and call for social justice and equality for all. They quite literally want to "level the playing field." Is this just a current bump in the road on our way to a better system of economic growth? When the road gets too bumpy and heavy repairs are due, do we repair the road or create a whole new highway?

History tells us that traveling a new course often leads us down a path we do not want to travel, and we discover unforeseen roadblocks that delay our progress and break the spirits of those pilgrims moving along the way. When we consider civilizations that have lasted thousands of years under a variety of government systems, is it a fair assessment to say that our system of experimental government, formed over 200 years ago, has provided the ideal solution for modern man? We have been raised to believe that we have the best Constitution ever written, and a Bill of Rights that provides the best continuous form of government in the history of the world to accomplish the supreme goals of Life, Liberty and the Pursuit of Happiness for all. Our perception has been that any road that takes us down a path that does not lead to this destination is destined to take us to evil places where we will ultimately suffer the bondage and misery as promised by Friedrich Hayek over seventy years ago.

The Road to Socialism

Since Hayek wrote his warnings about taking this road to Serfdom, we have lived another seventy years--a period of time that represents only one third of our history as a free nation. We will be examining what has transpired during the intervening period since Hayek's pronouncements. He warned us of the possible results of dramatically altering our course, a course which not only changes our socio-economic system, but will ultimately result in a significant alteration of our present form of government. We have taken a fork in the road that is heading us in the wrong direction: a road that abandons Capitalism.

When we examine the path we are on, pushed along by the forces of Progressivism in the past century, we discover that we are not just deciding between the road to more Capitalism, which has had its share of evolutionary bumps, bubbles, and recessions, versus the adoption of the road to Socialism. We are making a fundamental choice between a government whose sole mission is to preserve Life, Liberty and the Pursuit of Happiness and a socialistic form of government that professes to provide a heavily regulated world that defeats the will of the people by implementing controls and laws that replace personal freedoms with heavy-handed governmental programs and multiple layers of bureaucratic controls. A new ruling class is being formed that promises to ensure equality for all--but in truth, will lead us to nothing less than complete totalitarianism.

Socialism cannot be implemented by any other means than aggressive government coercion. When we select between Socialism and Capitalism we are also selecting between a representative form of government that allows personal freedom and a Big Brother system of ultimate and complete dictatorial control. Any type of control granted or seized by a central government automatically predestines the elimination, or at the minimum, a severe and caustic reduction of personal freedoms. So on a higher level, the progressive challenge of our day is forcing our people to choose between Freedom and Tyranny. Most of the people in our great nation are blind to this gigantic battle for our future. We are being told one thing, while the undermining forces in our government are preparing for another.

Economic models and specific forms of government are not picked at random. The complexity of evolving structures, both economic and political, are based on hundreds, and at times thousands, of years of history. The weight of this history influences the divergent schools of thought to determine economic societies and the necessary form of government to best control and monitor the chosen philosophy for the people. The rising to power of *Adolf Hitler* in 1919 in Germany is an example of the dramatic change in government based on philosophic views after the failures of World War I. We will discuss these influences later, but let it suffice to say, where we identify radical changes in economic philosophy we usually discover that it was preceded by a fundamental change in government under new leadership. These changes do not come about without heavy cost. We find that war is the ultimate trigger in this evolution. In most cases, if not all, fundamental economic changes are preceded by some type of involvement with a war effort whether it is intercontinental or internal, and usually accompanied by civil unrest. The desire to change systems can be due to the corresponding effects of war or it may be the very cause of war. To initiate revolutionary changes in our society requires a fundamental breakdown in the economic system. What is so tragic is that a very good, working system may be destroyed, and the blame placed on some phantom evil such as unbridled imperialism. In the past, it has been said that imperialism brings with it another domineering style of government, one less tolerant of other systems and values. The irony is, that in one way or the another, a new tyrant usually arises.

It is of great value to briefly review the history and evolution of European nations and the various forms of governments associated before and after the changes. By doing so, we can predict, with some reasonable certainty, the road we must travel to effect similar change in our own socio-economic structure. Clearly, different types of governments have different options. In each case, a problem must be identified, monitored, changed, and enforced through either regulation or sheer dictatorial power. The particular style of government determines the methodology for each course of action. As a government becomes more involved in the regulation of free economic activities, the people become less free. Freedom is stolen in the name of a "false freedom" --a promise made that is never kept. This is how it proceeds and it clouds the truth. Where individuals were once free to make their own personal choices, now the government steps in, with its propagandist style, and states that more government control will free individuals of the necessity to make hard choices. What goes unsaid is that the reformers believe that private individuals are not capable of making good decisions on their own. If that were true then explain, "How did we become the greatest nation in the world?"

Transformational language, the redefining of commonly accepted terms, is the tactic used to convince the naïve and blur their arguments. Never is true liberty enhanced or increased one iota by reducing freedom of choice. We are dealing with the very essence of our republic created by brilliant men at the foundation of our government. They realized that freedom of choice is Liberty with a capital L, and that when this basic liberty is thwarted in the name of freedom we have lost part of our mission as Americans: To Promote Life, Liberty and the Pursuit of Happiness. We must remember that we can never enhance one of the trio of our founding principles by stealing from another.

Consistent with our goals of freedom we eventually freed the slaves, the first and only nation to do it internally, and thus made it possible for all people to receive the product of their labor. Our goal as Americans living in a proud tradition of Constitutional Rule of Law is to maximize the opportunity for everyone to be free to pursue their own goals of freedom--while joining together collectively to protect those freedoms when they are assaulted. Over the course of our history, we have bravely sought to combat attacks and aggressors from outside our nation, but now it seems we are faced with an enemy from within.

History gives us perspective. It provides us with the tools we need and the mountains of experience we can sort through to form our view of the future. The United States has a glorious history by creating the greatest major form of government to successfully reach the stated goals of its Founders via the Constitution. It blends both harmony of thought and purpose. Our goals, coming from what is referred to as a young nation, challenged the aged and experienced older, independent nations of Europe and the Eastern Continent. As the youngest in the Western Civilization family, we were able to benefit from the experiences of our older brothers. Those older and definitely more tried brothers have lived through centuries with evolving types of governments which have all been distinctly different in their own realm--meaning almost every form of government was tried, from kings and tyrants, to the anarchy of the French Revolution.

It was recently stated in a seminar by the National Center for Constitutional Studies that out of approximately 200 countries in the world about 175 have written constitutions. The United States Constitution is the oldest continuous written form of government. As we move forward we have the opportunity to review modern history to draw conclusions about our form of government and predict, with reasonable certainty, the impact of any changes. We can evaluate the ultimate impact on the individual under any changes. The great pool of information and knowledge available today can help us evaluate the best road to travel. Today we are seeing civil unrest in Europe and the Middle East which gives us a preview of what happens when promises remain unfulfilled. Therefore, we are faced with a choice. Which road will maximize our personal freedoms and at the same time meet the needs of society? When making that choice we must realize that sacrificing freedom should be the last choice for America. In actuality, sacrificing our freedom should never be a choice.

From an historical point of view, we see that most nations experience similar evolutionary patterns, in the ebb and flow of time, as they borrow from their predecessors and fall under the influence of dictatorial rulers. Over time, as each system falters and fails some return to their former style of government.

Alternative styles of governance evolve depending on the leaders and they come in a variety pack, depending on whether they were elected, anointed by Monarchy, or gained power through violent revolution. Each style of government always encompasses a particular socio-economic structure. If we are to learn from them, we have to make a careful examination to determine if the form of government dictates the economic system or if the government is changed to implement a new economic system based on default or preconceived needs. What we have discovered is that without a democratic mechanism some form of dictatorship is required to significantly change socio-economic systems.

The founding of the United States as a separate nation was based on separating itself from its colonial roots under King George III. Our nation formed from this basis as it developed its uniquely American style of government. What was created out of the individual colonial rule was a representative form of national government. This united stand evolved out of years of debate and development and combined the very best and idealistic aspects which provided the greatest amount of freedom for the people. This distinctly contrasted with the history and evolution of every other nation on earth. *John Locke*, a 17th century English philosopher, is credited with influencing many of our Founding Fathers, including *Alexander Hamilton, James Madison* and, most notably, *Thomas Jefferson*. Locke had a profound influence on Jefferson's writing of the Declaration of Independence. It was Locke's belief that, "everyone had a natural right to defend his Life, Health, Liberty, or Possessions," the basis for the founding principal phrase in the American Declaration of Independence; "Life, liberty and the pursuit of happiness" which we will refer to often. America, living under these principles in the Declaration of Independence since July 4th, 1776, combined with a democratically elected representative system of government, gave birth to the concept that the people themselves were the controllers of their own fate. Rather than establishing a system where the government ruled the people, the very opposite was created: "We the people" would rule the government.

By comparison, there are governments that govern by means of a powerful military that dually controls the people and provides for the common defense. We see these dictatorships currently in Venezuela, Cuba, North Korea, Egypt, and Libya to name just a few. A strengthening of an internal army generally is a sign of anticipated unrest. By contrast, The Constitution of the United States adopted on September 17, 1787 outlines the restricted powers of the central government. Our military is limited to the "Common Defense".

America was patterned after the principle of the "Rule of Law." This means that rulers and dictators may not adjudicate arbitrarily and must follow the Constitution and the laws created to support it over the years to meet the needs of the people rather than the needs of the government or a ruling class. This concept alone was a very unique system of law. The Constitution clearly puts forth that that each State would retain its sovereignty initially developed under the Articles of Confederation. The Federal government would be responsible for duties not currently retained by the States, and specifically those of supporting international treaties, and raising taxes for military defense and navigation. Our current system of government is unique because it clearly states the basic principles of its Founding Fathers while establishing governance based on both State and National Constitutions that solidify our unity and purpose as the United States of America. (Initially, the 'u" in united was not capitalized.) While the concept of States Rights and a limited system of Federal Government was designed over time, this system of checks and balances has been derailed through the failure to interpret and legislate with strict adherence to the Constitution. Today, we are living with the results of flagrant violations of the powers provided in the Constitution, failures on the part of all three branches of the government.

Looking back from an historical perspective on the story of our nation we will examine some of the significant periods which helped to frame our nation. We will also examine the influence exerted by those who felt it necessary to begin altering and modifying our style of government to meet the current mood of the people. The *Progressive Movement,* not without some good intentions, is gradually eroding our freedom in the name of progress. The Progressives have been most active during the most difficult periods in our history. This movement attempts to gradually solve social problems that have often been misdiagnosed and at best, their solutions have been poorly designed. Problems when poorly or emotionally defined can lead to inappropriate solutions.

Improper social solutions can have the devastating effect of mis-directing an entire society. This is where we are today as a nation. We are at that fork in the road. One road will continue down the road of freedom where the spirit of the American free enterprise system has provided the greatest progress in the world, while the other, "progressive" road leads us down a path that carries us to excessive regulation and the global redistribution of wealth. It is now time to examine some of the significant events that have led us to this turning point in history.

The American Revolutionary War ended with The Treaty of Paris in 1783. Most of us view the victory through rose-colored glasses. We try to imagine the victory parades, the exultation of the new America and the joyous celebration of new freedoms. But there was a dark side as well. The prolonged war plunged the new nation deeply into debt. Untold devastation of farms and property left many in a depressed state. At that point there was no centralized form of government that could unify the individual states. The new nation was still very dependent upon its exports to the former mother country, and imports continued to be a problem. Quite understandably, the war had strained both trade and intercontinental relations with England although they improved with France and the Netherlands. Financial matters were complicated. No centralized banking system existed and the problem was compounded by the fact that each state had its own currency. States were mere shells of independent little nations Each state conducted its own foreign relations policy and all international transactions were subject to each state's own interpretations. Clearly the nation felt the need to unify its diverse approaches and depend upon a system of economic principles that were purely capitalistic. Above all, it was time to create a new and powerful guiding Constitution-- although that was not the original intent.

Europe, most significantly Great Britain, had lost a major source of revenue following American independence. England's problem was compounded by significant debt caused by the military operations required to fight the Colonies. Both the free nation and its former mother country were financially devastated by the costly, prolonged war. The post war period resulted in dramatic economic measures being taken on both sides of the Atlantic. The economic models at the time were pure, unbridled capitalism. There was an "anything-goes" mentality, described by the French as *laissez faire,* providing the impetus for expansion that was accompanied by heavy taxes.

England resolved its economic woes by launching, or rather erupting, into the Industrial Revolution. This expansive economic growth began initially in England during the last half of the 18th century and lasted about 150 years. England became the hub of innovation. Adaptation of labor saving technology improved the overall standard of living for its subjects. Quite notably, this is the first major "revolution" in history that had nothing to do with war. However, one could view it as another kind of conflict, a war of ideals set in motion by industry and technology. Great Britain innovated and leaped ahead, making significant advancements, while France limped along far behind its European neighbor. Germany had not as yet congealed into a unified nation and continued to import not only thought but patents and inventiveness. A new and unique brand of the Industrial Revolution emerged which raised the standard of living as well. But later, Germany would be stalled by a war of ideals rooted in the intellectualism of the time.

At the same time a grand technological awakening began in America. The young nation drew from the experiences of England and Germany. Over the centuries the mature nations of Europe had developed well formed communities both urban and rural, but America was predominately an agrarian society with only pockets of development that were almost exclusively centered around the sea ports. Advancement in technology during this peaceful revolution directly impacted labor, and more specifically, craftsmen. Gradually, and then with increasing force, hand labor was being displaced by mechanization. Factories were built by industrialists who grew ever more powerful. The national economy and society as a whole changed from a labor-based economy to a capital based economy. The movement required investment funds for land, equipment and labor: these were regarded as "the factors of production". Significant shifts in the means of production displaced some people. Both women and children joined the work force. This process was repeated throughout Western Civilization.

Friedrich Engels, a German philosopher and rudimentary economist living in Manchester, England, wrote a paper that ultimately had a major impact on the prevailing thought in Europe, and eventually the world. His study, *The Condition of the Working Class in England in 1844*, detailed the negative impact of industrialization on the labor force. Workers were being pitted against industrialists in what now might be seen as the first case of modern day class warfare. He used statistics to demonstrate that working conditions, specifically safety and mortality rates, were devastatingly and morally deplorable. He took the point of view that it was disgraceful to allow the plight of the working class to continue at the hands of "greedy industrialists." The war on the industrialist was about to begin.

Engels teamed up with *Karl Marx* in London soon after his study was published. Marx believed that there was a "normative process" in evolution where Capitalism replaced Feudalism and Socialism would replace Capitalism. In his mind, this would ultimately lead to a stateless, classless society called Communism. Marx believed that the working class would eventually be the agent of change bringing destruction to the industrial class. A natural evolution from this condition would be the final and ultimate revolutionary stage--the leveling of all people. This process and its implementation based on *The Communist Manifesto*, is known as *Marxism*. Marx's premise, based on providing justice and equality to the working class, whom he called the proletariats, placed workers in the same class as the capital investing industrialists. He discounted the value of capital and the resultant risks associated with entrepreneurship. He failed to acknowledge the creative talent and inventiveness of the people. Further, his theory was ultimately defeatist in nature because Communism by definition would end the period of industrial progress. Individual motivation to improve and innovate would disappear because it would have no reward. The issues that were popularly discussed in Europe by the intellectual class soon became issues impacting the rapidly industrializing United States of America as it recovered from the Civil War.

One example, which highlights the long term social issues in America caused by the industrial innovation, was the cotton gin. The new cotton processing technology in the South had a dramatic effect on the economic and social status of the United States. Slavery, a significant factor of production, provided the essential labor for agrarian operations and the support services for plantations. If we look at slavery as a "component of production" added to "capital," and both land and equipment, it is easy to understand the reluctance to repeal slavery. Slavery lowered the cost of production. The chattel ownership of slaves made slaves "assets of production," rather than "labor factors of production" in normal operations. In an economic sense, slaves were equipment: depreciable and expendable.

Examining the operation of a plantation under slavery gives us a glimpse into the future. Ironically, the plantation system was very similar to the French feudal system using serfs to work the plantations. The irony begins when we consider that Marx's abandoned method of labor management could be a microcosm of a future society rooted in socialistic principles, where a ruling class, called the government, controls the necessities of life in return for labor. In this case government becomes the plantation owner. When we compare the working class in Europe and the slaves in America we see an important difference. The working class consisted of individuals with individual rights, while the slaves were private property with no rights. In Europe, labor was paid directly and in America those on the plantations were paid in kind. Both groups under different systems were often purported to have similar working condition issues. But of course, the living conditions of the slaves were another deeply depressing matter.

This economic model reveals that both paid labor and free slaves, along with the associated costs of owning slaves, are both "factors of production." The improvement of working conditions in Europe and the repeal of slavery both had moral and social implications. The costs of both resulted in changes in the cost of labor in the short term while directly impacting the capitalist model and its profitability. Both sides of the Atlantic had to deal with social and economic upheavals, but no upheaval was more costly and brutally conducted than the "War Between the States".

The American Civil War was fought almost exclusively on Southern soil which meant that crop production was drastically disrupted for many years. As the Union Army pushed to the South the plantations were plundered in the name of freedom. The Union victory caused an immense upheaval in the life of the Rebel South. In the end, the result was freedom from bondage for 700,000 slaves. The economic impact of the war for all States was overwhelming, and further compounded by the overall economic loss of production. As the economist would say today, the economic heart of the South was battered and left drowning in red ink. The War for Emancipation stopped the collection of taxes, thus creating major deficits for both North and South. Tariffs were the largest source of federal revenue from the 1790s through World War I. The War Between the States hampered the collection of those tariffs for both the North and South. Overall, the ravages of war severely stalled advancement of the new nation which was then less than a century old.

Recovery was long and painful, but it did come about. The South ultimately revived financially and the Industrial Revolution continued in America with the expansion of transportation networks that were paramount for improving the movement of not only people, but of goods and services as well. This nation on wheels provided work for former soldiers and slaves alike. Newly created mechanical and motorized equipment helped to centralize factories which were predominately located in the North. Our country was originally founded by the early settlers who based their livelihood on the perceived future value of our vast natural resources: timber, mining, farming and livestock and the availability of open land. Now technological advancements led to the centralization of production and a rebirth of our prosperity. America was not competitive in many areas and tariffs were used as a tool to increase the price of imports to maintain an economic advantage. This resulted in the higher cost of goods until American Capitalism became more competitive. Early technology provided the economic advantages to become more competitive.

One formidable benefactor of this new technology was the meat packing industry located in Chicago, which was a hub of railroads near the shores of Lake Michigan. In the early1900s, Chicago claimed to be the meat distribution center for the world. At the same time, it became the poster child for the American worker, but in a negative way. American industry attracted tens of thousands of immigrants who elected to work for higher pay and better conditions than existed in their homeland. Much attention was drawn to the abuse of these workers due to horrid working conditions. Workers injured or even killed on the job were literally dragged from their work assignments and replaced on the spot from a pool of willing new recruits. *Upton Sinclair,* an activist expose columnist from Kansas, rose to popularity with articles about the squalid conditions in the packinghouse districts. His research led to the America classic novel *The Jungle,* published in 1905. Sinclair, a declared socialist, in dramatic fashion detailed the horrors of the life of the workers in Chicago's packinghouse district. He had a far more populist reach than Engels did in 1844. Sinclair, along with others, cemented the ideals of Socialism and Communism together as he highlighted the social injustices that resulted from poor working conditions and sordid living conditions offered by the company rental office. Once again the "greedy industrialist" was targeted and the populists were angered. Although this journalistic attack was clearly warranted, now all capitalists were painted by the same brush as the meat packers. This recurring theme of "social injustice" expanded into the mines and any industry that had significant amounts of labor. Yet, prospective workers stood on line for days hoping for these opportunities.

This was a new-age for the industrialists. Their key means of pre-serving capitalism, according to Sinclair, was collusion with unions, the bribing of the police, and the controlling, deep connections in local government. All these factors working together supported production growth and maintained the expansion of Capitalism. Not so coincidentally, these are the same tools being used today by the Socialists, but are being twisted to provide the destruction of our capitalistic economic system. Today we are being assaulted by the unions and the organized labor force to achieve this gradual destruction which was predicted by Marx. The *Progressive Movement* starting in the late 1800s is now seen as a "transformative" element bringing about the changes that move them closer to their goals. It is no coincidence that Chicago is again the center stage for changes taking place today. The notoriety of Chicago-style politics that once led to the disruption of one business culture has ushered in the advent of another. Over the next 100 year period the transition moved from industrialist control, and then to a depression-era mob mentality, and then old styled, anything goes, Chicago politics. At the same time, unionization moved to influence peddling from Wall Street to Main Street and the politicians were all too willing to oblige.

With the success of the Industrial Revolution in America, we were able to move away from financial dependence on Europe. Due to the unlimited opportunities available in the New World, European capital was attracted to industrialize America. America characterized as Miss Liberty became a preeminent player in the world of trade and commerce. This spirit of development blossomed and evolved in a country with only 150 years of history and surpassed the growth of other Western Societies many centuries older. The amazing progress of America from its start in the early 20th Century was made possible by one key ingredient: the almost unfettered belief in Freedom steeped in the Declaration of Independence. This spirit helped the United States surpass other nations which had developed their business models at a much earlier time. Our unique form of government reinforced our founding principles and made incredible progress possible.

With reference to Holland and England during the same period, Hayek memorializes in *The Road to Serfdom* the same point emphasized above in our preliminary study of the Industrialization of America, but with far more clarity:

"The result of this growth surpassed all expectations. Whenever the barriers to the free exercise of human ingenuity were removed, man became rapidly able to satisfy an ever widening range of desire. And while the rising standard soon led to the discovery of very dark spots in society, spots which men were no longer willing to tolerate, there was probably no class that did not substantially benefit from the general advance. We cannot do justice to this astonishing growth if we measure it by our present standards, which themselves result from this growth and now make many defects obvious. To appreciate what it meant to those who took part in it, we must measure it by the hopes and wishes men held when it began: and there can be no doubt that its success surpassed man's wildest dreams, that by the beginning of the twentieth century the workingman in the Western world had reached a degree of material comfort, security, and personal independence which a hundred years before had seemed scarcely possible."

While America had accomplished significant advancements on every level, the dark spots referred to by Hayek did indeed exist. In particular, there were heavy personal costs borne by the people and especially by the immigrants who were responsible for this remarkable advancement. Historically speaking, we note that during every period of significant growth there come unforeseen consequences that are not immediately discovered or easily rectified. In the case of industrial expansion and the centralization of work forces, workers were often victims during the interim course of progress and this was most apparent in the mines, the fields and the factories. As societies emerge, there is a sequence or pattern that all seem to follow: development that leads to exploitation, and then to a growing awareness of the excesses, which in turn aids in ultimately improved overall conditions for all. All this evolves as a result of the maturing of the capitalistic way of life. Capitalism breeds competition. Competition creates new and improved uses and methods of interacting with the essential factors of production. There is no formula or time table for how long this process takes. We have witnessed in our own history that, universally speaking, life is improved and society benefits from the process. History reveals that this evolution does take place when not impeded. But, paradoxically it seems, there are no major successes and societal changes without the accompanying imbalance and pain. The pain may be either the cause of the change or the impact of the change. Ultimately, the ebb and flow rights all wrongs and the benefits are eventually shared by all.

The advocates on the Left would want you to believe that the evolutionary process involved in all progress under a capitalistic system, or any other system they do not sponsor, is fatal and immoral. The first tenet of the anti-capitalists is that capitalists are immoral in the deceptive practices that take place in the pursuit of wealth, and that this is done at the expense of the working people. This automatically breeds the cry for unions to protect the helpless from the all-powerful capitalists.

Any argument founded on isolated examples, which when extrapolated to the whole, is intellectually dishonest. While Engels' study on the conditions of the working class in Manchester revealed increases in death rates in both adults and children and severe increases in injuries and disease, it was reported that there were other macro studies that detailed the exact opposite when viewed over longer periods of time. While it is outside the scope of this study, it would be interesting to determine if the entire Marxian movement was perpetuated by this type of fraud and deception. The short term problems during periods of development may be no different today. Quite possibly, the entire socialist movement was perpetuated on faulty or disingenuous research—with limited studies on time periods of their own choosing.

Karl Mannheim, a Hungarian born philosopher and sociologist, studied the sociology of knowledge in the early 20th century. His classic work, *Ideology and Utopia,* published in 1929 provides some interesting theories and ways to dismiss *Engels.* He prefers that the term "ideology" be broadened to expand beyond a particular point of view. He believed that ideologies that take the narrowest point of view obscure the total picture. Mannheim zeroed in on Marx's study of cultures and ideas, and believed that his view was too narrowly focused on the impact of a certain class, the proletariats. Mannheim asserts that dissecting cultures over only a brief period of time leads to inaccurate assessments. The methodology Marx used of segmenting various classes during short periods of time provided a false impression that gave unsustainable results when extrapolated to a larger population. Mannheim further stated that theories and solutions developed in response to temporary imperfections in society may result in solutions with far greater negative consequences than the original problem being addressed. To put it very simply, the cure is worse than the bite. Over reaction to a problem is like panicking in a theater when a small lighted match hits the floor. He says, in effect, wouldn't it be better just to stamp it out than to scream "fire" and set the entire audience into a panic?

Ideology should not take precedence over reality. It is feared that those with heart-felt allegiance to a cause, regardless of facts in evidence, dismiss data through their altruistic belief systems. They are blinded by their ideology and then reject the very facts that may contradict their belief system. Mannheim judged that, irrespective of the entire body of data, these firebrands continue their march for social justice in an atmosphere of denial when a short, simpler adjustment could have been the proper solution. This mentality can ultimately lead to civil unrest, and turn into violence after peaceful protests fail.

The key to keeping the Socialist troops in line for this suicidal march is continual propaganda. Studies have shown that to maintain this level of commitment for these zealots requires continued propaganda and indoctrination based on false evidence. This smoke screen clouds the facts and makes them much easier to convince. In many ways, the current "state run media" provides this cover for contemporary Progressivism. They pound at their perceived enemies, sometimes with hate and scorn, while excluding facts that could water down their beliefs. They reject facts to the contrary of their positions, despite overwhelming evidence. It's like saying that the economy is recovering nicely when stimulus packages fail, even as unemployment rises, and consumer confidence falters. This is more of an ideological pipe dream than "a fair and balanced" presentation of the events.

The indoctrination in the theories of Marxism is based on "class warfare." It creates a perceived enemy and attacks it: for example, "the rich Wall Street fat-cats" or the "failed Bush policies", and let us not forget the "greedy insurance companies". This type of rhetoric has been a long and insidious process that has gradually taken place throughout the 20th Century and is now accelerating.

The radical indoctrination of the Weather Underground and the Hippies in the Sixties, with their hatred of America and their long list of enemies including the "fascist pigs" as they called the police, and the conservatives to which they attached the moniker "neo", has continued to smolder for decades until they in unbelievable scheming could finally seize control of our government. In their patience, using extremely liberal educators and community activists, they have reshaped thinking and the meaning of history. They have subverted reality to fulfill an "American dream" that we believe is doomed to failure. When we look at the history of failure of this ideology in the Soviet Union, and the current examples in the European Union and former Eastern bloc nations we see nothing but the tragic failure of Socialist policies. Fidel Castro of Cuba is the most recent to admit they are having trouble with the State-run island paradise. They are in the process of laying-off about 700,000 state workers and re-privatizing many businesses..

Today in Greece, after years of overly generous Socialist, grand give-away-programs, we see a nation on the brink of national bankruptcy. Sweden has warned us, Russia has warned us, and the threats to the economies of Spain, Portugal, Ireland and so on, are all clarion bells sounding the alarm: move away from Socialism. Yet we, the most modern economy and most successful constitutional government in the history of the world, seem to be embracing it. Our leaders are pushing to level the playing field, to soak the rich through heavy taxation to give to others what they have not earned. As a nation, we are being pulled forward to this end. Daily we hear our elected leaders and their liberal advisors urging us toward deeper and deeper indebtedness, more "globalization" and more spreading of the wealth. When will they realize that the richest nation in the world is already bankrupt? It is as though these eggheads, hippies, and revolutionaries are trapped in a 1960s vinyl 45 recording in an age of I-pods. They are still demanding the changes from the 60s when we have moved past those situations. They continue to clamor for change, ignoring reasonable solutions based on long honored principles.

According to economist Larry Southwick, Capitalism and the market principles always result in long term growth. However, we need to keep in mind that for most of human history there was little or no actual growth. He further states that "people need incentives to invest in creating new technology and for the most of recorded history, there was no such incentive." This idea is also highlighted in *The 5000 Year Leap*, by W. Cleon Skousen who in 1981 revealed that starting with the founding of the first American settlement in Jamestown, Virginia in 1605 and over the next 200 years, more progress was made in the name of mankind than in the previous 5,000 years. It was a 5000 year leap! The ideas developed by freemen flourished-- based on freedom, Capitalism, and the idea of personal responsibility. These concepts began the heart of "American Exceptionalism."

The usual economic patterns and cycles take into account that there will be ups and downs in every long term economy, but the general trend line normally moves upward over time. Today, contrasted to the former tough times of the past with the exception of the Great Depression, our government tells us that we can stimulate our way out of economic downturns. A Socialist government believes that they have the wherewithal to solve all of our problems when they have more government control. It is precisely this "over control" that has caused the problems in the free market system. Significant changes in economic policy and regulation always result in changes to the overall economy: rarely with positive results.

Capitalism and greed have been blamed for our economic downturns. In actuality, it was the result of relaxed government regulation, without a clear understanding of how the financial markets worked that led to the crash of the US real estate market and the overall devastation of the world financial markets. This came at the same time that most major developed nations were suffering from the weight of ever increasing unfunded social programs. These nations were attempting to improve their portfolio yields by investing in unprecedented high yield American investments. High risk mortgaged backed investments led to the financial destruction of many economies. In response to the financial calamities, Capitalism, specifically Wall Street, is being bridled and stifled while the non-productive government is being overly expanded.

The industries that were based on natural resources, America's foundation in the 18th Century, have been thwarted by government intervention and more regulatory control. Our economic engines are stalling at the hands of government control. Normal business operations are being challenged. Economic progress is at a standstill because business owners do not trust the government. The business community isn't getting any sincere help and is being overregulated out of existence due to the problems ultimately caused by irresponsible government regulations. There is little hope ahead as huge tax increases have been planned for the coming years and the new Obama health care program of over 2000 "unread" pages became more about seizing power than providing health benefits. As the government seeks to make a more perfect world, we are challenged by its political hopefulness. The results achieved never seem to match their intentions.

Chapter 2   The Great Utopia

"In Ancient Rome it was the legend of the Golden Age of Saturn in the glowing terms by Virgil, Tibullus, and Ovid, and praised by Seneca. Those were the carefree, happy days when none had private property and all prospered in the bounty of a generous Nature." Ludwig von Mises, Socialism.

Utopia is a creative term first used by Sir Thomas More in 1516 in his book of the same name to describe a fictional community that was perfect in every way. The word in ancient Greek means "not a place". In English it is defined as "a good place". Based on definition alone, we see an immediate historical contradiction in the philosophy pondering an unachievable fictional community that nevertheless provides the basis for many pie-in-the-sky thinkers whose mission it is to create a perfect society here on earth.

Designing a perfect society is still one of the goals of the Progressive Movement dating back to the late 19th Century. Progressives believe that by eliminating the problems of life they could create a more perfect world. The immediate dilemma was that the people were thinking, learning and gaining knowledge on their own. They were circumventing the intellectual base who in their own conceit believed they were far more knowledgeable, and therefore, knew what was best for the people. The intellectuals believed that independent thinking should not be left to the amateurs. To counteract individual thought, progressivism was created as the prescription by which intellectuals who felt they better understood true idealistic goals of man then could prescribe the best methods to achieve them. Freedom of thought by the masses has always been the arch enemy of "managed" perfectionism.

The intellectual class determined that building a better society and moving closer to Utopia requires a better system of living for the masses. It has been decided by many social philosophers that Socialism provides that solution. The elements of change from an existing system to a totally different system of living must be based on solving significant weaknesses in the current system. The key problem is always purported to be that "the rich are too rich and the poor are too poor." To right that perceived wrong in their mind requires a massive change in ideology. The ideology must determine that equality in outcome must be separated from individual contribution. As we have seen, Capitalism is a system of competition based on personal incentives and free trade principles. Socialism is based on the theory of equality regardless of individual performance where we are obliged to take from the successful and give to the unsuccessful. The fruit of one's labor is shared regardless of the level of contribution. They foresaw, however, that to accomplish this transfer, from providers to takers, is not an easy task. Those who have worked hard to gain what they have are not going to simply hand over their cash to those who are less successful. So they devised a simple mechanism available to make the transfer payments possible. That mechanism is always the government and it comes in the form of taxation. As the need for supplementation increases, then so does taxation, the only viable form of legal exchange.

In 1789, The French Revolution erupted with its main purpose to change the structure of society that existed for many years. Prior to the Revolution, philosophers were detailing their theories on life and the roots of their idealism which was based on the teachings of *Plato,* and most specifically his philosophy on government in, *The Republic,* written in 380 BC. Plato believed that there was only one purpose in life and that was to support the State. Any individual who did not support that premise was guilty of treason to the whole of society. From that point on, all collectivist movements moved forward based on the underlying ideals of Plato. The French Revolution temporarily reversed the trend of organized planning and its movement toward Statism when it unseated the aristocratic system that was in place.

The French Government, called Estates-General, was composed of a tri-lateral set of groups that included the Clergy, the Royal Class, and the Peasants Worker Class. As an outgrowth of the revolution, the working class and peasants gained prominence above the other two upper classes. The working class had finally achieved power over the king and the feudal system and the religious hierarchy. The ten year struggle led to a warring of interpretations by the various philosophical schools of thought about the significance of the revolution and its impact on the peasant working class. *Alexis de Tocqueville,* a noted French government official and philosopher, sided with those who believed that the rising middle class overthrew the government. The conservatives believed that a group of unruly, radical conspirators forced out the ruling class, while the peasant working class, which made the most gains through the revolution, espoused that they truly influenced the government.

Fifty years later the peasant worker class was credited, by the historical "revisionaries" in the Marxist group, as the primary group responsible for the revolution. The Marxists stated it was purely a class struggle of the working class to overthrow the government. Marxist theory espoused an evolutionary process leading to Socialism. In actuality, the French workers overthrew the government because of its inability to meet the most basic needs of the people. It was not a working class struggle, per se, as much as a fight against starvation arising as a result of an ineffective feudal class system during a period of famine. The people were not ready to trust a new government for their survival. They wanted better access to food and they wanted it now. The primary form of nourishment at the time was bread and there were shortages. The peasants raged, "We want bread, we want bread". Their fury matched up against the infamously unsympathetic retort, credited to Queen Marie Antoinette, "Let them eat cake", and the mobs responded with their chant, "Off with her head," which soon followed.

The Marxist early theory on the societal evolution was in motion. Marx believed that there was a natural transition or evolution from Feudalism to Capitalism, to Socialism, and ultimately to Communism. The French people entered the second stage of evolution: Capitalism. The movement was more against the government and the church which jointly shared control. Capitalism was not a primary factor in the revolution as much as the anger at the lavish lifestyles of the ruling classes. As we said, it was less a worker protest than a people's war over government provided living conditions. The primary problem was the lack of availability of food and supplies. In comparison to other European societies, the French were not considered as industrious as other nations. The net result of the revolution was that the new found freedom provided the beginning of a capitalistic economy where people were becoming self reliant. Independence and self reliance was a new way of living for many and became a difficult adjustment without immediate overseers.

History classifies the French Revolution as "the dawn of the new modern era." This ended the "early modern period" which started in the early 16th century. It signaled the end the reign of aristocracy and gave power to the people. *Claude Henri de Rouvroy, comte de Saint-Simon* is viewed as the father of the Socialist movement in France. The French Revolution broke the people's trust in the old forms of government and required that a new structure be formed that was more suitable to provide the basic needs of its citizens. But Saint-Simon failed to ignite any following because the new free citizens placed their faith in a spirit of self reliance. This might be entitled the period when Utopia was delayed ...but not forgotten.

While the French were developing a new government, across the sea America experienced its own revolution and began a new life with a new Constitution and its first free government under the guidance of President George Washington. The struggles to establish a government of the people, by the people, and for the people had been bloody and costly. The former colonies were saddled with heavy war debts, a badly disrupted commerce system, and the contentious aftermath of the ratification process of the Constitution.

Comparison between what was happening in France and the United States offers some interesting conclusions. During this early period, all eyes were focused on America's relentless expansion, called its Manifest Destiny. The young nation expanded its trade with Europe under new terms. Americans were an industrious and adventuresome people. Growth and development blocked any move towards planting the seeds of Socialism because the agrarian society, with small pockets of industry, did not provide the basis for Socialist solutions. Those small pockets of commerce and industry were about to explode. During the expansionary period the second wave of Europeans, who were starving and sick from disease, began their migration to America inspired by the promise of free land and opportunity. This great influx of new citizens coincided with the beginning of the Industrial Revolution which soon was in full force in America. They immigrated freely by the hundreds of thousands with the hopes of higher wages and a better standard of living. Free market Capitalism was the driver of this expansion of opportunity for a better way of life for the new immigrants.

The combination of increased international trade and the expansion of the territories ultimately fueled a prosperous America. During the period of American expansion in the last half of the 19th century Marx and Engels developed their Socialist theories in England and were determined to implement them. Europe was ripe for change due to the many uneven economic conditions resulting from industrialization. The work force was changing in a modernizing world. Specialists, the craft workers, were being replaced by factory production workers. The principles espoused by *Adam Smith*, *In the Wealth of Nations* were being applied, on a large scale, which lead to increased levels of productivity. The changes in the working conditions and worker profiles, as a result of industrialization, provided somewhat easy inroads for Socialism. Organized labor began espousing the merits of Socialism as a result of the consequences of a changing and evolving work environment.

During the period leading up to the industrialization of America, President Thomas Jefferson acquired the Louisiana Purchase in 1803 from France. This added a huge territory from the Mississippi River to the Rocky Mountains. France, insufferably in debt, received $15 million in compensation which included $3 million in debt settlement from Napoleon Bonaparte. Napoleon had duped Spain out of the land in an imperial gesture of expansion and then resold it to America. This exchange ultimately resulted in the greatest land sale in American history and provided limitless opportunities for American settlers under one continental government. Ironically, the money sent to pay the French for the greatest real estate transaction in history was used by France to pay off their debt burden remaining from their participation in the American Revolution.

The quest for land as a result of the westward expansion by the early settlers provided the motivation for further development and Americans headed west to a new land of opportunity. Private ownership of property abounded, something unfamiliar to most people, especially the immigrants from Europe.

In both France and the United States, we see parallels in development that reveal an interesting point. Socialism, the glorified, planned economic system that promised to provide the best of all possible worlds, cannot exist in countries that are in the process of a full blown expanding economy. When a nation is in a period of high growth and prosperity, personal success becomes a national passion. There is no need for an idealistic Utopian solution if the developing nation already possesses the resources to reward both the workers and the leaders of industry. The theory of a Utopian world can only exist in a developed nation that has the resources to refund or redistribute from one class to another. With so much freedom in America for individuals to prosper through personal initiative, there was little room for Socialism to get a foot-hold. In order for Socialism to progress it had to lay in wait until the wealth was created as the primary funding source for redistribution. Interesting, isn't it, that once the capitalists have provided the necessary base of wealth then socialized programs can be developed to satisfy the requirement of the needy. Under a democratic system, the expansion of the needy class provides the power to essentially vote on 'great giveaway programs" promised by politicians. Alternatively, without the benefit of free elections, an angry class must be created to provide the impetus for socializing those programs. The revolutionary process can then be employed to confiscate wealth from the industrial class. Class warfare is one of the essential tools used to create the motivation for social change and without a democratic system in place it will ultimately lead to revolution. The confirmed Marxist-Socialist does not care how the revolution comes about.

Regardless of the method, the net result is always the redistribution of wealth. Short of a full scale revolution, an aggressive taxing mechanism must be in place for the transfers to take place. This can be combined with a state run program of confiscation of property to take away the assets of the industrialists, which includes all private businesses. Since Socialism itself has no track record for creating wealth, it must use taxing and outright confiscation as the only vehicles available to create the funding sources required to maintain the redistributive process. Capitalism is the only economic system known to provide the financial resources required to fund and convert a country to a Socialistic system of economics. Capitalism, Karl Marx' fat cow, must provide the milk to make the economic and ideological transition. But when the cow runs dry, what happens next? Today we are seeing in Europe what happens when the cash cow quite literally runs dry. Greece, Spain, Ireland, Portugal and other nations are witnessing what happens when the government runs out of money. Riots erupt in the streets as a result of the government's reducing any level of benefits to the people. Despite the pitfalls and shortcomings of Socialism many people, and most especially those with their hand out, are convinced that Socialism is a better economic system. It comes as a shock to them to see what happens when the government runs out of other people's money. Margaret Thacker, the former Prime Minister of the United Kingdom, when asked about Socialism replied, "The problem with Socialism is that sooner or later you run out of other peoples' money."

Liberty, the greatest threat to Socialism, is one of the greatest attributes we possess as a free society. Hayek again quotes de Tocqueville in emphasizing this theme using a technique that promotes ideas and beliefs that differ in meaning from what is commonly understood. "Democracy extends the sphere of individual freedom," he said in 1848; "Socialism restricts it. Democracy attaches all possible value to each man; Socialism makes each man a mere agent, a mere number. Democracy and Socialism have nothing in common but one word: *equality*. But notice the difference: while the true democrat seeks equality in liberty, the Socialist seeks equality in restraint and servitude." Socialism promises a "new freedom" which is meant to persuade people to believe that they will somehow discover of new level of freedom, a new sense of happiness, which places them closer to that imaginary Utopia. Nothing could be farther from the truth.

The use of transformational language, a common propaganda tool, is designed to sell new ideas by using the exact opposite meaning of current thought to infer that the new idea is similar, but better than the accepted belief. This often used methodology, a kind of bait and switch lexicon, is used to deceive the people in order to achieve the goals of a movement. Where the ideas of freedom and liberty were universally understood as the right of the individual to act, to work, select a trade, speak, take responsibility, and make their own personal choices, the "new freedom" was defined on its benefits rather than by its activities. Freedom, in its traditional sense, implies that the individual has freedom of choice. "New freedom," a nuance on freedom, promises freedom from choice while eliminating the worry and concern of making choices. Freedom of choice is transformed into a negative that infers progress. Eliminating personal choice is translated into "increased happiness" resulting from the elimination of worry and the tedium of making decisions and selecting between alternatives. When freedom of choice is eliminated it is replaced by governmental mandates that further limit the rights of people. The thinking here is that the benefit of not being forced to make choices would somehow eliminate the many struggles in life. Freedom of choice was transformed into something bad rather than a right. Hence, eliminating struggle would supposedly bring happiness by stripping away the liberty required to make many choices.

As a result, "new freedom" means that people would be able to rely upon the State by sacrificing their freedom of choice, which is redefined as a personal burden. As we will see later, to eliminate freedom requires changes in laws which when administered eliminate many choices. Today, after 200 years of true freedom, we clearly understand that an increase in laws and regulations always limits our basic freedom of choice.

Jeremy Bentham, a British philosopher said in 1789, "that every law is an evil, for every law is an infraction of liberty" and in discussing the preservation of liberty Bertrand Russell in 1940 believed that liberty was "the absence of obstacles to the realization of our desires." *The Road to Serfdom, pg 63.* Two simple sentences uttered centuries apart contrast the goals of true freedom and Socialism. The implementation of Socialism violates these principles through the manipulation of the masses by creating the false assumption that "freedom" and "new freedom" are essentially the same.   True freedom is based on the opportunity to make personal choices. In contrast, "New freedom" is based on the lack of personal choices. Choices limited by Socialism prevent self realization and lead to tyranny.

With the concept of the "new freedom" at work came the promise of freedom from financial worry through the "redistribution of wealth". This is merely taking from the "haves" and giving to the needy "have nots". It is not a wealth building formula because it does not create more of anything. At best, it punishes success and rewards mediocrity. Redistribution of wealth requires the initial possession of wealth and when it is transferred it becomes subsistence. Subsistence leaves no evidence of wealth after consumption. It is a form of "trickle up poverty". The money is taken from the capitalistic creator of wealth and given to the consumers of wealth. No one becomes richer in this transfer. The money is taken from the capitalistic system and it just seems to drain away. No one in the transfer, except maybe the manipulating and participating elite, gets richer in the exchange. Getting richer is not the goal. The leveling of all people is the primary goal. In the long run, less is available for the continued re-creation and recycling of wealth required for long term sustainability and a healthy economy. There is no greater threat to economic freedom and the continual creation of wealth than taking from the creator and giving to the consumer through either direct confiscation or taxation. The elimination of free capital will eventually erode the economic cycle until it completely disappears.

The fundamental principles required to build a true, self-sustaining Utopia depends on the endless creation of wealth. This socialist ideal demands the continuing use of what has been called "the evil capitalists." When capital

The Road to Socialism

creation is no longer available the cycle ends. Socialism at its core creates nothing of value other than endless regulations and taxes. The stagnation and suffering in Communist Cuba is a clear example of the elimination of the producing class. Therefore, the final stage becomes apparent: Communism. We can conclude that Utopia here on earth will never become a lasting paradise. The real intent of promising Utopia to the masses, who have their hands out for more, is to offer an interim stop on the road to Communism, the ultimate Marxist dream.

Government always promises to provide the necessary services to its citizens. To do so it must determine an acceptable level of services and then decide who the beneficiaries will be. Over time we see that no government has the ideal track record for adequately providing for its citizenry. One essential criterion to measure success should be the long term sustainability of these government programs. Using this criterion we see the failure of the Great Society promises developed in the mid 1960s under President Johnson. Today almost every major social program is severely underfunded, making long term survival impossible without dramatic and unpopular changes. This is the same problem that is causing riots and destruction in Europe today. Our social programs are bankrupt or living on life support with unsustainably high deficit spending. In reality, they were probably bankrupt at inception because the lawmakers never possessed the fortitude to honestly identify the true cost projections of our government run social programs. They also failed to establish the necessary reserve requirements to satisfactorily meet the continuing long-term needs of the programs. This will be further addressed in Chapter 13.

Therefore, the coined phrase "new freedom" is an inappropriate, deceitful propaganda tool used to convince our people to make decisions and follow a plan that, in the long run, has no possible means of long term success. Quite frankly, long term success was never its true intention. We are finally becoming aware of this hoax. Our elected politicians like it because it gets them reelected, and the recipients receiving the "entitlements" love it. There is a sad truth to all this. Many well intentioned programs were sold on the false premise that the government was providing a "hand up", yet our poorest people, the most needy and dependent, are the victims of the same programs that were designed to improve their lives. Through government participation and misguided social programs we have imprisoned, even enslaved, millions of people. Their jailers are the very same government that promised them opportunity. The Native America Indians are the poorest and most destitute society in America. Their plight is the result of massive government programs, restitution and reparation programs that keeps them living in squalid living conditions in government owned housing. Billions are spent on a variety of government sponsored Indian Affairs social programs, yet they have the highest level of alcoholism, drug addition, and unemployment. Their government created Utopia could not be worse if it were created in hell-on-earth.

Another common tool to gain populous support for socialized programs engages the use of the intellectual elite. To lend creditability to the early Socialist Movement, many of the best minds in Europe were proponents of Socialism. The philosophers, the social theorists of the time, were consumed with ideas of moral justice and anti-capitalism and guided the cause toward more government control. The thinkers in our modern time are not normally thought of as producers and many of the early ones had difficulty supporting themselves. Many of them gravitated toward the learning academies or writing where they have found cushy assignments and over paid teaching positions. Karl Marx, for instance, lived a shoddy existence until Engels gave him the financial support and the ammunition to improve his lot: thus helping him promote his thesis with their *Communist Manifesto*. Intellectuals, those with ideas rather than results, always seem to be near the inception of change and are always in the spot light in the move toward change.

Hayek points out an interesting observation about intellectualism. "The higher we climb up the ladder of intelligence, the more we talk with intellectuals, the more likely we are to encounter socialist convictions. Rationalists tend to be intelligent and intellectual: and intelligent intellectuals tend to be socialists." "One's initial surprise at finding that intelligent people tend to be socialists diminishes when we realize that, of course, intelligent people will tend to overvalue intelligence, and to suppose that we must owe all the advantages and opportunities that our civilization offers to deliberate design rather than following traditional rules, and likewise to suppose that we can, by exercising our reason, eliminate any remaining undesired features by still more intelligent reflection, and still more appropriate design and 'rational coordination' of our undertakings." *The Road to Serfdom, Pg 33.*

This observation supports the idea that massive transformation by intellectuals is a greater threat to success than gradual and continuing adoption of free market principles. I suspect that the fear of failure due to the absolute principles of Socialism is the underlying factor that requires the gradual and surreptitious implementation of Socialism. The techniques employed to sell Socialism are the same techniques we see in our homes everyday. Anyone who has seen the latest "slicer and dicer" on television, has heard the claims that for $19.95 they can eliminate every complicated problem in their kitchen while creating a Kitchen Utopia. The cost of a false Kitchen Utopia is $19.95. The real cost of a Utopian World is the loss of our cherished Liberty.

Socialism is an ideological myth perpetuated by a variety of false promises and manipulations of body, mind and soul. During the 19th century we witnessed progress in culture and living conditions. However the results of the socialist agenda produced much misery while trying to eradicate "social injustice." Social injustice is the polite name for class warfare based on class envy. The Left dredges up every anecdotal occurrence to justify injustice. President Obama jumped into the fray by castigating a police officer as being racist for accosting a black man in a Boston suburb, who happened to be a personal friend of the presidents. It appeared to the officer that he was trying to break into a home. It wasn't until later that it was proved that it was his own home. The President, without any facts at hand, claimed it was an act of racism.

Socialism, using other forms of "social injustice" presumes that people have been exploited and manipulated during the selfish accumulation of wealth. Their purpose is to stop the "greedy capitalists" and replace them with an alternate measure of government. We can see that the cure is worse than the sickness when we examine the first half of the 20th century in Germany and its profound debasements and death camps. In fairness to Socialism, the behavior of Germany under Hitler was not motivated by Socialism, but rather was caused by a megalomaniacal ruler whose secondary objective was to install Socialist principles after the annihilation of people during the holocaust. That mad man wanted as his ultimate goal to create a master race. In truth, is it any different if instead of eliminating a race we shorten the life spans of our senior citizens by limiting their access to healthcare based on their future utility? Only God should have control over life and death. Who is the ultimate authority that makes these decisions? It certainly will not be you or me.

The intellectual revolution in Germany that led to its political revolution resulted in the most violent, horrific and unthinkable behavior of any Western Civilization in modern history. To understand a society that does this one must examine the philosophic idealism that was pervasive at the time of the 1920s. *Emmanuel Kant,* an early 18th century philosopher, had great intellectual influence over the German Enlightenment. He promoted the idealism of the Platonian principle that it was every citizen's sole purpose and duty to serve the state. Kant quickly had many followers. His ideas impacted thought in every school of philosophy in Germany in the 19th century. These philosophers influenced The Social Democrats, the working class party which was in control. Their primary purpose was to destroy Capitalism and to revert all means of production back to the State.

In 1920, a new Weimar Constitution in Germany was adopted following the horrors and the German defeat in World War I. This new legislation gave the state massive and unlimited powers to control the people. Article 7 of their new Constitution throws light on the spirit of freedom, or the loss of freedom, at the time, in contrast to the freedoms we have come to take for granted in America. Article 7 outlined the responsibilities of the State. It included in detail the management and control of every aspect of human life. Curiously, a later article in the Constitution outlined the freedoms of the people which sounded on the surface like a version of our own Bill of Rights. However, the final condition to those rights stated, "the government reserves unlimited power, at its discretion, to attach conditions to the exercise of these rights." For instance, Freedom of Movement concludes with, "Restrictions can be imposed by federal law only." This restriction limited where one could work, live and where they could travel within the country. So with one sentence in the Article, it took away what it had previously promised." Well, so much for freedom. During that period the German Republic professed to be the "freest republic everywhere." Apparently, "everywhere" did not include the United States of America, which was practicing far more freedom than any other nation on Earth and it continues today with increasing exceptions. In the end, with a goal of creating a Utopia, the German people had no individual rights. There sole purpose in life was to maintain allegiance and total, unwavering obedience to the State.

This is not intended to be a comprehensive review of all the civilizations that attempted to seek Nervana by means of Socialism. It should provide a clear view from the examples presented that reaching the Utopian dream cannot be attained without coercion, manipulation, and the threat of violence. The intellectuals knew their goals could not be met without "dumbing down" the populists. The age worn tactics employed over the centuries are still required today to promise a set of false benefits to the people. Any movement that is based on fraud explicitly lacks the merits to adopt and sustain a long and sustainable life of its own. It will eventually result in some form of revolution. This should lead us to wonder: what are the true motivations of an intellectual class that survives purely on dishonesty? The grossest example of this mentality is the Nazis who had the Jews bathe and dress prior to marching them to the death chambers while playing German Classical music lulling them into a spirit of compliance.

To those who are not convinced that the loss of individualism is not a significant factor reversing the development of human nature, consider the history outlined above. Before we leave, let's look at our old friend Saint Thomas More and see how differences of opinion were resolved between leaders and their people.

"When a scholar and important man of letters writes a book about *Utopia*, a fictional community that is perfect in every way, we might wonder why he has his head in the clouds. But Sir Thomas More in 1516 knew exactly what he was doing. As Chancellor of England, he was creating an ideal literary place instead of the contentious one he lived in. While he continued to pledge his loyalty to King Henry VIII --during the time Henry broke from the church in Rome over his willfulness in taking multiple wives while executing some of them--Thomas proclaimed he served God first as a power higher than the King. For this, Thomas literally lost his head and now is regarded as a saint and a martyr." *Contributed by Russell J Huff*

Chapter 3   Individualism and Collectivism

"The common features of all collectivist systems may be described as the deliberate organization of the labors of society for a definite social goal. In many ways this puts the basic issue very clearly. And it directs us at once to the point where the conflict arises between individual freedom and collectivism. The various kinds of communism, fascism, etc, differ themselves in the nature of the goal towards which they want to direct all efforts of society. But they all differ from individualism in wanting to organize the whole of society and all its resources for this unitary end, and in refusing to recognize autonomous spheres in which the ends of individuals are supreme."   F.A Hayek, The Road to Serfdom

Our subtitle here could be "Adam Smith versus Karl Marx." Both their names are synonymous with the economic systems they developed. Adam Smith, author of *The Wealth of Nations*, is referred to as the father of modern economics. Karl Marx, with his *Communist Manifesto,* was the creator and founder of the socialist movement. Both of their economic systems have similar goals, but with methods so dissimilar that day and night have more in common.

Before we look at an overview of the two ideologies, let's look at the characters whose books have probably fostered as much debate around the world as the Holy Bible. Adam Smith was born about 100 years before Karl Marx, on June 16, 1723 in Scotland. Marx was born in Germany on May 5, 1818. Both had fathers who were lawyers, Adam's father was a civil servant and Karl's father was a capitalist, of sorts, owning a vineyard. Karl did poorly in school in the study of law and switched to social sciences, eventually getting a Doctorate. Adam Smith entered the University of Glasgow and studied moral philosophy. Oddly enough, Smith, whose greatest work, *The Wealth of Nations*, the economic guide book to Capitalism, never took a class in economic systems, yet is acclaimed as the father of economics. He devoted his life to that work. Marx, having written the *Communist Manifesto*, dedicated his life's work to the cause which is still popular today but he never received much credit for his influential work during his lifetime. Marx spent much of his time pointing out the evils of Adam Smith and his work whose full title is, *An Inquiry into the Nature and Causes of the Wealth of Nations*. Marx is synonymous with both Socialism and Communism. Adam Smith is still revered today for his documentation and explanations of Capitalism. Both of their books are alive and well in economics and social science classes in universities around the world. Marx' *Communist Manifesto* is less than 70 pages, while Smith's *Wealth of Nations* grew to over 1,000 pages. Oddly enough, to implement Capitalism only takes a willing buyer and a seller. In comparison, to implement Socialism it takes a revolution.

Over the next five chapters we will be presenting the various intents, goals, aims, and characteristics of individualism, referred to here as Capitalism, and the competing system Socialism, which will also be referred to as Collectivism. The terms in each camp are often interchangeable, but have slight interpretive differences in meaning over time due to both their evolution and castigation by their opponents. Marx created the term Bourgeoisie for Capitalists, who were the enterprising, creative entrepreneurs, yet portrayed them as evil and greedy. He referred to workers as Proletarians and portrayed them as the abused, the downtrodden and expendable by the Bourgeoisie.

Individualism was the popular term used through the 1700s and was later changed to "Kapitalism" sometime in the 19th century, no doubt by Karl Marx. Kapitalism was later translated into "Capitalism," which replaced Individualism to make "capital," the ownership of the business assets, the dreaded threat to society because it represented ownership by individuals. It's easy to see that it would be difficult to create a social war against "an individual" but the act of Capitalism and the "evil capitalists" were an easier group to attack and denigrate as they became the targets of a warring class. In the 1800s, communities were composed of individual merchants, cobblers, craftsman, and small associations of people, but for the most part they were individuals providing services within the narrow range of their neighborhoods. There was no collusion, price fixing or conspiratorial plan to take advantage of labor. They were not at war and there were no warring classes. Large corporations or tax incentivized organizations didn't exist. For the most part, a community consisted of buyers and sellers, producers and consumers. Trades and merchants were often family legacies. Legal institutions were developed much later with the need for a more definitive system of laws. The early use of the term "corporation" was in reference to feudal estates, which were separate business entities, usually specializing in farming and agriculture.

Economics is a social science that concerns itself with the production, distribution, and consumption of goods and services. The study of economics focuses on the various quantifiable factors that affect the various inputs and outputs of production and then traces the distributive process, and ultimately the consumptive ends of that process. The specific areas of concentration focus on the producers, the consumers, and today, the government which plays an important role in both the social and economic impact, through both monetary and fiscal policy. On the international front, the study of foreign exchange mechanisms includes the balance of payments between countries and the exchange rates of international currencies which are of significant importance in the study of international economics. The exchange rates between currencies, usually pegged to the US Dollar as the recognized medium of exchange, is used to determine perceived value of a specific currency based on its currency ratio. It is easy to see that business enterprises and the production of goods and services involve a variety of closely monitored disciplines.

Our basic study of the differences between competing economic systems requires a certain degree of understanding of economic principles. The capitalistic system, which is based on the need to make money or "make a living", and Socialism, a social approach with specific goals whose intent is to provide and distribute goods and services on an equitable basis without regard to contribution, have dramatic differences in application. The capitalist is concerned with profit. Profit generates the means for future development. The socialist is not concerned with development or enhancement, but rather social equality or leveling through the redistribution of wealth to fulfill the "essential needs" of the people. Government can be viewed by the Socialist as the engine used to facilitate the transfer of wealth and restrict the behavior of the capitalist. The capitalist views government as a necessary evil, and seeks to limit government and its over-reaching tendencies. Government, through the political process, is the arbiter between the capitalist and the socialist. Depending upon the outcome of our periodic elections, the emphasis of government may appear to favor one group over another or become more favorable to the capitalists or business, versus more social programs demanded by the Democrats.

Why is all this background important? Hayek, in *The Road to Serfdom*, discusses the impact of the various groups in the debate between Individualism and Socialism or what he refers to as Collectivism. His audience either appears to be fellow economists or else the average reader in the early 1940's was historically far more in tune with the events of the day, specifically in Europe. These topics were often debated and many had a better working knowledge of the important social topics of the day. Today it is paramount that students of social systems have an adequate background in the fundamentals of both systems to fairly evaluate them and make intellectual choices between the competing economic models. This requires a basic understanding of the mechanics and workings of each system. Our liberal education system no longer places a value on history. Without a sound knowledge of history it would be very difficult to make an educated choice between competing systems of government and the economic impact of those choices. Determining where one wants to go has a significant impact on the choices or alternatives available based on their ultimate destination.

For example, if you were in New York and wanted to go to Paris you would have certain choices regarding the means of transportation you could take. If you were going to California you would have many of the same choices, but you would also have additional choices depending on your time frame and finances. You could take a boat or airplane to both destinations, but your level of your expediency may determine your choice. You could drive, take a train, or even walk to California, but those options are not available on a trip to Paris from New York. There is no right way or wrong way to get to your destination, but based on a good understanding of your specific goals and the necessary means available to accomplish those goals, the most suitable choices would become obvious. In making choices between governmental changes, social reforms and changes in economic systems, one must decide where you want to go, consider all the options, and the consequences of each choice. Only then can they decide the best method to get there.

When examining Socialism, it is not just a destination because it incorporates and dictates a method to get there. The implementation of socialist reforms requires far greater power in the Executive Branch of government. The increase in power of this branch can be witnessed in the number of non-Senate confirmed positions added to the President Obama Executive staff. Expanding the role of the Executive Office and its powers, without Congressional approval and confirmation, violates the principles of checks and balances within our system of government. Our choice today is whether or not we should attempt to meet certain social goals and to select the best methods to accomplish those goals.

The backbone of our American way of life is rooted in the Constitution. Repeated violations of the Constitution could ultimately lead to a "Constitutional Crisis." The gradual and progressive usurpation of the Constitution by our elected leaders is in direct conflict with the oath taken by each person to preserve and protect the Constitution. Socialism, and particularly Marxism, concerns it self with means and ends. Changing our economic system will undoubtedly require changes in the Constitution starting with the unchecked violations we see today. This dilemma is understood by the Marxists who are progressively trying to destroy our Constitution in order to alter our system of government and make it more totalitarian. The average citizen is no longer aware of the basic tenets of our Constitution. Designed ignorance and learned bias are tools of the progressives. Many people are convinced that moral judgments are discarded when considering the means to an end. They focus on the end result, and are willing to use any means to get to that end. When we discuss ends, the topic of morality is always imposed to justify the ends. When the Socialist discusses means to attain those ends, morality is suspended for the "greater good." The Socialist and Marxist want to have it both ways. By abandoning our moral code the road to "social justice" is paved with "social injustice".

When choosing "social injustice" as a means, then we are deciding winners and losers, and in most cases, the losers become the "un-equals" in social equality. It's weird, convoluted thinking. Some call it "balancing." Others silently call it "retribution". Regardless of what it is called, it is the act of taking from the producer and giving to the non-producer to make social outcomes equal regardless of contribution. The pendulum swings both ways for the Socialist.

Capitalism, in its purest sense, is founded upon the principles of individual liberty and the freedom to produce goods and services to satisfy the needs of people. In contrast, Socialism believes that this individualism is a selfish act and never addresses the needs of social responsibility. To the Socialist Capitalism, by definition, is a selfish act. Yet, it is Capitalism that built this country. Capitalism is based on the laws of supply and demand and free competition. Capitalism is an economic democracy in the marketplace that seeks economic efficiency. Its roots are seeded in providing goods and services at the lowest competitive cost and selling at the highest price that the market will bear. Through the free market-auction process between buyers and sellers, the actual prices or perceived value of goods and services is determined. This can be a single transaction, or on a much larger scale, thousands of buyers and sellers can mutually determine the value of goods and services in a variety of markets nearly simultaneously, yet independent of each other. It is presumed that consumers determine value based upon their need. Proprietors, sellers, exchangers and providers offer products at the equilibrium price to maximize sales and to make a profit through satisfying people's needs. As demand for particular goods and services increases or decreases prices change. This is called the "efficient market theory". If prices are higher than the perceived value to the buyer, then prices will drop. If demand is higher at a certain price level, then prices will rise. Through this market bidding process the ideal prices are determined. This is a dually selfish system because each person in the market process, the buyer and seller, has the intention of receiving the most value in return for their exchange.

The Wal-Mart Corporation, whose footprint has a global reach, has expanded its merchandising around the world and successfully and consistently provides consumer goods at affordable prices through efficient buying and their own international distribution systems. Wal-Mart, formerly known for consumer goods, is now the country's leading supermarket providing food products—competing with Safeway, Albertsons, and other national chains. Competition has provided efficiency in the market place offering benefits to hundreds of millions of people everyday as both producers and consumers. Socialism implies by its mere existence the destruction of this type of free enterprise system with its private ownership of property. The means of production are assumed by the state and the free entrepreneur becomes extinct as the economy is taken over by a central body that creates a "planned economy".

Socialism is a totally comprehensive system based on specific goals requiring the adoption of necessary means to obtain ideal ends. Our capitalistic system takes place through the marketplace and only requires one buyer and one seller to negotiate and exchange something of value for something of value and then the transaction is completed. Socialism requires an entire government system to plan a "total economy" where the production and distribution of goods and services are planned by a centralized body. This body, actually hundreds of bodies as we have seen in the Healthcare Bill, seek to monitor the pricing and delivery systems of healthcare to eliminate waste then thrash out "excess value" also known as "profit" by the capitalist. According to Marx, the excess value is claimed to belong to the workers. Socialism comes in a variety of forms to meet the specific aims of the culture. The specific means used to attain those aims are often controversial and do not require the consent of the people. When decisions are made for the benefit of all people, in spite of their protests, we are no longer a true democracy.

In the ideal capitalistic society, the government would monitor and facilitate the exchange of goods and services and provide those services required that could not be provided by the private enterprise system. In return for this assistance, government would assess taxes and levy fees to cover the cost of the programs and services. Under a totally Socialist society the government takes over all means of production, either through ownership or stringent regulations, and becomes the sole or partial provider of goods and services and determines how to distribute those services. The General Motors and Chrysler bailouts are a perfect example of government interference in the affairs of private enterprise.

In the Spring of 2009 the government bailed out the financially cash strapped auto manufacturers, General Motors and the Chrysler Corporation, using over $60 billion of Stimulus Funds. Hundreds of privately owned auto dealerships were closed. According to the *Wall Street Journal on June 2, 2009,* the government took a 61% ownership of GM to help it emerge from Chapter 11 Bankruptcy. The Auto Workers Union Health Care Fund was given 17.5% of the private offering and the Canadian Government received 12.5%. The bondholders, normally given a priority of the assets based on Bankruptcy Laws, took a diminished stake of 10 % and were blocked from any further claims. As part of the restructuring plan, in April of 2009, hundreds of dealerships received a computerized list of those dealerships to be closed accompanied by a poor copy of a computerized letter stating in effect, "If your name appears on this list you will no longer be a Chrysler Dealership effective June 9, 2009." One Chrysler dealership owner, who spoke in confidence, said he attempted to contact Dealer Services to discuss his closure and never had a courtesy conversation with anyone at Chrysler Corporation prior to having his franchise rescinded. The personal losses endured by the private owners based on undisclosed edicts resulted in the loss of millions of dollars and years of investment for each owner.

Although the government and the new officers of GM and Chrysler denied that the selection of dealerships to be closed was based on politics, it was often reported that of the dealerships selected for closure, the ones closed were almost exclusively owned by Republicans. It was asserted that dealerships were closed to reduce costs. A question that plagued many people was, "If the dealerships were privately owned and paid fees directly to the automakers, where were the cost savings to the manufacturers?" In this callous and treacherous deal, each of the individual dealerships lost millions of dollars based on a photocopied letter with no recourse. Their customer lists and computer files, valuable assets, were turned over to the surviving dealerships. Many stories emerged during the dealership closures. It was often reported that highly successful dealerships were closed and less profitable stores with lower sales volumes remained open. Someone, somewhere, was picking "winners and losers." Was it the auto manufacturers or the Government Car Czar?

An oddity in the car market was discovered on the West Coast of Florida. Between Tampa and Fort Myers, there were more than six Chrysler dealerships spanning a distance of about 150 miles covering a population of over 1.5 million people. The two dealerships in Sarasota County with a population of over 300,000 were closed. The nearest dealership to the south was over 70 miles away, a long way to travel for warranty work. To the north there were two dealerships about 15 miles apart that remained open. Those dealerships were purportedly owned by Democrats while the two that were closed were owned by Republicans. Is this a coincidence? Stories like this were repeated all over the country. The *Wall Street Journal of June 14 2009* reported that Steven Rattner, the Car Czar and architect of the auto bailout program, resigned after six months. Ron Bloom, a labor negotiator, replaced Mr. Rattner. The WSJ article included this comment, "Jack Fitzgerald, an auto dealer who was mandated to close Chrysler and GM dealerships in Maryland and Florida, said the task force, under Mr. Rattner's lead, failed to truly grasp the nature of the auto retailing business." When the government gets involved in private enterprise then normal business practices are suspended and politics will always enter the decision making process. The stated goals and the intended goals may, and in actuality usually are, miles apart.

Recently, President Obama ordered that corporations bidding on government contracts release the political contributions of all of their employees. This was stated to be used to make sure that companies were not given preferential treatment based on political contributions. It appears to be the tool the President needed to make sure that his friends were adequately rewarded. When the government, a centralized political party and the business community become allies, then we begin to look for and more like Nazi Germany.

Capitalism to be effective requires the private ownership of property operating under free market principles, and this is in sharp contrast to government ownership, either partly or wholly, as in the case of General Motors and Chrysler. Following the "rule of law" allows the private system to work. The overreaching of government and the violations of the Constitution even during times of crisis do not make these decisions anymore valid. The fears associated with overpowering, privately owned enterprises pales in comparison to the routinely destructive nature of government interference in the operation of private enterprises and the confiscation or elimination of private enterprises.

What is permissible and perfectly legitimate is the public ownership of national and community parks, bridges, and transportation networks, and other infrastructure created on behalf of the people. Conversely, under the expansion of Socialism, the government will take larger and larger stakes in private business. It begins with regulatory control of the factories, mills, furnaces and the assembly lines for the production of goods and services and it will then creep into every other area of business. Added to this we will see the ownership and operation of community hospitals and health facilities. Socialism cannot exist without this massive intrusion into the lives of individuals and the corporations they work in. This intrusion also requires an equally massive system of planning and control by government. Where common people come together in meetings of exchange, under Socialism the same transaction requires a bureaucracy to plan, monitor, price, and control the transaction. It will also determine availability and rationing, if necessary. This revolutionary change in government is supposedly necessitated to meet certain social ideals: social justice, greater equality, and economic security. The "efficient market system" will be eliminated and the laws of supply and demand will be destroyed through the often bungled efforts to manage the production and distribution of goods and services to satisfy arbitrary ideals.

Meeting social ideals is never immediate and will never be achievable with the abandonment of the capitalistic economic model. True Socialism requires the transformation of every industry group to ensure compliance with the policies set forth by collective government bodies. These organizational boards, commissions and agencies will determine and establish rules and regulations to maintain consistency in meeting the supply needs for the basic services. The Affordable Care Act of 2010, commonly referred to as Obamacare, created 157 bodies to manage healthcare. They will have "unlimited power to control every aspect of healthcare". Unless this is overturned by the Supreme Court, this massive confiscation of private medical care will be just the beginning of socialized services dictated by the government.

Under a socialized type of government, the role of socialized services will be greatly expanded. They will determine the best means to produce goods and services, and decide by whom. They will determine the best methods to distribute those products and services to consistently meet the stated goals. This becomes more obvious when we look at the General Motors, Chrysler and the Healthcare Industry. Unfortunately, achieving stated goals has never been a task that government programs seem to perform very well. Efficiency, cost effectiveness, and customer service generally are not the first things that come to mind when considering interaction with government agencies. Monitoring business performance of government services does not appear to be a high priority. Our system of government requires Congress to oversee via "oversight committees" the various programs they pass into law. Very few social programs are later evaluated to determine their success or failure in meeting their stated objectives, yet every program eventually develops a perpetual life of its own regardless of its overall effectiveness. In the never ending life cycle of government programs, freedom of choice is minimized or eliminated at most junctures along the way.

Governments have an innate fear of monopolies because they believe they "unfairly" and "unjustly" take advantage of their size to overpower the consumer and result in price gouging. Under a Socialist society, government owns the monopolies and positions itself to create cost effective means of providing, controlling and distributing services. Government is the ultimate monopoly that has the power to allocate or restrict our services. According to Dr. John Moor, an Orthopedic Surgeon in Sarasota, speaking at a Tea Party meeting, "There are three criteria used to measure effectiveness of any service: Quality, Access and Cost. Further he said "Only two of the three criteria can be met at any one time, always at the expense of the third. If we have unlimited access we then must sacrifice cost. If we reduce cost, quality will deteriorate." When it comes to cost reduction, rationing is the quickest way to reduce cost followed by a reduction in quality. Regardless of our ideals, to accomplish these controls requires massive planning and the coordination of activities. The planners and coordinators who make the decisions are normally the individuals who are the farthest away from the point of service. These bureaucrats may not always be the most talented, yet they are assigned responsibilities to determine policies and procedures that affect millions of people.

The planning process is not unique to the socialist alone. The entrepreneurial capitalist is also a planner. The planning activities include: what to produce, how to produce it, where and how to obtain the raw materials; who will participate in the production of the product; and ultimately the distribution method and best market system to recapture all the costs to make a profit. Local, State, and Federal Taxes are paid to support government services and programs from the profits of the enterprise. As an aside, let's pose this question: if we have no profit from the free enterprise system where does the tax money come from to support our legitimate government services?

Under the free enterprise system millions of people participate in the planning process in tens of thousands of independent business enterprises simultaneously from product inception to product delivery, whether it is a can of peas, the production and sale of automobiles, or your local shoe repair man. Each venture or business enterprise, large and small, is in business with the intention of making a profit. Ingenuity is the method employed to reduce costs, improve production methods, design effective transportation networks and support the marketing of the various products and services we enjoy everyday. Whether one works in a factory or owns the factory or the corner shoe repair shop, the intent is to provide the best service and remain competitive enough to make a profit after paying wages and other expenses.

In contrast, in the Socialist environment, those who may be farthest away from the process will determine if you get peas or carrots. A tribunal may determine if you have access to an automobile. As in China, the Communist government decides who gets an automobile and even how bicycles are allocated. Not everyone is allocated a bicycle in China since it is not considered a toy, but rather State owned business property. If you have no business purpose in service to the state, you may not have access to a bicycle. Commissions and government bureaucracies make the determination of your true need based on the government's need for you to have transportation. Under Socialism the restriction of goods and services is routine. For those who are authorized a car, the old Henry Ford axiom will apply. "You can have any color you want as long as you want black." If you need the hole in your shoe repaired you will go to the Government Shoe Distribution Center and stand in line until someone determines if your shoe will be repaired or you are authorized to buy a new pair. But in this case you will have a choice. Your choices will be: brown or black. While these examples seem like exaggerations they make a clear point and emphasize the difference between the two economic systems: freedom of choice versus allocation. Socialism is not based on want or enjoyment: it is based purely on need and the government is the ultimate authority to determine your needs.

The reorientation of our children planned over the next few years is designed to change their belief systems. Our children and grandchildren will not have the choices we have enjoyed as they march down the road to Socialism. There are those who are naively charging along intending on changing our American way of life. Regrettably, they have been inflamed with anger and are demanding more and more change. They are convinced that more government is the answer. They are seeking happiness in an unhappy world and they have been told that bigger government is the answer. The pursuit of happiness is never a declared goal. It is unique to the United States of America and it rovides us with a basis for exceptionalism.

As we reflect upon the contrast between the two systems of Individualism and Socialism, let's pause to think for a minute: When was the last time you wrote a letter to a government agency or department telling them how happy you were with their service? Do you think happiness is one of the true goals of government today? Is customer satisfaction an essential criterion for rating and evaluating the quality of government services? Is happiness an expected or anticipated outcome of using government services? One of the utopian goals of Socialism is to provide a better, stress-free life by eliminating freedom of choice, which is then assumed to lead to a greater level of happiness. Under a free market, capitalistic system happiness is a by-product of enhanced customer service, quality, price, and access and the availability of a variety of goods and services. With the elimination of any one of these essential criteria, customers will run to the competition that provides better quality, price or service. In the event that you are unhappy with the services provided by your government under a Socialist system, what are your alternatives? Inescapably, the answer is "None."

The Road to Socialism

Chapter 4   The "Inevitability" of Planning

"The primary goal of collectivism – of Socialism in Europe and contemporary Liberalism in America—is to enlarge governmental supervision of individuals' lives. This is done in the name of equality. People are to be conscripted into one large cohort, everyone equal (although not equal in status or power to the governing class) in their status as wards of a self aggrandizing governments." George Will, Environmentalism as a Cover for Collectivism, 12/15/05

This chapter's title carries a hidden meaning. The quotation marks surrounding the word "inevitability" appear to be symbolism for Hayek's lack of conviction that planning is inevitable. If the goals of Socialism were to be evaluated on their desirability and studied in context with Capitalism, then other alternatives could be available that do not require a massive revolution. In examining social problems, Karl Marx was not content with modifying the status quo. He was not satisfied to improve life his sole desire was to change life. The purpose of revolutionaries is to support and promote revolutions. Revolutions must contain the element of anger to rally support. As we have learned, in developing support for a movement, one must create an enemy or target. Also, what must be presented is a rational argument. It appears that in the absence of a rational argument the changes necessary to support transformation were classified as "inevitable". This is like saying, "As everyone knows" preceding a statement, when in fact, no one knows. As we examine recent history, we can determine the success of some of these events. If the premise of inevitability were true then we should witness some demonstrative successes while, in turn, failures should be evident by their lack of successful development.

The purpose of government planning is to control every aspect of the economic process through development up to and including the satisfactory providing of a product or service and the distribution of that service for the social good. It is implied that government can provide the products and services better than the free market. Socialism is a "control process" rather than an "innovative process." Innovation connotes progress and improvement, which can be evaluated by on increased supply, quality, and reduced cost. Control is evaluated on consistency and equality regardless of cost. Cost in not a primary component of the delivery of government services: therefore there is no emphasis on innovation. In the area of what we call Public Works Projects, the creating and maintaining of parks, bridges, highways and mass transportation systems, there are no individual owners so government is the shepherd on behalf of the people. Without competition there is no cost comparison or process to inspire innovation.

In addition to general welfare concerns, "social services" are generally support services and supplemental services that are provided directly to individual citizens. The ability of government to provide these "entitlement programs", for the most part, are unique programs that often parallel the intent of private programs but are provided by the government. Common examples are "Social Security" retirement benefits versus private pension plans or Individual Retirement Accounts (IRA). In the area of healthcare benefits, there are a variety of medical programs available through the government. Low income housing and many other housing programs are also provided by the government. Often these programs are paired with the free enterprise system to provide services under the supervision and guidelines of the Federal Government. These services are not the specific topics of the "inevitability of planning". These are existing programs administered under regulations passed by Congress. Some work well and others have serious deficiencies. What we will attempt to furnish are examples of how these systems fit into the assumption of "inevitability".

According to our guide, Mr. Hayek, there are three major areas that have been identified by the Socialist proponents that lead to the inevitability of planning. Again, the assumption is that these areas cannot be satisfactorily provided by private enterprise or the capitalistic system. We must remember that the Socialist's dreams and desires were created over 150 years ago with the aim of protecting the working class from the "greedy and evil capitalist". Over that period we have experienced massive growth and development. Prior to many of our economic and lifestyle changing improvements in life, the socialists identified and often targeted the following categories for more governmental control: 1) the monitoring and controlling of the technological and scientific worlds for the benefit of the workers: 2) controlling monopolies to protect the people from unfair price increases and business practices; and 3) supervising any areas of development that are too complex to be left to private enterprise.

Before we examine some examples of this government control, it is worth considering the progress that we have successfully accomplished through the free enterprise system mostly without government support. In 1928, candidate Herbert Hoover's presidential campaign slogan was, "A chicken in every pot and a car in every garage." At that time we were about to enter the Great Depression. Since that time, we have survived the Great Depression, lived through World War II and came out victorious, endured the Korean War, Vietnam Conflict, and a variety of conflicts throughout the Middle East. Today our ten year old children are talking and "tweeting" on cell phones, while riding in a car owned and operated by their big brother who parks in the student parking lot at the high school which is often within walking distance from home.

The fear of famine and starvation, a threat 70 years ago, is replaced by obesity, supposedly caused by an overload of fast food, including fried chicken from fast-food establishment, non-sugar free beverages, and a lifestyle that is designed around inactivity. The lifestyles of the middle class and the poor have improved measurably, despite the protests of angry people who are against pollution, who are busy saving the environment, and supporting many other social causes. They have abandoned "the chicken in every pot" for loftier social goals. The "evil rich" have given us technology and science to go to the Moon and their next stop may be Saturn or Mars. Innovations in space science have given us Teflon, microwave ovens for our homemade fast food, and a myriad of other technical advancements, such as the home computer which was unimaginable in the early 70s and is now so miniaturized that it can be implanted in your latest cell phone. Regardless of income, every person in America can live in a home.

Our parents and grandparents lived in shared housing in the 1920s and 30s, an idea unheard of today. Many literally built their first homes in their spare time, without massive government interference, while living in apartments. Almost all children today grow up in houses, condos or apartments. In the 1950s, while in grade school, I mowed a one acre lawn for a dollar. I can not recall the last time I saw a child under the age 18 years of age mow a lawn. Most of them are at the Mall playing video games, texting or watching movies at $10 a pop at the local multi-screen Cineplex. None of these things existed when the call for the inevitability of planning was made. We went from silent movies In the 1930s to 10-15 screen multiplex theaters. We arrived in the 21st Century with a higher standard of living than any nation on earth even though some were still poor and downtrodden, many of those because of poor choices. With that said, let's review the benefits of "inevitability" on the improvement of our living conditions over the last 50 years.

It has been professed by the Socialists that science and technology are areas that should be nationalized for the benefit of the workers. This issue is particularly confusing since during the Industrial Revolution, labor saving devices were invented and implemented to reduce the need for labor. These advances obviously displaced workers and provided many repetitive and very mundane jobs that often lacked individualism or creativity. Adam Smith predicted centuries before that these advancements would indeed lead to the need for greater education and cultural studies to deal with the tedium and boredom created by technological improvements in the area of mass production. In addition to being the first economist, Mr. Smith was clearly a futurist. The planning that resulted in the early industrial period was not by government but by the unions. Karl Marx admitted that he did not want to learn about Capitalism he wanted to eliminate it. Marx was considered a brilliant researcher and studied 2000 years of history, governments, and economic structures but he refused to learn about his nemesis: Adam Smith and concept Capitalism.

The idea of collective bargaining provided a new class of workers who were united by a quasi-free enterprise system. Unions charged dues or fees for membership in return for contract negotiation. In this case, advancements in technology which resulted in labor saving devices became the enemy of the unions because of the loss of membership which drained the union coffers. Eventually, unions became a special interest group that denounced progress. They made it impossible, in many cases, to achieve the benefits of labor saving devices, thus driving up costs.

It was alleged and feared that technological growth would cause monopolies as a result of increasing efficiencies. This efficiency would supposedly reduce the cost of labor due to replacement of workers through automation or produce a new lower class of worker resulting from mechanization. The fear was that the jobs would become boring and tedious, lacking the need for craftsmanship and skilled labor. Karl Marx claimed the purpose of the development of this new technology was a "class war" against the workers. This is a false argument, but it resonated with many workers who refused to reinvent themselves. The steam engine and the gasoline engine provided significant labor savings through the elimination of hand powered boats, and then replaced the horse and carriage. Thomas Edison soon after invented the light bulb, combined it with Benjamin Franklin's electricity, and soon thousands of candle makers were unemployed. If Marx had his way, our children would walk to school, we would have a horse in every garage, hire a worker to shovel out the manure, and we would be shopping for our soft goods and buying candles by the dozen at the government run co-op. Marx still proclaimed that technology, and hence all progress, should be controlled to protect the worker.

Monopolies were also feared by Marx. He believed that cost reductions from lower labor costs gave large businesses an economic advantage forcing small businesses to be eaten up by their greedy competition. Did that happen? Yes, quite frankly it did. Just as in the jungle, the fittest survive. Those that failed to invest in capital improvements often struggled and some disappeared. Those that refused to develop better techniques succumbed to the more creative. Some businesses failed due to the change in demographics as people moved closer to better opportunities in the urban areas that housed the factories. Today we see our inner cities blighted due to changes in markets and locales of business. The government programs designed to support the remainders, living off well intentioned entitlements, become shackles that chain our poor to the most undesirable neighborhoods. Was this caused by the capitalist or the well intentioned but misguided social worker? It is assumed the problem was simply economic. Today we have "paperless" immigrants from Mexico who swim rivers, climb over high fences, and walk through blazing deserts at night just to find work, while many of our unemployed won't take a bus across town for a job. Yet, the capitalist is blamed. Or is the real reason that society cannot run fast enough to keep up with progress?

At the turn of the last century our society was losing its agrarian culture as fewer and fewer farm hands were required to produce our food supply. Monopolies were created. But then new opportunities also evolved. In the west, in Colorado, north to Montana and Wyoming, and south to Arizona, you saw the cattle drives on the silver screen, in old black and white movies, with the cowboys and the cattle rustlers in black hats. Cattle were physically moved from state to state to follow nature's food supply. Warren Monfort had the brainstorm to move the feed, not the cattle. In Greeley, Colorado fences were built, large pens were created, and cattle were no longer moved. The food came to them. The result: Far less expensive cattle prices. The loss of cattle through sickness and disease was reduced. Cowboys were replaced with transportation specialists. Food harvesters were needed to bundle hay. The cowboys were mostly eliminated not by automation, but through ingenuity. The consolidation and mechanization of our food supply reduced the cost of production. Range hands became farm hands. Along with cattle came high volume chicken production and hog farms. The grain and wheat silos were signs of progress. This progress not only reduced the need for labor but reduced the cost of the food supply. The cost of living in America was reduced for the benefit of all. "American exceptionalism" was the reason for our progress.

When Herbert Hoover pledged a "chicken in every pot," it was no ordinary chicken. We needed expensive chickens. During the Great Depression, government was fiddling with the economy, trying to stall a recession before it turned into a depression. One of the causes identified by President Roosevelt as a contributing factor to the depression was the low cost of food. In order to stimulate the economy, food prices were raised and fixed at certain levels. Those levels, not reachable by the unemployed, resulted in millions of chickens, cattle, and hogs being destroyed while many people went hungry. Purveyors were jailed for selling above their cost but below the parity price. The economic theory in the 1930s was that higher prices were good because they increased the gross domestic product (GDP). The evil capitalist was being paid not to produce to keep inventories low, and thereby artificially inflate prices for both the employed and the unemployed. This was our first experience in government controlled "trickle down poverty". One may say "planning" was inevitable. Other are still debating 70 years later whether government aided in increasing the length of the economic depression or shortening the length of its misery. We have a similar debate going on today stirred by "experts" of the Great Depression who are following the model of prolonged recession. There are many that believe the free enterprise system will solve problems more quickly than constant government intervention. What we have noticed is rarely, if ever, does a detailed autopsy of government intervention ever indict government for its interference and impatience in dealing with cyclical economic problems. Those "intellectual eggheads" with the least amount of real experience and practical expertise, but with ideological theories, are the first to rush to solve problems they do not understand. Proponents for smaller government prefer using the free enterprise system where people spend their own money rather than contribute to a large, self-serving government. Free enterprise can move quickly to employ resources for the overall, long term benefit while government interference often causes the exact opposite of its intent.

Another fear of the Socialist was the fear that monopolies would lead to higher prices and lower quality service. The breakup of the AT&T monopoly by the Justice Department caused the AT&T giant to divest itself and breakup into smaller companies in the1970s. The government feared that the famous American and Telephone and Telegraph Company was becoming too big for its' britches. They had to be stopped. This is a perfect example of misguided government creating the exact problem they attempted to forestall, but only quicker. The break up of AT& T by the Justice Department led to higher prices and lower quality of service under a government managed plan that took over ten years to implement. The government usually gets the exact opposite of its intent. This is a classic example of government causing the problem it feared the most. With patience, technology would have alleviated the problem. With the advent of cell phones and increased competition the feared problem would have disappeared based on an all new industry which was barely on the drawing board during the lawsuits that cost the tax payers and the stockholders hundreds of millions of dollars less than 20 years later. Traditional phone companies are becoming today's dinosaurs. At the same time, 40 years later, phone companies are reintegrating despite government warnings because the fear never materialized.

Now, however, the government has diverted its attention to power plants and fossil fuels. We have a government and a political system that cannot sit by idly and allow the status quo to remain undisturbed. If left alone, progress in the economy over time seems to solve most problems. But the government always seems to need a bad boy to whip. It needs an enemy somewhere to make elections more fruitful. Someone once wrote that "war was the result of politics". It can also be said that "politics is the result of war" whether it be foreign or domestic issues can be ginned up for political aggrandizement.

Today we are voyaging into the realm of the unknown with Star Trek intensity in the area of healthcare reform. Massive legislation, most of it passed in the dead of night, has been recently adopted to "improve" healthcare. The fear is that greedy capitalistic insurance companies are controlling the healthcare system causing higher costs and lower quality service. A government bureaucracy is being created to attack an insurance problem that is labeled a healthcare problem. That is like blaming the wagon for the ills of the horse. Marx knew that progress for his agenda, to be successful, required time and patience deriving slowly from evolving changes in the attitudes of the people. Progressivism, the mildly patient tactician of this kind of change, has become impatient and its followers are demanding immediate change "for the good of all people." There are many that assert that the failed policies and management of insurance companies, based on poor regulations and administrative follow up, led to the increased cost of healthcare. The greedy drug companies and other inventors of life-saving technology have been blamed for running up the cost of medicine while the true reason is that the billions invested in scientific progress must be recaptured. The life changing discoveries from penicillin to the creation of artificial limbs, and the discovery of cures for cancer were not products of government. The major "contribution" to medicine on the part of government has been overly targeted regulations and constant monitoring of Medicare under outdated procedures, all the while using archaic systems. Do they provide good services to all? The standards that the government adopts for their own systems are lower than the standards they demand of private enterprise.

We have examined some of the major events in the last century and the progress that has been made which is enormous, but this improvement has been intermittently interrupted by government interference. We see no evidence of technological advancements as a result of government regulation. Actually, just the opposite is true. The best government is the one that builds the roads and dams, provides our basic infrastructure and protects the peace, while standing aside to let the creative juices of an enthusiastic free enterprise system do what it does best: provide solutions through inventiveness and creativity that in the long run aid in the advancement of life. To answer the opening question and challenge to Karl Marx, "Is planning inevitable?" We can only surmise that it is if government legislation insists that it is. Our common goal is to make sure that it never happens.

Chapter 5 Planning and Democracy

"A social system is a code of laws which men observe in order to live together. Such a code must have a basic principle, a starting point, or it cannot be devised. The starting point is the question: Is the power of society limited or unlimited. Individualism answer: The power of society is limited by the inalienable, individual rights of man, Society may make only such laws as do not violate those rights. Collectivism answers: The power of society is unlimited. Society may make any laws it wishes, and force them upon anyone in any manner it wishes." Ayn Rand, Textbook of Americanism.

Hayek opens this section in *The Road to Serfdom* with the following definition, "The common feature of all collectivist systems may be described, in a phrase ever dear to socialists of all schools, as the deliberate organization of the labors of society for a definite social goal." He goes on to say that society lacks the "conscious" or conviction to meet social responsibilities and tends to deal with lesser issues. He states this is the argument of the Socialist.

In America, our Congress has many declared Socialists. Under our republic system of government we have elected representatives with differing beliefs. Those elected officials charge off to Washington not merely to deal with the current problems of the day, but to develop systems they believe are in the best interests of their constituents. From afar, it does not appear that the ideas molded and installed are always in the best interest of "all the people" but often there is a targeted class of people who do not necessarily fit into mainstream society. Many of these people are the ones that government appears to be serving, at the expense of others.

Often it appears that Socialistic solutions are adopted in exchange for social reintegration and the basic argument comes down to planning versus democracy. It is easy to assert that many solutions appear to be based on political goals rather than strictly benevolent goals. A misdiagnosis of a societal problems can automatically be responded to by the far Left as a money issue based on hoards of compassionates who respond to needy people. If and when such problems are determined to require solutions, the different approaches, ends versus means, are developed based on the goals of the program. Those on the Right tend to extol the virtues of self reliance. In contrast, the left seems to believe that making the unfortunates accountable is cruel and unusual punishment. Perhaps the difference in opinion is purely definitional. If the problem is ill defined, then the answers may result in solutions that tend to go forward into perpetuity ever increasing over time due to their failure to meet any minimum standards to accurately address the real problems. Do we ever go back and correct the mistakes of the past? There is no conscious evidence of that ever taking place. Congressionally designed money pits run eternal.

The War on Poverty was declared in January 24, 1964 by President Lyndon Johnson in his State of the Union Address. This war has gone on for almost five decades with no end in sight. Other wars are usually won or lost in a decade or less. If we continue to extend the war rather than attempt to win it, our only weapon is tax dollars that we are borrowing from other nations. As the victims and casualties of this war increase, our revenue base decreases and is diverted taking away long term ammunition used in an unwinnable war. The vast sums in this effort could and should be available for more productive purposes to address the problem. By not dealing with the issues of self reliance, we continually rob a portion of society who most dearly needs it. If money were purely the solution would it not be fair to assume that the war should be over by now? Yet, the battle ground continues to expand. Once again, it is time to mention that government programs rarely, if ever, are reviewed to determine if they have met their original objectives. The failure of our programs to meet their intended purposes leads to the need for even more untargeted socialized programs. After a barrage of propaganda, they are usually adopted through the democratic process. They are designed through a variation of the "planning process".

Our American charter "To promote Life, Liberty and the Pursuit of Happiness" is based on the principles of entitlement for everyone to be able to pursue these goals. These are not just arbitrary, lofty goals. They form the character of our nation. What comes into play is when certain groups come up short for one or more of those paradigms. The response is always to design programs to meet "social goals" for these special groups. These are often justified based on "our common purpose" or the "common good" and best of all, finally, by invoking the Constitution. Any program that can not stand on its own merits generally falls under the loosely interpreted "General Welfare" clause. There are those who believe, particularly the Socialists, that happiness is created through the elimination of a particular set of problems. And there are others who believe that happiness is attained in spite of a problem or a particular set of circumstances. Once again we can look to Hayek to highlight and enunciate the situation.

"The welfare and the happiness of millions cannot be measured on a single scale of less and more. The welfare of a people, like the happiness of a man, depends on a great many things that can be provided in an infinite variety of combinations. It cannot be adequately expressed as a single need, but only as a hierarchy of ends, a comprehensive scale of values in which every need of every person is given its place. To direct all our activities according to a single plan presupposes that every one of our needs is given its rank in an order of values which must be complete enough to make it possible to decide among the different courses which the planner has to choose. It presupposes the existence of a complete ethical code in which all the different human values are allotted their due place." *The Road to Serfdom, pg 101.*

Hayek not only stated the aim, but the problem and its solution. There are too many human variables, limitations, and aspirations, in society to arrive at government planned solutions to every situation that could lead to unhappiness. Today, when a child loses a soccer game, the solution is to stop keeping score. Instead, the loss should be a call for more training, knowledge, and skill development rather than tearing down the scoreboard. There is a pervasive attitude that it is society's responsibility to cure all ills. Assuming that all children will be happy if they don't lose a soccer game, we ignore those who gain a sense of accomplishment through winning, a key factor in the development of self esteem. Instead, individual defeat is a call to set up rules to deny eleven winners thereby reducing twenty two children to a system of mediocrity. This is the Socialist's planning system for fairness. What we forget is that character is not often developed through winning, but through dealing with adversity and overcoming challenges. The politically correct coddling by the tearing down of the scoreboards in life denies many of the opportunity to develop character. In this case, social meddling creates social injustice just by the very act of attempting equality in a system that evolves around winning and losing. When every child receives s trophy for attendance rather than the successful display of ability, we have reprioritized social skills making attendance more important that outcome. When we diminish the value of our goals we also diminish the value of our society.

Hayek came to America and shared his vast experiences that he learned in Europe. He spent his later life in America studying and researching. During that time period, Abraham Maslow, a New York born psychologist, was developing his humanistic theory on self actualization based on what he called the "Hierarchy of Needs". There is no evidence that Hayek and Maslow ever crossed paths, but it would have been interesting to see the interrelationship between the Austrian refugee economist and the Jewish-American born psychologist. Maslow's theory asserts that there is a hierarchy of five categories of human needs starting with the basic "Physiological Needs": food, water, and other subsistence needs, the next level is "Safety and Security Needs", which includes housing and protection, then we move up to "Love and Belonging", followed by "Self Esteem" issues, and ultimately "Self Actualization" of the individual. Maslow believed, through his life's work, that these were common needs for all people to feel fulfilled. The Socialist may not deny his theory, but only approaches happiness through the first two levels of the hierarchy. Maslow asserts that mere life does not result in happiness. We have a higher purpose. Man must ascend to that higher level. Those aspirations are not a goal of any social programs. It is probably an unknown and unquantifiable hope that can not be addressed through the planning process because it is based on individualism. Happiness is not gained from reducing toil and the complexities of everyday life and the elimination of financial responsibility as claimed by Karl Marx. According to Maslow, people must rise up through a higher level of self esteem leading to the satisfaction of attempting and sometimes achieving higher goals. When we provide for the basic needs we have not even gone half way to creating happiness. If it were true that satisfying man's basic needs resulted in happiness then all prisoners would be happy. It was never government's responsibility to create happiness, but rather to protect the right of all with liberty to pursue happiness. Today we have a created a system of long term subsistence for almost 50% of our citizens and we have families who have been trapped in our systems that do nothing other than perpetuate the problems they deplore.

Ayn Rand's remarks in the header comments of this chapter clearly highlight the differences between individualism and collectivism and the beliefs that accompany the rights of the individual versus the powers of government. The democratic process in America is the method we have adopted to level the power of government. Again, it is "We the People" not "We the Government." The goal of our Founders was to retain the idea of individualism rather than collectivism. Collectivism stamps out a cookie cutter ginger bread man approach to governing. Individualism believes in the uniqueness of each man, rather than we all be cut from the same clothe. Individualism rests in the freedom to do anything that is not prohibited by law. Democracy is the arbiter between those two schools of thought. A democratic-republic has great limitations. Once the ballot lever is pulled the voter has little influence to direct the activities of their elected officials. Each of our U.S. elected congressional representatives has a constituency base of approximately 700,000 people. They are old and young, and multi-racial, of varying economic classes, diverse in every demographic category. It is often hard to meet the needs of all the people. Yet, is it fair to punish certain groups to benefit others? The purpose should be to protect the rights of all people not to choose some over and above others.

There are many who believe that the United States Constitution is a weary old document that no longer meets the needs of the people. There are others who feel that the original parchment meets the needs of the people but, Congress does not adequately accomplish our goals due to their self aggrandizing intentions that ignore the Constitution Many would like to see stronger constraints on government based on its original design. The guilty one on both sides of this argument is the Supreme Court which referees the scope of activities based on their role in the checks and balances system of governing. There are those who feel that the Court is too liberal in its interpretation of the Constitution. Others believe it is too restrictive. If that be the case, then maybe it is "just right."

What are the limitations in governing under a democracy? An often heard misconception is that The United States is a democracy. We are not a democracy. We operate under a brilliantly designed representative form of government whereby our representatives are elected under the "democratic process." Our system of individual state constitutions was craftily united under the United States Constitutions deferring specific powers to the Congress under Article 1 of the Constitution and retaining all rights not specifically conferred to the Federal government. The specific importance of this differentiation has been overlooked since the adoption of the 17th Amendment which gradually allowed for the transferring of more power to the Federal government.

Until 1913 the US Constitution specified "that state legislatures would elect U.S senators. Article 1 Section 3 reads: The Senate of the United States shall be composed of two Senators from each State, chosen by the Legislature thereof, for six Years: and each Senator shall have one vote."

In giving the elective power to the states, the framers of the Constitution hoped to protect state independence. Our fore fathers were suspicious of majority rule and sought to restrain what they regarded as the potentially destructive forces of democracy. While providing for direct election of the House of Representatives, they countered this expression of the people's will by allowing legislatures to select members of the U S Senate. When the electoral components of state elected representatives, were combined with the direct elections of US Representatives, and the representative elections of U S Senators, the people were offered the greatest form of a representative style of government. This provided the greatest amount of protection to the people. During the late nineteenth century, the political mood was changing and the 17th Amendment was ratified in 1913 which resulted in the direct election of Senators. This innocent change resulted in the shifting of power from the States to the Federal electorate transferring accountability from the States. What resulted from this change was the greatest expansion of government in the history of the United States. In hindsight, the Founding Fathers, with their vast amount of historical wisdom, knew exactly what they were doing. Aristotle warned us that the most dangerous form of government was a "pure democracy." The 17th Amendment moved us one step closer to his warning.

Karl Mannheim, the Hungarian born sociologist who lived in Germany during the 1920s, was exiled to Great Britain due to his work and studies that threatened the Marxists. His observations of society in relation to government action make his remarks noteworthy. While the parliamentary government of Great Britain varies from our Constitutional system in America, Mannheim's point is important in understanding regulatory power in regulating under a democracy. "The only way in which a planned society differs from that of the nineteenth century is that more and more spheres of social life, and ultimately each and all of them, are subjected to state control. But if a few controls can be held in check by parliamentary sovereignty, so can many…In a democratic state, sovereignty can be boundlessly strengthened by *plenary powers* without renouncing democratic control." *Man and Society in an Age of Reconstruction.* Under United States constitutional law, plenary powers are granted usually to boards, committees, and regulatory agencies, with the power of Congress, under the Commerce Clause of Article I, Section 8, and Clause 3. These bodies are empowered by Congress under this section with the ability to develop rules, regulations, taxing authority, and the methods of penalty for violations with the same authority as Congress who gives this authority. This is an assignment of unlimited power which should not be done capriciously. As we move on we will see how this power is being used today in many areas of government.

The implementation of Healthcare Reform and the over 150 associated departments created by Congress place the total control of our healthcare under the Secretary of Health and Human Services who has been awarded the sole plenary powers to make all final decisions on healthcare. This makes the Secretary one of the most powerful individuals in the United States Government with the authority to control every aspect of health care representing over one sixth of the US Economy. The Secretary, and the many boards and committees created to control the department, have all been given plenary powers at various levels. There are many states who have challenged the Constitutionality of the unlimited authority of Congress to even pass such legislation. Two courts have ruled against the Affordable Healthcare Act. In the meantime, the Secretary, under a phased-in implementation plan, holds the purse strings and the regulatory control of every aspect of healthcare dipping into a $105 billion budget. The United States government, with the stroke of a pen, switched their role when they became the primary purveyor of healthcare services when they were formerly its largest customer.

When we consider our former argument regarding the "inevitability of planning", in this case we see it is more than inevitable, it is said to be essential through dictatorial-like power for the implementation and development of our new healthcare system. Rather than approach the reformation of our healthcare systems with a gradual conversion to the single largest provider of government services, we are being overwhelmed by a total conversion of every aspect of healthcare. This massive change, if improperly implemented and released, could possibly stall every aspect of government healthcare resulting in disastrous results for our citizens.

Many still doubt that the program will be able to even meet its minimum goals. This negativism is based on experience gained over the last fifty years. Additionally, the massive regulations required to implement such a plan were born under massive legislation. It is estimated that the Healthcare Reform Program will require hundreds of thousands of pages of rules and regulations: the details of which are yet to be worked out. The enforcement of those regulations will be made possible by the plenary power that vests their unchallengeable power in each person appointed. These appointees will make the rules and determination the eligibility of individuals for a variety of programs, the specific methods and types of services, design payment vehicles and methods, and provide for the quality control of services. It will also include a new automated, national system to relay and monitor patient data.

At this time, the IRS has not been able to fully implement their nationwide centrally controlled system. The FAA's new automated system, designed to provide more protection in the air, is still not fully operational around the country. What is the likelihood that the same government will be able to develop and maintain an on-line data input system for the health records of 300 million people? Eventually, if the healthcare reforms survive the Supreme Court, a little less than 200 people will have the authority to make healthcare decisions instead of the decentralized methods composed of tens of thousands of insurance and service providers under the current free enterprise system. It is estimated that hundreds of thousands of additional government employees will be required to monitor and control the healthcare economy. Any savings attributed to the consolidation and centralized control of healthcare will be transferred to a government bureaucracy which is already unable to pay its bills. The promise to turn the "healthcare cost curve downward" has already been erased by further Congressional Budget Office analysis. If the more accurate cost figures were available prior to the congressional votes maybe the situation would be different today? Or was all this obvious to a powerful core of far-Left Socialists who ignored the costs in their lust for power and control over American healthcare? Each person can decide for themselves. Those Democrats who are up for re-election in the next cycle are hinting at their remorse for voting for the healthcare reforms. This may be merely political jockeying or it may be guilt and fear of reprisal from their enraged electorate in 2012.

The coming election cycles in the next few years will be a testament to the opinions of the voters who have the ability to remove or reinstall their congressional leaders. The Congressional elections of November 2010 were a referendum on healthcare and out of control spending. The Republicans made significant gains in the House. Many begrudgingly gave credit to the Tea Party Movement for the successes. Almost a year later the Left is continuing to blame the Tea Party Movement for the ruination of America. It has been reported that some of the elected officials who voted for the healthcare overhaul regret it today. As our elected officials come up for reelection over the next couple of years, the issue of healthcare will continually be a topic as we gradually witness the formidable impact of healthcare reform. The subject of healthcare reform provides us with a perfect example of excessive government planning under a democracy as it relates to a single issue. It is the largest single issue under the governments control with the exception of Social Security Retirements Programs. The democratic process was used to surrender our democratic process. The voices of the majority were not heard. In essence, we were told that government knows what is best, not the people.

At a time when we are feeling insecure about our medical futures, Great Britain and other European nations are analyzing their options regarding a failed socialized healthcare system. Daniel Hannan, a Member of the European Parliament, warned emphatically in his book, *The New Road to Serfdom, on page 85* when he was asked on Fox News in August of 2009 if he would recommend the British health-care model. He replied, "If you look at the international comparisons, Britain fares badly. Our waiting times are longer than in the Western nations, and our survival rates are lower. Britain is pretty much the last place in the industrialized world where you'd want to be diagnosed with cancer, stroke, or heart disease." When I recently asked a visiting British subject about the quality of healthcare in England, he retorted, "It's great, if you have a suitcase full of Euros." He said the Black Market healthcare in Europe parallels the Black Markets of Russia under its Communist regime where the wealthy have better access than the average citizen. It might be time to pull that old suitcase out from under the bed and fill it full of rainy day healthcare cash.

This discussion is not merely an argument for capitalism over socialism. The capitalistic forces will remain in play as long as we let them. The real threat is the amount of government regulation that intercedes in the product development and delivery of services under a heavily regulated "planned" program. We have discovered that the "Rule of Law" can be transferred to non-elected officials using plenary powers, with no power of recall. Those appointed have the ultimate authority to control and maintain a system with irreversible power. The choice of Socialism over Capitalism is simple: do you want to relinquish your power of choice to the power of the government?

Chapter 6   Planning and the Rule of Law

"True law is right reason in agreement with nature: it is of universal application, unchanging and everlasting: it summons to duty by its commands, and averts from wrongdoing by its prohibitions...It is a sin to try to alter this law, nor is it allowable to repeal any part of it, and it is impossible to abolish it entirely. We cannot be freed from its obligation by senate or people, and we need not look outside ourselves for an expounder or interpreter of it. And there will not be different law in Rome and in Athens, or different law now and in the future, our one eternal and unchangeable law will be valid for all nations and all times, and there will be one master and ruler, that is God, over us all, for he is the author of this law..."   Cicero defines Natural Law. (106 BC-43 BC) (Great Political Thinkers p.133)

Topics such as the law and its interpretations can be very dull reading. We admit beforehand that this chapter could bore you and put you to sleep. However, it touches on a vital subject: the Rule of Law versus Case Law, the case by case, touchy-feely interpretation of the Law used by today's Progressives. If you want to understand what is going on in America today, you need to plow through this chapter. What is at stake is the very essence of what makes America great—her adherence to the Rule of Law. So good luck, get a cup of strong coffee, and read on. You will be rewarded with information crucial to understand today's struggle for the control of America.

According to Hayek, nothing distinguishes more clearly the conditions in a free country from those in a country under an arbitrary government than the observance in the former of the great principle known as the Rule of Law. Stripped of all technicalities, this means that government in all its actions is bound by rules fixed and announced beforehand –the rule of law which make it possible to foresee with fair certainty how the authority will use its coercive powers in a given circumstances and to plan one's individual affairs on the basis of this knowledge. *A.V Dicey, in Introduction to the Study of the Law of the Constitution. 1915.*

The rule of law is the codified rules of the game that allow people to know in advance what they can do and what they can not do. This provides people with the guidance to know what is acceptable or legal versus those things that violate the people or the State. The parameters of law provide the context of what can and cannot be done in many areas that are regulated beyond the level of the "thou shall nots". In general, those things that are not specifically prohibited are in turn legal until someone decides that someone or something provides an unfair advantage or discovers another method to corrupt the system. They then file a lawsuit and, if they win, create another law or set of laws. Those noted as prohibited provide the exclusions to activity. All laws are based on rights. Early law was based on Natural Rights and our system of laws was handed down from England. Our nation was not developed with a "Rule Book" but something close to it since we started with the works of Sir William Blackstone.

Blackstone published the first comprehensive record of the laws of England in a four volume set called *Commentaries on the Laws of England* in 1765. This was the key document for the basis of law in the United States until our own system was developed based on case law. Blackstone was cited in law cases before judges in America as the law of the land although its basis was rooted in English common law and its principles. Students studying law in the late 1700s did not attend formal schools of law but read Blackstone and apprenticed under practicing lawyers. The length of study ranged from under a year to three or four years depending upon the amount of time spent studying Blackstone and the time assisting with cases with their legal sponsor.

The Rule of Law versus the system of law used to enforce "planning" is a departure from our normal system of jurisprudence. Hayek contrasts the two. The rule of law principles leaves the individual free to act, work, and enter any endeavor not deemed illegal, while the planned society is heavily regulated by detailed rules and regulations constantly requiring arbitrary decisions to deal with specific cases not documented in manuals that cite thousands of rules and regulations. It can be assumed under this system of law that precedence does not affect the outcome of the next similar decision, hence, it becomes arbitrary with "on the spot" decision making to meet the needs of individual situations. The area most significantly impacted by regulatory law is in the area of business and commerce. The business regulations of today's government, in its ever expanding role, are expansive, far reaching laws and rules that supposedly serve the best interests of the people. Our regulations cover Interstate Commerce, International Trade, the Food and Drug Administration, Transportation and thousands of environmental regulations which have become the umbrella of rules over everything we do. Just these areas require hundreds of thousands of pages of rules and regulations.

The granddaddy of them all is the Internal Revenue Service's set of regulations which agonizes over 70,000 pages and is growing as a result of the healthcare takeover. Any government departments dealing directly with the citizenry rely heavily on regulations. With all these regulations many still have difficulty getting the proper answers to questions. If you have ever had the opportunity to contact the Internal Revenue Service, the Social Security

Administration, or Medicare or any other large administrative bureaucracy for advice, you may have been told that the administrators are not liable for the information they provide. That means that rather than provide accurate information on your situation based on rules and regulations, your advice may be arbitrary based on the best knowledge or interpretation of the service person on the phone at the time. If you call more than once with the same question, you may receive contradictory information from another agent. Unfortunately, you are ultimately responsible for your actions, although you may base your actions on information you have received from the government.

It is plain to see, our country's legal system is a combination of individual laws on one hand and rules and regulations for "planning" or the administration of the various industry groups and government programs on the other. Industry regulations include anti-trust legislation, Security and Exchange laws, and Food and Drug Administration to name only a few. Social programs for Housing, Social Security and other programs for the aging, and a variety of social programs to help the lower income groups also require massive legislation. Regulations are required for aiding and controlling a variety of special groups of people whether it be for business or for individuals. These areas add several hundred thousand pages of rules and regulations. It is interesting to note that Hayek spends a significant amount of time referring to the law and its role in both areas. He was a student of Ludwig von Mises, the noted sociologist whose encyclopedic anthology *Socialism, An Economic and Sociological Analysis,* never addressed the topic of law. Hayek not only included the law in his book *The Road to Serfdom* but then went on to dedicate eight chapters to the subject of laws in *The Constitution of Liberty* in 1960. When operating in a democracy under a representative style of government, as opposed to a dictatorship, laws are the foundation for any fundamental change in our American culture. It is the law that advances the agenda of change. This often results in response to events and in many cases provide a prelude to our "coming attractions."

The significance of the two approaches to law, the rule of law and "planning" are paramount to the particular system of economics and the activities permitted. When we think of Socialism, we assume that it is an all or nothing proposition. A nation can have Socialist programs within a free economy. The programs are isolated outside of the free enterprise system and are funded through a variety of taxing programs, either directly or indirectly. These amalgamations do not change the nature of the law in total but are designed through legislation, which is law, to supplement the development, implementation, and regulation of specific programs or activities.

It is easy to see the complexity of planning versus the free market system. In summarizing the significant differences between the two styles of law it becomes apparent the higher level of complexity involved in legislative planning. The laws must be specifically targeted, but the powers must be broad to make the necessary adjustments and modifications to apply the law to a large and often diverse population.

Under the rule of law, the free market system government confines itself to determine conditions to use resources, both public and private, leaving the choice up to individuals to determine their ultimate purpose. Rules are known in advance which do not divert the aim and purpose of outcome to meet the needs of designated recipients: the capitalist, the entrepreneur, and the stockholders. The result in the outcomes based on the effectiveness of the use of resources is always a change in capital, which is either reinvested or distributed. In the event of a loss, the loss is shared based on the ownership hierarchy in a specific order of priority. It is normally assumed that the "greedy capitalist" always makes a profit. Often that is not the case. The buggy whip factories are gone, along with the vast numbers of chimney sweeps. The large maker of main frame computers, the "evil and rich" IBM, the first name in computers in the 1960s and 70s, is phasing out of the computer business to concentrate on the service business and is now becoming a large software consultancy rather than a large computer maker. Those areas that we have been quick to regulate tend to go through their own life cycles shorter than the restrictive lives being regulated.

Can it be possible that the next invention to preserve human dignity or save a life is thwarted by government regulation to protect the few from the many, the small from the large, the slower from the quicker or some other oddity? Today, in the San Joaquin Valley in California we are protecting a purposeless fish by withholding water in an aqueduct designed as a water supply for agricultural irrigation. Tens of thousands are unemployed as a result of our misguided Environmental Protection Agency regulations, not to mention the vast amounts of harvests lost that would increase our level of exports. As a result of over regulation, we are importing rather than exporting our crops. "Social justice" as the Socialists use it is at war with true justice for that social group. Unfortunately, the social justice is for a fish which supersedes the needs of humanity. The farms workers of the San Joaquin Valley are the victims along with the communities they live in. The law here has perverse results that seem immoral.

The law, whether it be under Socialism or the "Common Good" clause of the Constitution, gives government massive powers through its expanded definition to direct and control private resources. Under Socialism the government directs the use of the means of both public and private production to achieve specific ends or purposes. In referencing private resources, land may be confiscated or appropriated by some means. In Germany in the early 1900s landowners were allowed to retain ownership of their private property. Unfortunately, they were not able to retain the income or use of the property. Under the rule of law, land carries with it by definition, a "bundle of rights". While the German government did not confiscate the property they confiscated all the rights, thus rendering the property valueless.

Our government today has many unchecked options to confiscate private property. The most notable method is Eminent Domain whereby private property may be transferred to the state for a higher and better use for the common good; i.e. "for the people". This method was normally used in the past to create major highways and public works projects. In some cases, property has been appropriated from an individual and resold to another private individual or large corporation for a higher and better use. This is legal confiscation in the name of this ostensibly higher and better use, which was merely to expand the tax base. Recently, a golf course country club in New York was taken by Eminent Domain to resell to a developer to build condos. During the building boom of the early 2000s many municipalities appropriated property taking it off the tax rolls only to find that there were no longer buyers for the property. In their infinite wisdom, the municipality became a "real estate flipper" on behalf of the tax payers. In many situations those taxpayers are de facto landlords of worthless property that used to be supported by the previous private owners. Not only did they lose revenue, they now have to carry the burden of maintaining the property through additional taxation. Case law has no problem with this coercive power. The law only looks at the right to acquire property for government benefit, not the creditability or worthiness of the reason. When we look at Socialism, we discover that government already has massive powers to acquire assets from private citizens with little or no justification of purpose. Purpose is irrelevant under the case law system.

We have examined some of the aspects of the law that effect everyday decisions. Next we will look at the complexity of planning in a couple of common scenarios. When we extrapolate this complexity in common areas we see the magnitude of the planning progress and its inevitable failure to meet any standards of efficiency in our daily lives. We must remember that efficiency is not the main goal under a Socialistic style of government. Redistribution of wealth and their interpretation of social justice trump economic efficiency.

Under normal circumstances, collectivism and the act of planning combine the resources: labor, public capital, and other resources to attain a specific goal or end. Let's look at food production for the state, i.e. the people. This process is dictated by specific rules and regulations concerning the use and application of the resources to meet a stated goal. The idea of planning is normally a centrally controlled activity. The process determines which resources to use, often the cost of those resources, the labor to be used, the equipment requirements, and the ultimate distribution of the products or services. Included is the forecast or budget for the production of goods and the estimated production levels required to meet the needs of the end users. In the area of agriculture these activities are normally borne by individual farmers or corporate enterprises on an incremental and local level based on a variety of integrated analysis. The geographic diversity of similar crops in different regions requires detailed localized analysis of the various factors of production in relation to market projections. Some of the factors of production are variables as a result of climate, soil content, and changing weather patterns. Local farmers are reactionary to localized conditions. Their primary intent is to maximize production by taking into account all the variables and respond to local conditions year over year.

Imagine for a minute, the complexity of determining the resource requirements, production levels, and distribution methods for produce, livestock, and granary products like wheat, corn, barley and soy. To compound the problem these products have both retail consumer destinations and a wholesale or bulk destination as raw materials or additives to other consumer products. The net result is differing distribution systems normally managed at the producer or co-op level based on specific market conditions. At the same time, there are heavy regulations to cover both the agricultural and food industry requirements. In addition to regulations, there are subsidy programs for farmers on what not to grow and other program to instruct what to grow for the same products. Corn is a unique product because it is regulated by the Department of Agriculture and the Department of Energy. Corn, a component of ethanol gasoline, has many regulations depending upon whether it is a food source or an energy source with added incentives to promote the production for alternative energy thereby increasing its cost as a food supply.

It appears impossible for local bureaucrats to manage farm production on a regional basis or even at the local level. Those closest to the farm are the most accountable for the results because it is their money, their families, and their lives. For the bureaucrat and planner, it is just a job. This is the fate of the US farming industry today. Ironically, China recently announced that it is removing many of their regulations for remote rural farmers. Cuba is also in a transition from exclusive government control to privatization. What they have discovered, after many years of effort, is that they cannot manage the production of agriculture. Both the largest country in the world and one of the smallest countries in the world have both arrived at the same conclusion: they cannot manage agriculture on a regional basis. They seem to be able to manage all of the key components of agriculture except one: the weather.

Rather than look any further at the complexities of this process from seed to consumer, and the necessary laws to govern the process of food production, let's examine a local process that most of us are more familiar with to highlight the difficulty within our own communities.

Let's look at the complexity of operating a school bus network which should be far less complicated than operating a farm. In most communities, with the exception of some urban areas which utilize public transportation, student transportation is a very difficult process to manage. The goal is simple-- to get students to and from school in an effective and safe manner while trying to minimize the cost to the school district. School buses, to achieve maximum efficiency, may be used to service more than one school resulting in staggered schedules with different beginning and ending times. Routes are developed based on the projected population of a particular school and a particular route. Due to demographic population shifts, the addition and termination of some routes and buses for some schools makes the scheduling of school buses a never ending process. The numbers of students for a particular bus may shift plus or minus 5-7% or more resulting in under utilization which is tolerable or overcrowding which is a violation of state laws.

Bus routes are based on projected ridership numbers affected by pick up and drop off points in the community for a specific route. It normally takes 2-3 weeks of history to smooth out a route. Other contributing factors are students who may be dropped off at school in the morning and take the bus home in the afternoon or vice versa. Pickup times are elastic or adjustable for the first route for a bus in the morning, but relatively static for the 2nd route. In the case of dozens of buses, and hundreds in some communities, this is a massive logistical problem. As one can see, managing a school transportation system has a variety of variables at the local level. GPS systems have been added to many school buses. It allows the parents to track their child's bus along its route to minimize the amount of time waiting at the bus stop to pick up their children. This is in response to the bus scheduler's inability to predict drop off times with reasonable accuracy. These multi-million dollar tracking systems were sold to school systems and the public as child protection systems to locate hijacked buses. Since the movie Dirty Harry in the late 1960s I cannot recall a school bus full of children being hijacked.

When we consider the magnitude of planning involved in a routine, repetitive process, guessing right is nothing short of a miracle. When we think about the centralized planning requirements for key factors of services in our total economy we can not rely on wholesale miracles. As the government takes on the role of expanding Socialism in our society it takes on more power and control of our lives. Whether it is school buses, growing peaches and getting them to market, or establishing healthcare clinics, and reimbursement systems, Socialism requires massive regulation and a systematized method of bureaucratic control. This control is based on laws, laws that direct affect our lives.

The real purpose of the Law is to make the system work by minimizing arbitrary judgment calls. We need laws that provide the flexibility for decision making, yet provide the controls to make the system consistent from community to community. Those are the arbitrary decisions warned of by Hayek. When we consider the fact that Socialism was installed in most European countries, we have to remember that many countries in Europe are far smaller than the State of Texas. The vastness of America with her fifty States requires States rights to prevail under our federalized system. Our government structure was designed to be bottom up starting with the states, and it should provide a system that guarantees equal protection under the law. Under the rule of law, all people must be treated fairly and in a consistent manner. However, and ever more tragically, there are those who believe it can only be done through massive regulation and intense government control. For example, under current government regulations when obtaining a loan from a bank, we fill out and sign lengthy regulatory loan documents that guarantee we will not be discriminated against, but we don't ever read them. We walk through crosswalks carved out for wheel chairs that we never see. Our elevators and the drive-up windows are clearly marked with Braille for people who cannot find the elevator without assistance or drive to the bank, much less find the drive through lane. We have laws to protect every class, and cover these situations in minute detail, yet without any structure two people who might be completely unprepared can marry and have children without ever doing anything more than get a license and visit a judge.

Too many today even skip those steps altogether. Yet, we let them have unlicensed children but they can not drive an unlicensed vehicle. Many areas appear overregulated while others go unchecked. Apparently it all depends on what an advocacy group demands. Frequently, we notice that while one law provides one person access, it denies the freedom of another. That doesn't seem to matter to the zealots in an advocacy group.

The loans that led to the major real estate boom and bust resulting in millions of foreclosures required putting down the color of our skin, but a credit check, income verification, and many of the things required to get a credit card with a $500 Limit were suspended to promote homeownership. While we were guaranteeing equal rights we forgot about equal protection for the banks and investors that put up the money for marginal loans for people that often didn't even have adequate identification. The result was massive regulation of Wall Street firms that sold unregistered securities, securities backed up by undocumented mortgage notes. Congress, the guilty accomplices to the financial crisis, washed their hands of the blood of the largest economic disaster the world has known and their members walked away clean. The Dodd- Frank Financial Reform Bill which was designed to control the problem will result in tens of thousands of pages of new regulations to control the financial institutions that were blamed for the problem. At a recent Congressional Financial Oversight Committee meeting the people responsible for writing the regulations admitted it will take 7-10 years to write the regulations to satisfy the requirements of the bill. On July 29,2011 Congressman Barney Frank, the co-author of the bill, stated to Bret Baier of Fox News, that the rules would not be enforced until the rules are written. As we move farther away from our founding principles, our system of laws becomes far more complicated in a world of growing complexity. When we consider that those who are elected to govern are politicians and the specialty many of them bring to the table is their ability to get elected, not necessarily to govern. Sadly, most of them have never run a business and have no practical sense of how things work in the real world. After all this, it becomes apparent that the skills for planning have to be far more fine tuned than the skills required for governing.

Planning under collectivism has little to do with fairness and equality and are not issues that have a high priority. Socialism calls for equality in the distribution of wealth irrespective of contribution. Socialism is the leveler that requires different classes to receive different distributions. The goal is to equalize all people. Hence, the role of planning includes determining winners and losers based on economic outcome. Who are these winners and losers? Are there special classes or categories of winners and losers? Hayek's discussion appears to focus on Europe whose experience varies based on each country. He seems to tip toe about Germany where he talks about certain classes who are nationally discriminated against, obviously the Jews. The examples drawn indicate that class struggles and workers versus capitalists and different cultural groups have received different treatment based on their strata in the realm of Socialism. Thus, on the specific orders, lesser developed minorities can be elevated through arbitrary distribution, while other societies are punished or "equalized". This is a polite way of saying "reduced". Socialism in its implementation can be used as an equalizer over time, but there is no long term record of success of the process or the methods required. The methodology assumes that certain classes have had excess advantages over other classes over time.

Since Socialism is an economic concept that is not based on freedom, then governments must arrive at Socialism from an ideological perspective. The decision to adopt Socialist programs is not random or arbitrary. It is not a conscious choice between alternatives. It is the only choice for many. Today it appears to be a pervasive thought held by certain groups. When those groups attain power more programs are developed and presented to redistribute wealth. The government and its followers decide who has "too much". The rule of law under the current system of government appears to be overlaid by comprehensive programs. Those programs are sold to the populous with the intent to solve certain or specific economic shortfalls in certain classes of people or for the common good. The plenary powers we discussed before become the cornerstone of unstoppable power within the government.

The rule of law is then superseded by the veil of satisfying the general welfare. With the passage of any law that contains plenary authority the people will inevitably suffer the loss of freedom from the arbitrary administration of justice. It is no longer justice for all, but social justice for some. What kind of government must we have to achieve those goals? The answer is: Totalitarianism.

Chapter 7   Economic Control and Totalitarianism

"The Control of the production of wealth is the control of human life itself." Hilaire Belloc

"Most planners who have seriously considered the practical aspects of their task have little doubt that a directed economy must be run on more or less dictatorial lines. That the complex system of interrelated activities, if it is to be consciously directed at all, must be directed by a single staff of experts, and that ultimate responsibility and power must rest in the hands of a commander-in-chief whose actions must not be fettered by democratic procedure, is too obvious a consequence of underlying ideas of central planning not to command fairly general assent." *The Road to Serfdom, Hayek*

Up to this point, we have dealt with some of the goals and aims of Socialism. Its aspirations are seated in beliefs that some people have too much of the world's goods and others have too little. To make life fair, a mechanism must be in place to assure equality of outcome for all. The reason is presumed to be that the inequality is the result of some systematic flaw in national character that allows some to far exceed others in opportunity and gain, while holding down others to achieve that gain. There seems to be a wholesale belief on the Left that blames a conspiratorial plot of exploitation of the working class. The salesmanship of Marx superbly conveyed the idea that Capitalism and its proponents are solely responsible for the inequities of life and there is only one ultimate authority that can right those wrongs. That authority is an all-reaching, dictatorial style of government composed of the working class who have been exploited and thus entitled to all future reparations. Often the change from a free-style economy to a government controlled society is a gradual and slow process. The management of change usually accompanies a financial crisis where excessive power forces the change in government. The financial revolution of Socialist programs is usually accompanied by a series of carefully engineered steps turning over using increased control and influence of the government. This is followed by heavy regulation and an increasingly progressive tax system. The support is provided by those more fortunate beneficiaries who are identified as victims of the evil capitalistic group.

Class struggle is the keystone of this revolution and is fought with ideology rather than guns, and its prisoners are those who have previously succeeded in their abilities and have accumulated unwarranted success. Those societal "captives" are the ones who ultimately finance the revolution for the downtrodden and underachievers. In the process, Totalitarianism is the prince of darkness that makes the transformation possible. Oddly, those societies around the world that have never developed have traditionally been raised under Totalitarian rule and lack the greatest amounts of freedom. Those more developed nations which have enjoyed more freedom in the past appear to decline under the same kind of rule. To make our points absolutely clear we should start with a common definition of totalitarianism. Wikipedia, the on-line encyclopedia, provides a good basis for common understanding.

"Totalitarianism or totalitarian rule is a where the state, usually under the control of a single political person, faction, or class, recognizes no limits to its authority and strives to regulate every aspect of public and private life wherever feasible. Totalitarianism is generally characterized by the coincidence of authoritarianism, where ordinary citizens have no significant share in state decision-making, and ideology, a pervasive scheme of values promulgated by institutional means to direct most, if not all, aspects of public and private life."

When we think about planners, assuming they can actually perform the function of developing a systematic assignment of responsibilities on a national level to achieve certain economic goals, a valid question is "Who decides what is planned and what remains under the control of the people?" We have been told that only the part of society concerning economic life is controlled. All other activities will remain just the way they are. Currently, our air quality is regulated, our waterways and highways are regulated, we have food safety standards, and the paints we may use on our furniture are regulated, along with many other laws to protect our communities. The length of our work days and the minimum amount of pay considered fair for a worker is decided... just to name a few of the tens of thousands of things that are already regulating our daily lives. When we are told that controlling our economic lives will provide us more freedom to enjoy life and achieve happiness, which of those regulated items in our daily life will the government be willing to sacrifice? Answer: None! Rarely does a government ever sacrifice its control willingly. On the contrary, controlling the economics of life requires controlling the inputs and outputs of the entire economic process for any particular category of life. The gradual or progressive loss of freedom is undetectable from generation to generation. It is like gradually dyeing your hair. If one does it very slowly, over time it appears to be a natural progression and ultimately it is viewed as natural. To use a play on words, Socialism is the gradual dying of society under the increasingly greater influence of Totalitarianism.

The Socialist's discourse tells us that the removal of concerns for our economic well being will provide more freedom in other areas. For the average person, this "freedom of thought of economic issues," is the primary issue of controlling and spending disposable income. Disposable income or discretionary spending is that portion that exceeds one's basic needs. Allocating the remainder after paying necessary expenses is next. The people have the choice between savings and discretionary spending. Discretionary spending may include going to the movies, attending sporting events other entertainment, choices, vacations, a new car, a college fund, and a whole host of other personal choices. Today we have the freedom of choice to spend or save based on our performance in our occupation. We start with the freedom to choose an occupation. For some, the choice may include a second job to increase the amount of discretionary spending available. For others, the choice of supplemental employment may be based on the need to meet basic living expenses. Each person manages his or her own "private economy". Under the "promise" of Socialism, we are told that we will achieve freedom from the worries about our own economics. This freedom may not include a choice of occupation or careers. It may not include making choices of discretionary spending. Our choices may be made for us. The lack of choices equates to a lack of personal freedom. To achieve that freedom we must be able to make our own choices and decisions. We must have the ability to manage the process. Any process designed to manage any set of activities for a large group requires standardization. Standardization dictates that millions of individuals live under the same rules within their class and receive equal benefits within the means of society's ability to provide them. When resources are scarce, all will suffer equally. When resources are abundant they should be shared equally. But will they be shared equally? Our experience is that government is like a hungry lion: it never gets enough to eat.

Our neighbor Cuba, only 90 miles away, guarantees equal access to goods and services for all, but after many years under Communism they have nothing left to share. Cuba in the last fifty five years under President Castro has had a stagnant, declining economy that results in wholesale poverty. This is a prime example of the failure of Totalitarianism under an economic system of Socialism. A Canadian friend recently visited Cuba. Canada has free access to Cuba, where the United States has an embargo with travel restrictions regarding visits to Cuba. He said that he only had to visit Cuba one time to realize outside of the beautiful beaches there was no reason to visit Cuba again. He was curious about the healthcare system and visited a local hospital where he had heard there was some of the best healthcare in the world. Unfortunately, they have some of the worst medical equipment in the world and their facilities were not very clean. He was impressed with the fact that all medical care is free. He mentioned that he spoke to a college educated scientist who was now a bartender, and that the average citizen with free housing and many subsidies earns about $20 per month.

The Road to Socialism

In the spring of 2010 a delegation of our US legislators visited Cuba to review the same healthcare system. They returned with glowing remarks for a system which, at its best, is third rate, compared to our system of medicine which is truly second to none. Apparently cleanliness was not one of their criteria in terms of evaluating the healthcare system. The major benefit, touted by our misguided leaders, is that the system was totally free under a Totalitarian system. They failed to comment on the total life style of the Cuban residents. Many of the delegates were self-proclaimed Socialists. Should we wonder why Cuba raises some of the best swimmers in the world? We never hear reports of Americans climbing into homemade boats on the shores of Miami Beach to paddle to Cuba for better healthcare. A recent article confirmed that the average worker in Cuba makes $20 per month, and gets free healthcare, free housing, free education, and food vouchers. This is consistent with the reports from my Canadian friend. With a show of hands, how many of you want to get into the next boat leaving for Cuba?

Many criticize the cost of the best healthcare in the world. That is like criticizing a handmade Rolls Royce based on its sticker price. Hayek professes that the road to Socialism is a return to serfdom. Cuba in half a century never escaped it. As long as the Totalitarian elites are comfortable, there is no priority other than equalization. That means all suffer equally except the elites on the top.

When we view our individual goals and choices, we often limit ourselves from an economic perspective. But, in reality, our goals are not valued by the attainment of a certain level of financial achievement or a particular level of subsistence. Our true goals, whether stated or not, are often buried under our focus on economic realities. Our heartfelt goals are our personal aspirations, which are totally irrelevant and ignored by governments, but often times patronized. These goals and activities are things we do in our free time: attending sporting events, belonging to civic organizations, and spending time with our families. Our true ends are not the money we make but the opportunity it provides to do other things. Abraham Maslow highlighted the point that once our basic needs are met we must deal with self esteem and reach the pinnacle of self actualization. Many people under Totalitarianism never rise above the satisfaction of basic needs. There are still many who do not reach those minimum levels. In our country no one is allowed to starve or go homeless, yet our politicians try to convince us that is not the case. Hence, they want you to believe that more money is the solution to our social ills..

But, you may ask, "What about the homeless issue?" Suffice it to say, most have swept this issue under the rug. The level of minimal success in many areas of society notes that the Socialist's goals fail to recognize the importance of raising our communities to a higher purpose. Under Totalitarianism a higher purpose can never be achieved because its sole purpose is to provide the basic minimal needs of government subsistence. It is a style of government designed to implement and manage an economic system that ultimately impoverishes everyone. It is based on the philosophy that there is never enough to go around. It is the minimalist's philosophy, "where less is more". In truth, more, much more, could be produced without the interference of government. The laws of supply and demand regulate price in the free enterprise system. The government, thinking it is the center of the universe, approaches problems from the viewpoint that it needs to meet the demands of society rather than to provide a platform of self reliance and individualism for solving economic problems.

Many people who lead this Socialist Movement believe that there is enough money to go around, but the excess money happens to be resting in the wrong wallets—our wallets. The government pick-pockets feel it is their duty to remove our wallets through taxation and solve the plight of others. Government always believes that more money is the answer but in reality taxation does not provide sufficient resources to meet their inexhaustible quest for money. Then they must employ stronger measures to raise money. Borrowing from investors and other nations seems to be the easy answer. Confiscation of personal property as we have seen in Nazi Germany is always an available means if all else fails.

If we review some of our more popular social programs we can get an idea of the success of some of these programs. Take a drive through our government housing projects, visit our blighted neighborhoods, or drive by a school yard where drugs are routinely sold, and we can get a preview of a total society whose single concentration of efforts is on the management of economies rather than focusing on the elevation of the self esteem of a society. The poor living conditions and the increased societal burden is the result of failed socialization. We have politicians who love to give money away but they never solve the problem and eventually destroy those they proclaim they are helping. We never see photo ops of our government housing projects. After spending billions and billions on the poor we have not improved their lifestyles appreciably or helped them to become productive, self-appreciated people. We often hear from our politicians that something is consistent with or opposes our "national values" but there are few who know or understand these code words. What are our "national values"? Are they printed anywhere? When we hear that "we are the richest nation in the world and the rich must pay their fair share," who are the ones that have mismanaged the fruits of our labor? The people don't cause deficit spending of trillions of dollars per year, but our elected politicians do. The people don't make laws that create havoc in our economic system, but once again, our politicians do. It is our elected officials who make the judgment calls to provide services that are reckless and unaffordable. The social services we are providing do not serve the best interest of the people. They are not providing real solutions to our social problems but rather just a basic level of subsistence in hopes that the problem will take care of itself. Politicians have a habit of providing unsustainable tax-and-spend programs with little forethought of "who pays tomorrow?" The Debt Ceiling Crisis of the Summer of 2011 is a perfect example of dealing with the financial aspects of government spending after the fact. The lack of honest and realistic cost projections, and rosie, unrealistic revenue expectations hid our financial secrets in the halls of the US Treasury Department until future generations were required to meet the challenges of the lies of the past. The elections of Tea Party Candidates in 2010 brought the first signs on honesty to a self-serving government. Those who committed to doing "what was right" rather than what was "politically expedient" brought a new generation of politicians to Washington who appear incorruptible. The Left and the Main Stream Media blame the Tea Party Movement for being uninformed and providing candidates who are unskilled at Washington politics. They are often reminded that business-as-usual politics are the cause of many of our problems today.

Socialism is not the answer to poorly designed and administered social programs. Believing that Socialism can provide the solutions is like putting out a fire with gasoline. We have Blue Ribbon commissions and special bodies addressing the solutions to a variety of social programs. The emphasis is economic. The aging population, with its increasing reliance on Social Security and Medicare, was born into the system that promised it security at the end and so far they have been receiving it. Today, Baby Boomers are retiring and filling out Social Security and Medicare forms. For some reason, the government is surprised to see them standing at the door waiting for their promised entitlements. We knew they were coming for over 50 years. Government planning failed us. As a nation, we are unprepared to meet our promises to the people. Will more planning solve this problem? Isn't the true problem our elected officials with their heads in the sand and their ostrich-like tail feathers in the air?

In November of 2010, a liberal politician from Vermont, Bernie Sanders, was interviewed about the Social Security crisis. He touted that it is not a crisis and that increasing the retirement age is unfair. He said that it won't be a crisis for 27 years and it would be unfair to those who have paid into the system to be forced to increase their retirement age. Walk through any Wal-Mart and count the number of people in their seventies who are not shopping, but working. Is it unfair to them to force them to work as a result of a failed system? I admire their stamina. But, in contrast, we have other, much younger people who are retired. Many are public sector workers. They have direct access to tax payer funds with generous pensions and early retirement systems.

These are the same systems that private industry cannot afford.

Should able bodied people be given retirement benefits at a high percentage of their salary after a mere 20 years of service? Providing subsistence programs and early payouts in retirement systems robs society of the productive capability of those who no longer contribute. Actuarially, often those receiving benefits often get far more than their true capitalized value when we use conservative rates of return. Sooner or later they become our "unfunded liabilities". Much of this is a result of extended longevity reaping the benefits of technological advancements in medicine. We can pretty much assume that our retired school teachers, firemen, safety officers and government workers are not those saying "Paper or Plastic" behind the check out counter at the superette. The current financial crisis, whose cure is touted as Socialism, is blamed on the capitalist when in reality government is far guiltier than those who have made a success of themselves.. Our elected officials can not seem to restrain from spending and continue spending far too much. "Trickle down poverty" can not be solved by more spending or by taking from the rich. Eventually, the money will run out.

Today, more than a year after the passage of the massive healthcare bill that promised to reduce the cost of medicine and "bend the cost curve", the private sector is experiencing increases in insurance premiums as a direct result of the healthcare laws. At the same time doctors are talking about leaving their field and retiring. Others are relocating from low Medicare reimbursement rate areas to higher paying areas. The arcane Medicare reimbursement methods combined with outdated methodologies further deepen the divide between the government run healthcare system and good standard practices. The initial impact and further analysis of the true future costs of individual healthcare is revealing that we are about to experience a true redistribution of wealth for many. Many think this could be the true goal of the healthcare reform bill. The Affordable Health Care Act is becoming unaffordable. Today we are seeing the signs of increasing prices in healthcare policies under a climate of reductions in service. At a time when people are struggling, due to a failing economy, government is imposing higher costs along with more administrative control. But we have to remember that government, through their altruistic purposes and high flying promises, was concentrating on lowering the cost of healthcare. They are the largest single customer for healthcare services. The primary focus of the healthcare bill was not to lower the cost of insurance. Yet, the insurance companies, targeted as the greedy capitalists, are today responding to the government controlled and mandated increases in the minimum requirements of healthcare coverage. At the same time government spokesmen blame the insurance companies for raising rates, which for most of us was a foregone conclusion.

The healthcare legislation had some unique provisions in it. In addition to requiring certain mandatory benefits, it requires charging consumers immediately for benefits that would not be available for three years. That is like making car payments on a car that won't be built for 3 years. This is just another legislated tax disguised as healthcare improvement. To satisfy the mandates of the government many people are going to have to reprioritize their spending plans. Many will have to make very difficult choices. Others will be required to look for additional employment in a very difficult economy. The benefits of healthcare come at a price that will be impossible for many to pay. If we remember that the benefits of Socialistic programs are supposedly to provide the freedom from economic worry to gain time for other non-financial pursuits, then we immediately are disillusioned by the first promise to be broken. We were promised better healthcare, but the average person gets no additional healthcare for a higher price. In turn many need additional employment just to pay for their rising healthcare costs. Many will receive improved benefits but better access will still remain a key component for many years that has not been addressed.

Along with managing healthcare services and its costs, and establishing additional insurance requirements, the basic healthcare services available will also be dictated by ruling committees and special boards. There are some 157 new boards and commissions set up to help regulate our lives. Recently, a TV talk show Doctor reported that a 10 pound loss of weight can result in a 60% decrease in the risk of heart disease. Any bureaucrat that saw that show on television may be penning a new regulation under their plenary powers that all Americans will be required by law to lose 10 pounds. You must remember that the designated administrators have been given unlimited power under the healthcare bill. They may be considering having Food Guards at the exit doors of supermarkets whose job it is to eyeball the cart pushers on their way to the parking lot. Imagine these "health police" removing illegal items from the carts of overweight shoppers. Do you think this is far fetched? Talk to the people in California who have had sugar enriched beverages substituted with only sugar-free drinks in vending machines or the restaurants in New York City which no longer provide salt. A Totalitarian government, through the passage of a series of less than a half a dozen bills in Congress, can ultimately control every aspect of human life in America.

With this control of the many, they always find room to make exclusions for a few. In the case of "Obamacare", there are more than a few exceptions. Besides the law makers themselves in Congress and the branches of government, over 1451companies have been given waivers by the White House exempting them from obeying the health care laws according the ABC news as of July 16th 2011. Companies have until September 15th 2011 to apply for waivers. It may not come as much of a surprise that the majority of the workers are union workers who are allowed to keep their "Cadillac plans". Those with the best benefits are given exceptions to the law. We know there are the chosen ones in this system, but you may not be as fortunate. If you are lucky enough to be one of the few, you may stop reading. If you aren't that lucky you must provide a watchful eye over your elected leaders. It starts in your Town Hall with vending machines and table salt and moves up the line to mandatory diets and any other regimens that the government deems necessary to control the economics of healthcare.

In the 1970s under President Carter we had gas rationing resulting from a lack of a comprehensive energy policy. Forty years later we are still waiting for a plan. Carter's response to the gas shortage was the Odd/Even System for purchasing gasoline. If your license plate ended in an odd number you were allowed to purchase gas on odd days. If your license plate number ended in an even number then you were allowed to purchase gasoline on even days only. Under the current President and his "Obamacare" reforms there may be a similar program to legislate weight loss. Those who live in housing with odd numbered house numbers would be required to jog 5 miles on odd numbered days and those who live in even numbered housing would run on even days. This may sound absurd, but no more than many of the regulations already passed in the healthcare reform bill.

Another example of failed government policy that we never hear about that is the unintended consequence of failed EPA government regulations regarding the automobile industry and its relationship to higher incidents of death and injury due to emission standards. Emission standards and mileage standards (CAFÉ) are established for auto makers to meet minimum fuel efficiency standards. To achieve the increased mileage standards parts are no longer made out of metal but lightweight plastic. Cars are also becoming smaller and some vehicles are not much larger than a standard golf cart. They provide no protection in the event of even a minor traffic accident. The results are like falling dominos. The protection lost due to EPA standards results in higher medical costs, not to mention increasing death rates due to the higher incidence of fatal accidents. The resultant effect is higher automobile insurance rates which is the by-product of increased EPA standards. It won't be long before the connection is made and the Air Quality Board will be assigned healthcare responsibility. Healthcare in this day and age is just another code word for controlling life itself. Most of us begin our lives in the healthcare system and our lives, for many, will terminate somewhere in the healthcare arena. What happens in between those two book ends of healthcare will be government regulation of your total life. Life will not be based on liberty and the pursuit of happiness, but it will be suppressed by your total economic cost as a result of your healthcare expenditures in comparison to your overall contributions to society.

There is the old story about the Army recruit who was walking through the line to receive his new uniforms. A line of sergeants, each with a pile of different sized uniforms, Small, Medium, and Large, were throwing stacks of uniforms at the soldiers as they walked by the long counter. When one young recruit got his pile of uniforms he mentioned that he was a Medium not a Large. The quick reply was, "Not today". For those who thought they were going to stand in front of full length mirror for a perfect fit discovered that they were in a One-size-fits-all World. Following that, they learned the military lived by another concept: "Hurry up and wait." The early days in government-run military provide us with a peek into what we will see with government-run healthcare.

In the case of Totalitarian styled military units, where anyone who out ranks you is your master, one lives under a system of total control. In the military it is required for discipline, with its demand for precise and consistent conduct. There are serious consequences when that discipline is broken. The same structure will be required to administer the one-size-fits- all approach to government programs under a totalitarian system. There will be two classes: those who rule and those are who are ruled. Most of us will be outranked on many levels. We will be the sacrificial lambs giving up any sense of control of our own lives. Is this the America we love and are devoted to? How could this be happening to us? Who actually controls us?

Chapter 8   Who, Whom?

"Collectivism holds that the individual has no rights, that his life and work belong to the group (society, to the tribe, the state, the nation) and that the groups may sacrifice him at its own whim to its own interest. The only way to implement a doctrine of that kind is by means of brute force -- and Statism has always been the political corollary of collectivism." Ayn Rand

"I believe it was Lenin himself who introduced to Russia the famous phrase, 'Who, whom?' during the early years of Soviet rule, the byword in which the people summed up the universal problem of a socialist society. Who plans whom, who directs and dominates whom, who assigns to other people their station in life, and who is to have his due allotted by others? These become necessarily the central issues to be decided by the supreme power" *Hayek, The Road to Serfdom*

In Communist China, thousands of children as young as six years old are selected each year to leave their families with the hope to represent their nation in one of the highest honors of their nation, the Olympics. These mere children, those chosen by some criteria, are selected to train for many, many years. Only a handful of those selected each year will go on to represent their country. Those who succeed and receive the medals will rise to temporary greatness. Those who fail will return embarrassed to their villages and towns. The Chinese system of competition is similar to the competition employed in America in our businesses, our schools, our playing fields, and our arts and science programs. The Chinese, regardless of their politics, realize that competition leads to greatness. Winners are not chosen at random. They are developed. To develop greatness requires grit, determination, training, and sometimes luck. Few of us ever achieve greatness in our daily lives, but those who operate under the system of competition often develop a sense of character that produces above average results.

Those who do not develop and manage the right combination of resources often fail to reach their mark. Usually there are one or two ingredients or skill sets that are deficient and impede success. Napoleon Hill, the author of *Think and Grow Rich,* based on his masterful study of what he calls the *Laws of Success,* states that success is the result of doing the right things over and over again. Is luck involved? Yes, without a doubt. Luck is also involved in winning the lottery. The point is that by following a plan the results almost always depend upon some system of competition. This competition generally provides results that contribute to the betterment of society. We experience failures during competition, that's for sure. But as an overall system, competition that provides the opportunity for greatness far exceeds the mediocrity of any other system.

No doubt, some people are born into greater opportunities than others. The Socialist expects those who 'over-achieve' should refund a portion of their success. When we examine the winners and losers in life's lottery, it is true that those with better educations and access to capital have a better chance of achieving greater success in a free society. By comparison, those with the same advantages under a system of Socialism have no opportunity to achieve personal greatness, while those with limited abilities have even less of a chance. Today in America, a person with an bright idea for an unusual solution to a problem can achieve phenomenal success. Bill Gates and Robert Allen created Microsoft in their dorm room. Google and Facebook were both founded in dormitory rooms. Today these under thirty year old billionaires employ thousands of people. The older techies, like Bill Gates, who is one of the richest men in the world, have contributed mass fortunes to charities supporting causes in education, healthcare, and cures for diseases in third world countries. This "evil capitalist" is one of the larger employers around the world and has contributed more to society than the entire GDPs of most small, totalitarian countries. He and many others in the "Billionaire Club" are making a pact to donate a good portion of their mass fortunes to charitable ventures. In so doing, they will ensure that untold billions of dollars will escape the tax system and thereby go to directed causes where they may do the most good. Under a heavily confiscatory tax system this type of philanthropy becomes impossible.

When people talk of the failures of Capitalism and the free enterprise system, they are still hung up on stories of the robber barons of the 20th century. Those powerful industrialists who built our railways, mined our coal, and drilled for oil are blamed for the disparities in life. Names that come to mind are Andrew Carnegie, Henry Ford, J.P. Morgan, Joe Kennedy, and the Rockefellers. Today, detractors point to the Wall Street "robber barons" who they say mine riches from behind a desk or provide services in our financial markets that the average person can not begin to understand. Those trained risk takers are some of the richest 3 to 4% who pay the bulk of our taxes. They not only contribute to the GDP, but help stimulate a significant portion of our economy with their consumer spending. At the same time, plastered all over our television sets, we see the lifestyles of the rich and famous who are our entertainers, youthful beauty queens, child actors, and our sports celebrities who make tens of millions of dollars providing entertainment on and off the screen and in our sports arenas. The capitalists who provide the forum for these persons of fame are criticized as the evil ones, while those spoiled stars with their multi-millionaire contracts are envied through their fan clubs and are often guests of our envious politicians.

Ironically, many of our sports stars who achieve greatness in America come from second and third world countries where they played sandlot baseball and many ultimately make more money in one year than their entire suffering villages back home. When you look at the rosters of our baseball teams, one realizes that they don't learn English until they get to America yet more often achieve the American dream in greater numbers than those born in this land of opportunity. Many people living under repressive totalitarian systems immigrate to let their talents shine. On the other hand, those living in our inner cities in government housing and supported by other government programs have been made dependants of government handouts--many who simply cannot climb out of that system. The sandlots in the Dominican Republican, Puerto Rico and other lesser developed Latin American nations to the South produce people with great potential. While only a few achieve greatness, many have successful careers and go on to other endeavors. They appreciate the opportunity.

In comparison, many sandlots in America are full of gangs, drug traffickers, and other criminals under the cover of a non-caring government who misconstrues drug dealing for freedom of expression, and rioting in our streets for freedom of speech. At the same time peaceful protests in Washington by Tea Party members are classified as anti-American, racist, and propagandizing. A phenomenon that most people cannot understand is the burning down of the ghettos in both the winning and losing cities of Super Bowl contenders. The fires, riots and the public destruction of property in these cities is considered routine and is symptomatic of a culture that has misguided ethics. The rioters are not the only ones to blame. They have been defeated as surely as the Super Bowl loser with their jealousy for the winners. People in the areas with the most squalor continue to live in the neighborhoods with the most government subsistence. When we hear the cries for racial equality and social justice it is for those who are living under the shackles of failed government programs whose misguided aim was to promote social equality.

Today, we have cradle-to-grave social programs that perpetuate the problems over generations. Capitalism is blamed for its failures. It is often touted that Capitalism is not spreading the wealth. Joe the Plumber heard that message loud and clear. His conversation with Candidate Obama led to a wholesale investigation of this ordinary plumber by an unscrupulous State Department Office in Ohio. Is that a preview of what is to come when one disagrees with the government? Unfortunately, the failure is falsely blamed on the greatest payers of taxes whose payments are used to create solutions to societies' problems. The government seeks capitalistic riches, but spurns capitalistic solutions. Increasing government subsistence payments does not provide a higher quality of life. They ultimately provide a lower depth of poverty through the perpetuation of the problem.

At this present time, in a very bad economy brought on by a variety of government missteps, we hear the protests and anger against Wall Street, the insurance companies, the oil industry, and any company whose board of directors thinks it is appropriate to award large contracts to their management teams. Where are the cries against the person who is paid equal amounts for hitting a small round ball over a fence 400 feet away, or the middle linebacker who can knock down a person the size of a Mack truck? We spend $75, to $100 to watch these people perform in person. We also have the option to spend endless Saturday and Sunday afternoons watching the same feats on our digital, big screens television sets. The multi-million dollar ads, paid for by the "evil capitalists," indirectly pay the salaries of the brutes in our arenas. When we destroy the corporations we will in turn sacrifice our national past time heroes, and more importantly, our national engines of success that pull the entire economy along.

Ken Feinberg is not a household name to most people. There are few who know his achievements, his rise to greatness, or his role in our current form of government. Mr. Feinberg has the distinction of being the first Pay Czar to be appointed in the White House. He is one of the "grand levelers." He was recently replaced by his protégé Patricia Geoghegan as the Acting Head of the Office of the Special Master of Compensation, according to the Associated Press. Feinberg has been temporarily reassigned with the duty of distributing $20 billion to the victims of the BP Oil Spill. Both the creation of these governmental positions and the extraction of funds from BP Oil are visible signs of a totalitarian style of government at work. The primary responsibility of both Pay Czars has been to peg executive compensation to some arbitrary payroll criteria and to distribute equitable cash distributions. These are examples of the arbitrariness of their positions. Remember, a critical indictment of Socialism is that it administrates through multiple levels of arbitrary decision making. Both Feinberg and Geoghean are reported to be executive compensation experts. It is unclear if those credentials are based on their understanding of executive compensation or their dictatorial administration of executive compensation. Either way, these types of positions place us on a slippery slope. It may even be a testing ground for future arbiters with powers over life and death matters.

The Pay Czar positions were created in response to the failed government Bailout Programs that negligently, though some say conveniently, forgot to limit the usage of over $700 billion dollars given to banks and insurance companies that were deemed, "too big to fail". Congress and President Bush, in their almighty wisdom, literally wrote blank checks to the financial entities that more than likely, were the most responsible in our largest financial crisis since the Great Depression. Handing over billions of dollars of "bailout money" with no strings attached is like handing over a candy bar to a small child and saying "don't let this ruin your dinner". The unthinking parent is an accomplice as surely as the government is in handing over a bag of cash to a starving bank.

Later, it was discovered that those weak banks and corrupt Wall Street firms were giving out huge, unjustified bonuses to their top employees. In an effort to deflect criticism of the government the actual names of the recipients of large bonuses were leaked to the press. When it was publicly revealed what had happened, angry mobs protested Wall Street firms, and the homes of their executives and the recipients of large bonuses. The mobs were bused to their homes by ACORN and SEIU union members. There were no reports of protests against the legislators who crafted the poor legislation that resulted in hundreds of billions of dollars being misused. While the child may or may not go unpunished for the deeds of the parent, our well pampered Congress never steps up and admits any shortcomings.

The Pay Czar, one of dozens of newly created White House advisory positions, was appointed to regulate executive compensation for firms receiving bailout money including the newly reorganized General Motors. The new GM is not so affectionately referred to by right wing conservative personality Rush Limbaugh as Government Motors. The President then called for the resignation of Rick Wagoner, the Chairman and CEO of General Motors. White House Press Secretary Robert Gibbs claimed this was a "one-off situation" and was not going to start a trend. Apparently, the removal of three CEOs from GM in 18 months is not classified as a trend.

The Pay Czar has total control, one might say totalitarian control, over the salaries and executive compensation packages of those companies who have received Bailout or Stimulus Money. Ironically, while the Pay Czar targets executive compensation, the Stimulus Fund companies are most often required to use only union employees who routinely cost far more than non-union employees. In regards to the arena of compensation and spending, we have a dichotomy in the administration of payrolls by the White House and Congress. We decry excessive spending on one class yet promote it in another. On August 1, 2011 Congresswoman Michelle Bachman talking about her "No Vote" to increase the Debt Limit on Fox News highlighted the out of control spending on the part of the White House. When President Obama took office in 2009 there was only one White House staffer making over $170,000 per year. Today the number has been increased to 1761 staffers indicating that reducing spending is not a priority of the White House. It should be noted that most of the jobs added by President Obama did exist in previous administrations. Those on both perimeters of the economic stratus are victims of exclusion. The free market system is thwarted and accused of being unfair, while the government promotes the highest level of injustice with our tax dollars. These high profile examples exemplify a pervasive new style of government that operates with totalitarian precision, yet it may be only the tip of the iceberg as law suits shed more light on the backroom deals worked by this administration.

The reorganization of General Motors and Chrysler Corporation defied all rule of law. In the name of expediency, the laws of bankruptcy were suspended. The corporations were reorganized and the bond holders were dismissed while priority was given to the unions. Once again, winners and losers were decided by a controlling government, which dispensed with the rule of law against the rightful owners of government regulated secured and unsecured debt. The far reaching impact of this type of governmental behavior causes fear and suspicion in the capital markets. The capital market is the stalwart of the Capitalism system. They raise funds to expand business, start new businesses and refund existing debt in corporate America. The doubt created by government intervention needlessly generates fear and insecurity in our financial markets.

In September 2010, amidst poor job creation reports, President Obama chastised corporate America for sitting on the sidelines with over $1 trillion of cash in this unstable business environment. One year later it has been reported by Wall Street pundits that cash reserves offshore have grown to over $2 trillion. In basic economics we learn that businesses must manage and evaluate various types of risk: business risk, price and market risk, and add to that government risk-- that risk created by the decisions of governments that effect business operations. Historically, "government risk" was normally limited to the risks associated with business decisions involved in investments with other nations. Today our corporations find better investments in other countries because their "government risk" is less volatile due to the predictability of their governmental behavior. The predictability of our own government has vanished--gone with the wind. Investors are not flocking to Cuba, Venezuela, China or the United States to invest in corporations. The cash reserves held by our own corporations is a tempting prize to capture. The President's "jawboning," using verbal threats or recommendations, is a warning to corporations that he wants to see more investment in America. We have seen what has happened to those who were "too big to fail". The next category may be those "too successful to succeed".

When the famous career bank robber Willie Sutton was asked why he robbed banks, his answer was, "That is where the money is." Our next series of robberies may be against the most successful corporations because quite clearly "that is where the money is". If a government can steal a little old lady's retirement bonds in GM, they can surely steal the cash out of a uncooperative corporation's vault. Simply by accusing the stubborn company of wrong doing should be enough to extort more cash. All the government has to do is employ the skills of a crafty community organizer and convince a naïve public that it is in the best interest of America that the vaults of corporate America be raided.

When Stalin talked about the "Who and the Whom?" it was evidently clear that he believed in government appropriation for the good of the underclass, thus identifying half of the "who question." The "whom" are the cash barons and those with the highest incomes. A dictatorial government now was emboldened to seize the cash for redistribution in the name of a greater society. This is the kind of totalitarian government which decides the fate of winners and losers, without regard for the secondary consequences, while it usurps freedom and destroys the rule of law through the unchecked administration of government. Herbert Spencer, the19th century English philosopher, prominent classical liberal political theorist, and sociologist was credited with coining the phrase, "survival of the fittest" which was often used in context of the spirit of Capitalism. In actuality, he claimed that his comment referred to government policy which often led him to oppose programs to assist the poor. It was his theory that misguided government programs cause more harm than good. One hundred years later his pronouncement has been realized. Tragically, history has proven that when the number of recipients of government handouts outnumbers the producers in a society, then the democratic and capitalistic system will fail as the non-producers gorge themselves At that point our system of democracy in America will more than likely be compared to two wolves and a lamb voting on what is for dinner. The metaphor does not stop there. Once the lamb is gone, the wolves must turn on themselves and, ironically, conform to the law of the survival of the fittest. After the wholesale failure of these totalitarian social policies, in an historical cycle that lasts about half a century, the wolves themselves become the next targets of society.

The Road to Socialism

Chapter 9   Security and Freedom

"If you want total security, go to prison. There you're fed, clothed, given medical care and so on. The only thing lacking.... is freedom."
                                        President Dwight D. Eisenhower

Security and freedom can be viewed as polar opposites.   Another way to view it is that "security" is on a straight line on the far left and "freedom" is on the far right. This imaginary Security-Freedom Scale, developed to give more clarity to the discussion, provides a visual understanding of the co-relationship between the two terms. Total security is the absence of freedom and total freedom provides no sense of security.   Of course, there are degrees and variances in these terms. Our individual sense of security, or insecurity, is more of an emotional response and not always a rational choice. The level of comfort felt at any particular point requiring any level of freedom is dependent upon each individual's personal situation. When the Socialist talks about a "new freedom" he is relieving the individual from any personal responsibility.   To obtain a greater sense of security requires, in almost all cases, the sacrifice of freedom.   In America today, we are not at a point where we relish the wholesale loss of our freedoms for the benefit a small segment of our population who appear to lack the confidence, willingness or ability to provide for themselves. They may have lost their motivation whereby they tend to accept a lower style of living then rise up to the occasion to improve their skills or accept some responsibility for providing the personal effort to achieve a higher standard of living.   The debate on the extension is a perfect example.   Did the extension of long term unemployment benefits result in longer unemployment or was the benefit response the aggravated economic condition? While the Bureau of Labor and Statistics maintains a whole host of statistics they cannot determine if extended benefits is the cause or the effect of long term unemployment.

Each person's level of comfort surrounding a variety of economic matters is unique to that individual.   The variety of issues faced by the populous are based on different needs with varying requirements to supplement different levels of reliance on social programs. There are others who have very little dependence upon government.   They are usually the net givers rather than the takers of society. The Socialist condemns those who are net givers. They are most often the capitalists who are blamed for the failings of the economic system often out of envy or spite. Closer examination reveals that in today's world the problem is not the age worn argument over the control over workers as claimed by the Marxist. The new accused appears to be the capitalistic enterprises that generate mass fortunes for corporations and their captains who amass huge fortunes relative to the wages of the average workers they employ.

During the time of the financial expansion of industry we have created a greater dependence on government for both the worker and the non-worker. In the last eighty years we have gradually eliminated the concept of individual self reliance. Progressively we have exchanged our freedom for security through greater involvement of government in our daily lives. The ideal appears to be to flatten the large producers or earners while redistributing corporate and individual gains to through government or planned long range entitlements. The Left has determined some undisclosed criteria whereby leaders of industry make too much money and the excess incomes based on a very non-precise application that some unknown amount is "too much". There is no application or appreciation for of the vast amounts of assets and resources under the control of those who have "excessive incomes" relative to the level of responsibility and accountability of the individual line workers. Yet, the attacks on the capitalists who drive our economy persist through rhetoric and after-the-fact regulatory control.

The hit and miss attacks on corporate America lack sophisticated planning and implementation strategies resulting in disruptions and unintended consequences on outcomes. The corporate lawyers and accountants employed by the corporate giants are estimated to be five to ten years ahead of the regulatory agencies whose intention is to restrict or redistribute profits and add the safeguards to the public. The ill-planned gains hoped to be extracted from corporate America often never seem to materialize. In many cases they cause interruptions in the marketplace providing neither security nor freedom. Passing legislation like the Dodd-Frank Financial Reform Bill is a perfect example of the failure of new regulations. In the seven to ten years required to write the regulations to enforce the new bill based on recent testimony of the regulatory authorities, the corporate legal departments will have sufficient time to circumvent almost any new legislation. In the long run, the government will continue to create more insecurity into the business environment while imposing massive regulations and restrictions on those enterprises not large enough to defend themselves against poorly designed regulations. This in turn gradually imposes more limitations on freedom and disrupts the economic flow of commerce caused by either complying avoiding government regulations. Those corporations and industries that have access to the best lobbyists will circumvent the new legislation while putting up smoke screens in concert with the legislatures that provide cover for the most egregious violators. The most regrettable aspects of cumbersome and unwieldy legislation is the billions of dollars spend by both government and industry to tap dance around the legislation to solve problems that no longer exist imposing layers upon layers of unreadable regulations. The revolutionizing of the real estate mortgage and monetization of pooled mortgages could have been averted with simple measures to limit the number of issuers of securities and loan originators. A far simpler method to address the problem would have required minimum income and down payment standards on all pooled assets. This could have further been reinforced by requiring "seasoning of loans" whereby each loan within a pool should must have a minimum payment history of at least one year prior to being eligible to be pooled. These common sense changes would have eliminated worthless mortgages to be created, it would have slowed or placed more control on the flow of funds into speculative securities, and averted the mortgage meltdown that was the primary cause of the global financial disaster. While the industries that took advantage of the relaxation of mortgage and securities rules was a major contributor to the problem, irresponsible government intervention both aided in causing the problem and is further responsible for the delay in cleaning up the mess. Governments desire to increase home ownership to those who could least afford to purchase a home lead to the destruction of the economy. This debacle resulted in the global loss of trillions of dollars in the global economy. In this case, government was the root cause of both our loss of freedom and loss of financial security.

As the demand for security increases on the part of the people, then the level of liberty is diminished at the expense of those valuing their freedom. It appears that with the reduction of individual liberties, in response to the need for economic security, those who demand more security never seem to elevate themselves to the point where they can accept more liberty: in this case they lack personal responsibility. In a sense, they have been permanently debilitated. As more become dependent upon government for their basic needs, fewer citizens will regain a sense of personal responsibility to ultimately provide for themselves. We see this in Greece where workers who labor 35 hours per week and take two hour lunches are protesting over the increasing of the retirement age by two years due to the lack of financial reserves to meet the nearing requirements to pay their retirees. We have the same structural problems in our Social Security and Medicare Programs that are looming n, yet our politicians have failed to deal with the shortfall which has resulted in the recent write down of our credit worthiness. Government is the conduit to transfer wealth and security from the provider groups to the user groups. Along with this transfer we tend to transfer our freedom. Those on the right side of the Security-Freedom Scale, who cherish freedom and are the providers are forced to fill the pipeline for the government transfer system, are the most effected by the transfer of freedom for security. Unfortunately, freedom is always considered the villain in the story by those who lack self reliance as a national character trait. Freedom is then sacrificed in the name of security, whether it be financial or personal.

Hayek describes two levels of security: they are limited security and absolute security. Limited security includes providing minimum levels of assistance based upon individuals needs. Absolute security guarantees a specific minimum level of life style. Based on the Socialist's assertions, this can be achieved through the conversion of productive assets to the State thereby transforming the economy to redistribute wealth to provide an equitable style of living. This is the ultimate goal of Socialism. The exact nature and level of entitlement programs has never been clearly defined. Today, we have a limited type of security where entitlement programs provide both long term and interim benefits to meet the economic needs of differing groups of people. Unemployment benefits, food stamps, and free medical care at our Emergency Rooms are examples of interim benefits. It is assumed that sooner or later the individuals who depend upon interim programs will once again climb the economic ladder and ultimately become self-sufficient again These temporary programs should not be confused with other long term government benefit programs that are designed to fill the gap for those who have long term situations. At this time there are about 40-50 million people in the United States who are receiving permanent or long term benefits. This represents approximately 15% of our population. Recently, during the Debt Ceiling Debate, the Secretary Giethner reported that the Treasury Department issues 80 million checks per month. This indicates that 25% of the 310 million people in America receive some form of benefit from the government. The most common long term programs providing security are benefits for disabilities, retirement benefits, Medicare and Medicaid. The percentage of government dependents is rapidly increasing as a result of the wave of "baby boomers" that are entering the Social Security Retirement System

The limited systems for security are the temporary programs with built-in flaws. These programs, considered temporary, are not designed to be supplementary. They are usually all or nothing programs. These safety net solutions provide interim support until the person or family can regain their former position of self reliance. For instance, persons who receive Unemployment Benefits based on a former high level of previous earnings will not receive any benefits if they accept another position. In today's difficult employment climate, many people can only locate work that pays significantly below the level they were previously paid. There are many who now hold two or even three jobs to replace the incomes they have lost through the recession. There are others in the willing and potential pool of workers, who are collecting unemployment benefits at very high levels based on their previous employment higher levels, who often elect not to accept employment because when they evaluate the incremental increase in total income compared to the Unemployment Benefits they are receiving the difference between working and not working is negligible when viewed on a total income basis. There are others too, who are willing to accept employment if they are paid "off the books" in order to continue receiving their Unemployment Benefits. The gratuitous extension of unemployment benefits has resulted in many to game the system.

A system which results in this type of decision making provides an injustice to "the people" by those who are robbing the system. It is clear that our jobs programs are not aligned with our unemployment programs. Take for instance this proposal: if those who accepted wages lower than their previous level were able to receive a reduced unemployment benefit based on their new wage level, then both the individual and the government would receive a common benefit. The person would be productive again and the benefits paid to the individual would be significantly less while still providing a partial benefit. This seems to be a logical solution which benefits both "the people" and the individual and has longer term benefits resulting in the emotional well being of the family.

Another area included under the category of "limited security" is healthcare. The massive healthcare reform passed in 2010 provided a jolt to those on the right who do not view healthcare as an entitlement, but rather a threat to freedom. There are many who hold the opposing viewpoint. One problem is that with the massive on-line record system controlling all medical care will violate the Doctor-Patient Privilege, thus making all records accessible to anyone throughout the network. Many believe the increased availability of your personal information will lead to better care. Others fear the loss of personal freedom is an abuse of the right to privacy. This is another example of our loss of personal freedom which is sold as a benefit leading to better healthcare. As we approach the implementation of the program, if it is not overturned by the Supreme Court, there are many who suggest the implementation should be far more gradual beginning with public health clinics to provide services to those in the lower income areas where the highest need exists. These appear to be the group who have the highest need and is the cause of some of our most expensive services. If healthcare clinics were combined with government sponsored major medical policies, a significant segment of our population could be served. Again, this assumes that better healthcare is the objective. If these two suggestions were adopted then the most of the arguments from the Left would be addressed.

The debate over government's role as an insurer has created polarizing views. An argument can be made that our existing government sponsored insurance programs, i.e. Federal Disaster Programs, Flood Insurance, and other public sector insurance and federal relief programs substantiate the fact that the government is already in the insurance business. It provides insurance and insurance type relief programs offering assistance during periods of catastrophic losses for both the people and industry. Examples are hurricane and tornado relief, flood damage and protection, and less often but essential, earthquake relief programs. The argument presented is that our failure to provide national healthcare services is the next catastrophic financial disaster that is looming around the corner. If we view all insurance as a safety net, then healthcare insurance appears to be the next logical step in providing additional security for the people. Justifying healthcare coverage as "a right" is a long stretch of the General Welfare Clause.

It has already been discussed that there are significant changes in healthcare coverage and under the healthcare reform bill there will be many mandated medical services to be provided in the future. The issue of healthcare insurance and the regulation of medical services are complex issues. The government has artificially blurred the problem by combining the issue of the cost of health insurance, with its many flaws, and the act of providing healthcare services. It has been argued that insurance companies are responsible for the high cost of medical care. The combining of the insurance aspects with the service components does not reduce the cost of the service. In fact, insurance premiums are sky rocketing since the passing of the reform bill to meet the mandated requirements imposed by the government. Insurance companies have been blamed for the high cost of medical care. This will be the basis for a Single Payer System. If insurance companies are the cause of high medical costs then does it make sense to blame the high cost of auto repairs on the insurance companies too? Insurance companies react to cost they are not the drivers of those costs. By the end of 2010 many large corporations were experiencing 15 to 30% increases in their costs to provide group insurance plans to their employees. During the summer of 2011 it was revealed that additional mandates will be placed on insurance companies to cover the cost of birth control thereby adding more expenses to be ultimately transferred to the tax payers who are paying for insurance.

Unbelievable to many caught in the system and paying heavily for the changes, the government is providing interim waivers to over 1400 companies on portions of the healthcare reform act in response to the fears that businesses will be dropping or reducing coverage for their employees. The government is assaulting the insurance companies for "arbitrary cost increases." We have already witnessed some companies dropping out of the healthcare insurance business. This may lead to a national insurance crisis under the new, heavy handed government regulations designed to solve the medical cost problem by targeting the providers. This could be the strategy to arrive at a Single Payer System, the system of last resort. During the interim period, until this mess is sorted out, we will see turmoil in the insurance industry, the healthcare provider networks, and ultimately the people who will be faced with unaffordable increases in healthcare insurance, and limited access to services. The loss of freedom as a result of mandated changes by the government are providing the "insecurity" rather than the "security" that most people believe is needed. The net effect of the implementation of the healthcare bills will have far-reaching ramifications that will affect our overall sense of security.

After the one year anniversary of the passage of the Affordable Care Act, tens of thousands of businesses are evaluating the impact of their healthcare coverage and a major calamity is brewing in response to the poorly designed healthcare reforms. The additional costs required to provide coverage may render many firms unprofitable and will have a negative impact on the unemployment situation. The many fears presented by large employers prior to passage of the Bill, which were all dismissed by Congress, are coming home to roost much sooner than expected. In the government's misguided effort to increase the level of security to employees by improving access to health insurance is offset by the pending fear of losing their livelihood. The constant fear of losing one's job in a bad economy further adds to the high level of anxiety and insecurity caused by the healthcare regulations. The reality is that the overall operating cost for each employee for many firms will be impossible to absorb making many companies unprofitable resulting in closure adding to the all ready high level of unemployment. The best alternative for many will be to elect to pay the fine for non-compliance rather than continue to provide insurance benefits. The loss of freedom on the part of business will result in a loss of security for the employees. The increase in the cost of providing healthcare may have had the intended or unintended consequence of transferring the wealth of companies to their employees via increased healthcare costs. Unfortunately, the outcomes of a mismanaged attempt to socialize medicine will be paid for on the backs of the employees if the Reform Act is not revised. Revision of the bill and the various amendments required to shore up the weaknesses in the healthcare program will be difficult, if not impossible to incorporate into the regulations. From all accounts, the 2000 plus pages were written by an outside source. Congress has few, if any, fingerprints on the healthcare bill. Congress has delegated their responsibility, as is often the case, negatively impacting our most cherished assets: our people.

It is anticipated that significant changes will be made to our senior healthcare programs as a result of the new legislation. We know little about the changes being considered. On the surface, the programs appear re-distributional, consistent with Dr. Donald Berwick's stated views. Burwick was appointed by President Obama to Head Medicare and Medicaid. In a 2008 speech in Great Britain to the National Health Council, he touted the greatness of their socialized healthcare system claiming that "excellent healthcare by definition is re-distributional". This can be heard on the U-tube video, "Donald Berwick on

Redistributing Wealth". Two years later Great Britain, who Berwick touted for their effectiveness of their heavily socialized medical program, is vigorously rethinking their approach to healthcare because the costs under their socialized system are unsustainable. Whether healthcare is a right or a privilege does not change the cost components of healthcare. The single greatest factor in controlling cost is through social limitations of the availability of healthcare to certain classes of individuals. Under Socialist principles, the system relies on determining the overall future contributions possible from an individual to society in relation to their overall cost of maintenance. With the aging of our "baby boomers", the future costs will be significant. Many are anticipating the reinstitution of the "Death Tax" or Inheritance Estate Tax to provide additional pools of funds to funnel into the government coffers sooner along with the limitation of healthcare for the elderly.

As President Obama said recently, "I wasn't elected to make popular decisions. I was elected to make hard decisions". Those hard decisions may state who is entitled to specific services and who is not lucky enough to be included. These hard decisions could have life and death implications that negatively affect both freedom and security.

Some level of security is required by all people. One factor that affects an individual's level of security is their level of confidence in their ability to remain productive and continue their current level of employment. Employment and wealth are key components that effect a person's feelings or sense of security on our imaginary Security-Freedom Scale. The third factor is an emotional-behavioral response to actually how comfortable an individual feels in terms of Security. Two different people with the same income and net worth will normally have different feelings regarding their security based on several factors about what they personally determine is an adequate level for both, income and available assets. Their spending and saving patterns can significantly affect this response, which for both individuals, can be very different. Their outlook for the prospects of future continued income and future returns may also be different depending on their individual circumstances. Two families with the same income may be living paycheck to paycheck with one family having 3 children and the other no children and their level of security may be a function of the future possibility of continued employment. In addition to family size, other contributing factors to their sense of security include age, whether they have one or two income in their families, and the amount of consumer debt, and of course, personal lifestyle. These are the key areas that impact one's feeling of security. Many of the factors are determined by freedom of choice by the wage earners. This assumes that the individual will retain some level of liberty to make those choices.

Prosperity provides opportunity which is a function of the economics climate. One of the most significant factors to be considered, but is outside the control of the worker, is the economic environment that he works in. Whether we are in a boom period or a bust period, many households are directly affected by changes in the economy. During upturns and downturns there is a group of people who experience the least amount of gains or loses. These are the individuals living on fixed incomes and government subsidy programs. During downturns or recessions, all participate, but those on fixed guaranteed government programs see less impact. Therefore, those on fixed guaranteed incomes have only one enemy: increasing prices or inflation. Recessions and inflation are a normal result of changes in the economies, both here and abroad. They are cyclical, routine, and predictable. The predictability is often interceded through government influence trying to manage normal cyclical patterns in the economy. We no longer have the ability to regulate a global economy, yet that is what we are attempting to do. There is a whole school of economists who optimistically, some say arrogantly, think it can be done. Statistically, there is no evidence to support that theory.

Recessions are one of the biggest threats to personal security due to the negative impact on everyone's income. According to the National Bureau of Economic Research (NBER), there have been 47 recessions in the United States since 1790. The definition of a recession provided by the NBER is, "a significant decline in real gross domestic product (GDP), real income, employment, industrial production, and wholesale-retail sales". They summarize the causes of a recession in a variety of categories, but foremost, it is the result of changes in government's regulatory, fiscal, international trade, and monetary policies, which are the common tools used to regulate growth in the economy. On a macro-level, these areas both impact and cause some degree of change in the relative direction of the economy. The inputs include cycles in agriculture, manufacturing, consumption, and business investment, and the health of the banking and investment communities. There are many institutes and government agencies that provide detailed tracking of the various inputs and outputs for each category in determining economic impact. Weekly and monthly reports are common for reporting changes of activity in GDP, unemployment, producer indices, and a variety of other economic indicators. One critical indicator is the Consumer Confidence Index because it represents the hometown sentiment of the people. While not scientific, the index measures consumer attitudes which directly impact consumer spending behavior. When times are good, people spend. During tough times, they save. This psychological index provides an indication of near term consumer spending trends, a primary driver of our economy.

Our broadest modern day indicators are the GDP and unemployment figures which were not developed, tracked, or recorded until 1945. The actual information regarding prior periods before 1945 is based on subjective evaluation derived from historical information available at the time. These indicators provide a snap shot of the overall health of our economy. During robust periods GDP goes up and employment levels increase. During down periods, when GDP is declining then unemployment increases. Therefore, one of the key areas effecting individual security are recessions due to their impact on employment. The current 2009-2011 recession follows a period of massive expansion. The cooling off period which always follows a boom period was inevitable and foreseeable. The government failed to react to the many leading indicators that warned of the impending decline. Due to its laser-like focus on healthcare and financial reforms, they over looked monitoring the economy and depended upon an anemic stimulus plan that lacked any long range specificity to guide the economy. Doling out stimulus funds to public entities had no impact on growing the economy. Its primary result was delaying the inevitable. The result has been long range unemployment with no plan for recovery.

Government intervention is usually at the forefront of attempting to jump start the economy through a variety of methods. Unemployment, the human factor, is one of the most critical factors impacted by recessions which result from downturns in overall economic activity. The patterns of recessions indicate that resumption of hiring is not immediate when associated with the upturn of business activity that marks the recovery of a recession. Unemployment figures begin to improve following what appears to be a sustainable recovery. If we eliminate the 12 years of the Great Depression and subtract out those12 years since 1900, then we see that the average recession has a length of about 2 years. Therefore those 24 recession and recovery periods both have average cycle lengths of about 4 years. The most significant impact is unemployment. In the area of economic planning, this places an immediate burden on government to support those on unemployment benefits regardless of the economic system we operate under. Recessions are predictable but the actual length and intensity are frequently unpredictable without the analysis of significant amounts of data. The data accumulation and analysis is often a trailing indicator due to the time required to analyze the data and study trend lines.

In 1938 President Franklin D. Roosevelt signed the Fair Labor Standard Act of 1938 which was composed of the Child Labor Law and the Minimum Wage Act. These companion acts were passed based under the philosophy that children were being hired and, in effect, stealing jobs from their parents. The associated Minimum Wage Law, with its many exemptions, stipulated the minimum wage payable for a 44 hour work week. These depression acts were designed to improve wages to eliminate exploitation of workers and increase income levels at a time when they were most needed. There are very few Acts that drew more ire than the minimum wage laws which were offered to guarantee security to the worker while interfering with the free market system. Walter E. Williams, the noted Professor of Economics at George Mason University and author, provides a detailed analysis of the impact and effects of the minimum wage highlighting the racial impact of the laws. While legislating racism was not the intention of the Act in 1938, its unintended consequences revealed that Blacks and Hispanics are the casualties of a law that was intended to improve wages, yet studies have revealed that the minimum wage has had a direct negative impact on low wage earners, those with the least amount of education and work experience: the Blacks and Hispanics. As Congress mandates increases in the minimum wage, wages at all levels are pushed upward. As the cost of labor increases, employers seek automated alternatives and varying work methods to offset the increased cost of labor input. In Dr. Williams, latest book, *Race and Economics,* March 2011, "Chapter 3- Race and Wage Relations, he reveals through a series of historic studies that over time the lowest paid workers are the first to be eliminated. This is based on the "inelastic" cost/price ratio between the cost of production and the revenue generated for a particular unit of production. In layman's terms, it means, that as the cost of low price labor is increased it contribution toward profit is diminished resulting in alternative methods of production. To lower the overall cost of production. Hence, government in its attempt to regulate the cost of labor increases unemployment. Doctor Williams provides a complete overview of the intent, impact, and associated negative outcomes that directly affect those in the most need of work.

The free enterprise system is the primary driver of our economy. Over the last 50 years our economy has changed in complexity. Today we have fewer production type jobs available and we rely on hundreds of thousands of small businesses which make up the fabric of our economy. The hundreds of thousands of jobs that were in the "Industrial North" are now in "Industrial China" and other areas where they have lower costs of labor. As we have shifted away from an industrial, production type economy to a service economy, we have lost our standing as a nation of producers. Manufacturing has fled from the United States to countries with lower wages and production costs. The unions, who can be thought of as havens for factory employees, are losing their hold on employees and are shifting their emphasis to service employees. Unions were formally thought of as manufacturing representatives for our production workers. Today we see more union members in the service sector and government sector jobs then we see in manufacturing jobs. Due to improvements in working conditions under a variety of Federal workplace rules and regulations, the need for union protection no longer exists. Instead, the primary role of the union appears to be class warfare against employers to continually increase wages and benefits for their members.

It appears that unions have become an industry group that seems to have escaped regulation. They have become de-facto fund raising arms of the Democratic Party. The Center for Responsive Politics, located in Washington, DC, is a non-partisan research group that tracks large donor political contributions. Their website, OpenSecrets.org reveals that between 1989 and 2010 Unions have contributed hundreds of millions of dollars to political candidates. Almost without exception, over 90 percent of those contributions have gone to Democratic candidates. It is no wonder that most preferential treatment is given to them, especially when it comes to waivers for compliance with the new healthcare The level of security afforded their members seems contractually higher than for others so that now it is the Unions who are the protected class. Those who are protected and coddled, who fight for increases in the overall level of wages and benefits of union employees are a contributing factor for companies as they flee in search for lower cost workforces for manufacturing. Our automobile industry, once the greatest in the world, will soon be trailing behind Japan, China, and India –the latter two are now gearing up to produce our cars of the future.

The shift from a manufacturing economy to a service economy has resulted in the closing of many factories--negatively impacting the towns who relied on providing support services for those who were directly involved in production. Transferring from being a net exporter of our production to an importer of production from other nations has had a negative impact on our Balance of Payments with our international trading partners. When we import more than we export we must send money overseas. When we export more than we import then other nations send money to us which goes into our economy. It is feared by many that we are soon going to be turning into a second rate country based on our dependence on others for all our consumer items where we were once King. Those whose jobs have been displaced are the first to learn the lesson of insecurity. These economic victims are a result of government becoming accomplices in wage and price increases, most noticeably at the behest of unions as adeptly noted by Dr. Walter E. Williams in his previously mentioned book, *Race & Economics*. The same government whose role it is to protect the rights and liberties of individuals has sold out our industrial complex to countries that under bid our overpriced labor. The only way to repatriate those jobs is to become more competitive in the global marketplace which is probably a political impossibility.

In 2011, we are seeing a shift in employment practices around the country. We are in the midst of a recession following a dramatic increase in business activity fueled by an out-of-control real estate and construction boom.

The National Bureau of Economic Research (NBER) reported in September 2010 that the recession ended based on their economic indicators in June 2009. The people in the 9.6% unemployment category do not have the confidence in the recovery based on their continued unemployment. We are offered a false sense of security when the state and local governments are provided Stimulus Cash to fight off the needed reductions in staff to match their revenue shortfalls. At the same time, the Federal government is expanding by hiring to support massive government programs to provide more regulation in our lives. The loss of freedom is directly associated to the false sense of security by the expansion of government employment figures. When we consider that the "recovery" is fueled by international debt from China, our largest holder of government securities, it is like saying one's income is up because he charged more on his credit card. The skimpy numbers that are used to classify our recession as "officially dead" do not indicate a true economic recovery. Those who have been hired by any local, state or the federal government may feel some sense of recovery. Those still standing on the unemployment lines who are looking for jobs have little faith in the recovery. While the government touts the end of the recession, the number of people living at or below the poverty level is reported as the largest number in history. The recovery, which is supported by government plans and entitlement programs, provides no immediate hope for individual recovery in these financially trying times.

The greatest threat to our personal freedom is a result of government's changing role in the world. Our Federal Government has been assigned the duty to protect our pursuit of Life, Liberty, and Happiness but now acts to limit our freedom.. At the expense of our economic freedom, the government has elevated its role to be the protector of not only the United States environment, but has joined in with other nations to be the "environmental police" attempting to regulate global environmental standards. With the elimination of many of our production industries through excessive air quality regulations and many imposed standards, jobs have fled to lesser developed nations. The industry groups that made this country great will soon completely disappear. We have lost much of our manufacturing base, with coal mining, forest industry and the steel production industries under attack. Associated with the loss of those industries we have hamstrung our transportation network, thus eliminating the need for rail and highway transportation, and limiting shipping along the shores of the Great Lakes. These have been the historical stalwarts of our nation. We have increased our cost of energy through our reliance on foreign oil. We are purchasing our needed supplies from countries that hate us as a nation and are working to destroy us. Our partially secular nation is "turning the other cheek." We are not only losing our production capabilities through a contrived series of government policies intended on killing our oil industry, we have been blocked from the land available to drill for oil through a series of land purchases combined with excessive governmental regulations. Our rich mining areas will soon be off limits as well. The capitalist is blamed for the sins of our nation, while the true enemy is our own government—the enemy within. Between unionization and governmental clean act regulation, it is open season on the "American Golden Goose." which is almost extinct. As we are forced to march toward a planned economy based on service sector "clean jobs," we are increasing our level of "dirty unemployment."

What is described above is nothing less than an American tragedy. Freedom has been the basis for our free enterprise system. By eliminating our access to the nation's natural resources, a national treasure, and one of purposes of our original founding, our government has eliminated factors of production that once made America the greatest nation on earth. In a misguided longing for security, our government is stealing our greatest treasure ---our Freedom!

Chapter 10   Why the Worst Get on Top

"Revolution is not a dinner party, nor an essay, nor a painting, nor a piece of embroidery. It cannot be advanced softly, gradually, carefully, considerately, respectfully, politely, plainly, and modestly. A revolution is an insurrection, an act of violence by which one class overthrows another." Chairman Mao

Dictatorial systems required for the implementation and the on-going operation of Socialism demand a different set of rules from the ones to which we have become accustomed. In this chapter we will review the birth of beliefs and actions that create and maintain a Socialistic society. We are familiar with the free market system that is based on the differentiation of products using persuasion through marketing, salesmanship and developing good customer relationships. Coercion replaces salesmanship under Socialism. Capitalism operates using a completely different set of values. If the capitalist were to conduct business under the same rules as Socialism, in all likelihood the business owner would be fined or jailed. Those activities condoned and required to operate under a Totalitarian system defy rules of ethics and acceptable behavior. If customer service is a key differentiating factor in a competitive society, under Socialism the level of customer service will suffer because "good customer service" is not a national value and is no longer a key component in a non-competitive environment. The true Socialist views this as a big advantage of Socialism, since good customer service carries a cost with it that is no longer required. Ultimately, in a Socialistic society the process of consumerism will cease being a pleasure. It will be viewed as a chore due to the creation of a very sterile shopping environment with a limited number of choices in the marketplace. The ability to satisfy wants will disappear and the total concentration will be based on meeting government determined needs.

In the free enterprise system, employers and employees in private companies work under a system of formal or implied contracts. The two parties in a wage-labor contract actually trade or exchange wages for labor. The employee has the right to freely leave an employer and the employer normally can only terminate an employee for just cause. The employer establishes rules of conduct and performance standards. However, under a coercive Totalitarian system all normal ethical rules are suspended. In many countries individuals are assigned occupations that offer little or no freedom of choice. Work is assigned based on need regardless of personal preference, as we have seen before in Cuba where the scientist is now a state supervised bartender

When we consider the vastness of our economy today, with its variety of choices and the hundreds of millions of consumers and the millions of providers of goods and services, it is easy to see the complexity of the free marketplace. On the surface, each transaction may appear independent and impossible to regulate and control with any degree of consistency and uniformity. Under our growing brand of Socialism, micro-management of businesses is being eliminated, for the most part, through an elaborate system of regulations. Rather than manage and control each business and individual transactions, the government appears to be regulating through two distinctive approaches: the taxing authority and heavy handed regulations of industries. If they can control economics via taxing authority and control the social aspects of air, water, energy, and the use of natural resources, then fewer individual business regulations are required. Therefore control of the natural resources is paramount and reduces the need for individual regulations of many businesses. When the impact of the total control of healthcare is added to the environmental impact based on the laws regulating individuals and business life, we then will realize that the government controls almost every aspect of our lives. There are so many non-healthcare issues built into the Healthcare Bill that we can no longer doubt that the healthcare bill is a "Trojan horse" providing still more repressive regulations.

Tax policy changes related to healthcare are our newest form of regulation. With the passage of the Healthcare Bill both small and large businesses have the added burden of providing increased business reporting for tax purposes. These requirements are in the process of being rescinded, but sooner or later they will reappear unless the Affordable Care Act is overturned by the Supreme Court. What follows is the unwieldy requirements for compliance as of April 2011. Each vendor action that supplies goods or services to any business totaling $600 or more per year must be reported. The actual minimum dollar amount may be increased in the future. This additional reporting requirement will require new tracking systems of expenses by vendor. Each transaction will require obtaining Tax ID information, and reporting 1099s for each vendor if the sum total of business exceeds that $600 threshold. For a very small business this burdensome reporting requirement may require dozens of separate tax documents filed with tax returns. For large companies, it may require hundreds of thousands of additional filings. The process will involve sending letters to obtain tax information to each vendor, following up for compliance, and then recording and maintaining name, address, and dollar amounts for each vendor. Imagine for a minute the interstate trucker who purchases diesel fuel three times a week, with each fill-up in a different town or state. This will require tracking and reporting as many as 150 reports to ensure compliance with already heavily regulated oil companies. For a single, owner-operator trucker, this will require a separate tracking system just for fuel purchases and the receipts filed by vendor. This is just one example of the tax policy changes related to healthcare that is our new reality—massive forms of new regulations. Welcome to Socialism!

Many common areas in our lives are already regulated. The fisherman is regulated by season and catch limits. The auto maker is regulated using EPA standards for air quality control. Air quality control is enforced both during the production phase of the automobile and after the fact when the car leaves the assembly line through pre-determined emission standards. The fertilizers our farmers are allowed to use are heavily regulated for both the amounts acceptable and the timing of their use. Our neighborhoods are regulated by zoning laws and building codes that have been predestined by "long range, comprehensive plans" where boards of elected officials decide what our neighborhood will look like in fifty years. Our small businesses require multiple licenses. Often minimum education requirements are established and "standards of ethics" are dictated. All these common activities and rules come with direction and enforcement tactics that ultimately reduce our level of freedom. This gradual loss of freedom has become reluctantly accepted for "the common good." We are neither strangers to regulation nor their enforcement by local, state and Federal governments. So what is different under a Totalitarian style of government?

When we hear the word "Totalitarianism" for many it conjures up thoughts of mass murderers like Stalin, Hitler and Mao. For others, it brings to mind many of our current day dictatorial leaders like Fidel Castro, Hugo Chavez and Ackmud Ahmadinejad of Iran. These manipulative leaders are the "Poster Presidents" for everything that is wrong with dictatorial styles of leadership. As governments gain more control and the dictator becomes something of a god, military force is required to exert more power over daily activities. Those who admire Socialism from afar most likely fail to realize the excessive powers required to administer a Socialistic society. Those who regard a coercive, dictatorial style of management as an occasional by-product of implementation tend to oversimplify the process and are simply wrong. This kind of forced coercion is not a secondary issue. Coercion is an essential requirement of a Totalitarian style of government. Those who fail to recognize it as a necessary requirement to move people beyond the point of resistance will ultimately sacrifice most of their freedom. Morality will no longer be the cornerstone of law and order. The true ends of the Socialist Mission is to satisfy pre-determined social goals through a variety of coercive powers which supersedes all moral implications. Those elected to the highest positions usually rise to that level based on charisma and charm, but ultimately rule with their boots placed firmly on the necks of the populace. As President Obama said when dealing the Wall Street Bankers and the oil company executives, "I will have to keep my boot on their necks." This is not the tone and tenor of a business friendly president. As the business climate deteriorates, President Obama will become more dependent upon support from the business community. His short sightedness has not endeared him to the community he needs the most.

In September, 2010, during the Gulf of Mexico oil spill, Ken Salazar, made a similar statement saying to the New York Times, his " primary job is to put a boot on the neck of British Petroleum." These types of statements are very telling about the attitude of government toward business. Citizens living and working under this new style of government will be required to adopt a new set of standards and moral values. Often we hear references to Nazism that certainly are not endearing to anyone except the anti-capitalist sympathizers.

The changing of morals from traditional beliefs to a value system that views government as a supreme power is another key ingredient in moving people toward the acceptance of Socialism and a hard-line Totalitarian style of government. This can be accomplished gradually over several decades by continuing to bend the Constitution or more immediately through violence. To pull off a major transformation generally requires an internal, military-type operation to support the transformational government. Those chosen for military duty are often the youngest and most recently indoctrinated. Class warfare and the targeting of social enemies is essential for the development of sufficient hatred to overthrow the status quo. This ingrained hated is required to replace our long cherished belief in morals that stem from the Natural Law and are guidelines for acceptable behavior based on the ideals of protecting others and doing no harm. These teachings are based, for the most part, on religious principles, indicating our founding and our trust in "One nation under God" that provide the tenets of our moral culture. These ideals have become "progressively" declining values in America leading to the gradual deterioration of our collective moral well-being.

Traditional moral values are in direct conflict with Totalitarianism which demands quick and immediate compliance, or at the very minimum, quiet and submissive obedience. A solid foundation in a true system of morality under God is the biggest threat to Totalitarianism. Religious teachings on virtue and positive values have historically been the greatest threat to collective change. With the abandonment of religion and morals, those who are the most easily influenced can be moved to perform unmentionable acts in the name of altruism once a viable enemy is created. Those who make this transition must sacrifice any self interest and be willing to perform any service. This reminds us of the SS guards in the concentration camps of the Third Reich, where horrible things were done to innocent victims based on a policy of hatred that is still pervasive today in the world.. Needless to say, when Socialism reaches this stage, any means can be used to achieve their twisted ends.

The Road to Socialism

Through a long term, gradual reeducation process started over 100 years ago, our religions have been attacked by a strategy bent on weakening the moral fiber of our nation. This gradual decline in our morality has resulted in successive generations buying into the "Hollywood code" of violence, promiscuity and the destruction of family values, and the result of this breakdown of morality is overflowing our jails and prisons. These are graphic examples of the "thuggery" which Hayek refers to when he talks about "the absence of a moral center when an authoritarian style of government implements its schemes to achieve perceived other social benefits". It is quite odd that anti-social behavior is not a reason to rally to Socialism, but it is one of the key prerequisites in developing and implementing social change—that kind of manipulated change that cannot be sold to the people based solely on its merits.

Another sad contributing factor related to our decline in moral values is the gradual deterioration of the family unit. Throughout history the family unit has been the central stabilizing force in building a society. Historically, the family unit brought stability to homes with the adherence to the Fourth Commandment and the teachings of churches urging honoring thy mother and father. Belief in God, should be paramount in society rather than total allegiance to the State. The motto "In God We Trust" provides guidance to people who have a strong religious faith and a good moral foundation. There are those who disagree. This concept is lost for millions and millions who are treated as "victims of society" while living under social safety nets, in fatherless homes, with children that learn their patterns of moral conduct and "code of ethics" in the streets rather than the church pew. As our prisons overflow and our school graduation rates decline, our failed social safety net programs are bursting at the seams. The Progressive Movement, which is against a laissez faire doctrine in business, is quite comfortable with the "anything goes" attitude that is becoming more prevalent in our homes and our communities. All this deliberate demeaning of religion and moral principles results in the demoralization of a growing portion of society. This weakening of moral fiber has led to a permanent, victimized class who becomes a growing sector of society and the benefactor of our tax dollars.

Think for example of the tragedy of New Orleans during the aftermath of Hurricane Katrina. The crime, the violence, and the mayhem was caused by seedy people and perpetuated by a lawless, local out of control government. In turn Ray Nagan, the Mayor, blamed the problems on President Bush and his failed FEMA Disaster Recovery efforts. Had the Mayor sounded the alarm and the residents evacuated The Big Easy, many problems could have been averted and would have resulted in a more orderly evacuation of nearly 1 million people. The problems escalated from the Parishes to the Mayor's Office, up to the State Capital, and ultimately to Washington D.C. Big government, at every level failed the people not only in Louisiana, but in Mississippi, and Alabama. These unfortunates are not the victims of Capitalism gone astray. The victims of this natural disaster and the aftermath of the savory citizens attempting to capitalize on the disaster are a result of the failed Progressive Movement that results in lawless behavior based on the lack of any moral code. Further, the response by Big Government, at every level, was unable to respond through their integrated system of "red tape" in a timely manner. Five years later there are over 5,000 unused mobile homes that are rotting on vacant lots awaiting government approval to utilize them for housing for the displaced people of the Gulf region.

As our social norms deteriorate, our need for social responsibility is increased to support a morally declining society. This comes with great expense. The new system feeds off itself, and we are creating a permanent welfare state for over fifty per cent of our population which pay little or no taxes and is perfectly content with living with their hands out for more. The large numbers of participants in social programs then become a central core group in favor of more social programs. When the government creates a large constituency group that is dependent upon government for its sole survival, it is certain that the same group of dependents would never vote against the programs that they have become dependent upon. When it comes to voter support it would be like having your kids vote on whether they would like ice cream or spinach for dinner. Our vast numbers of poor are rapidly becoming an organized voting block and a key component for the transformation to a more Socialistic society. Ignorance and programmed poverty are essential ingredients in building a more Socialized society.

Hayek asserts that there are three primary strategies employed "to enlist large scale support groups for a social transformation which may not be composed of the best of society, but rather the worst". The first strategy requires controlling the education process and information flow to insure that our children will become sufficiently indoctrinated for future manipulation. The second strategy relies on manipulating the lesser informed and undereducated who Hayek calls "the docile and gullible." They hold no views of their own but allow themselves to be force fed by their providers. These are the sheep who are herded by the government. These submissive people become more susceptible to believing in common enemies, which the Socialist government willingly supplies and identifies. Creating the actual enemy groups is the third critical strategy. Together these strategies aid in uniting a large common segment of society while training them to succumb to the decisions made by their government. At the same time, the elite Socialists provide activist support for the instigated changes. The docile and the under educated, influenced by the elite or ruling class, become the pawns of the movement against intentionally, yet falsely vilified targets.

Take for example the hatchet job performed on Sarah Palin and her family by the press and bloggers and even the White House Czars. Their attacks, lies and personally damaging remarks were meant to discredit her and her moral standards. In some ways it worked since her candidacy for President seems to have been derailed. On the other hand, these tactics by the Left have further endeared her to the Tea Party members who share her values. Her support in the 2012 elections may just help to derail President Obama's quest for a second term.

The pawns of society, those who are carefully taught to hate and fight for their "rights," gradually gain a sense of unity. The coordinated strategies make it compelling for large segments of the population to unite to conduct a social war against the powers that have made our country great. Look what happened with union support in Wisconsin. Among the protestors were paid agitators sent to stir up the dedicated teachers, healthcare workers and the firemen and police who stood to lose some of their rights bargained for when the state was financially sound. The recent recall elections of republicans organized by the unions resulted in unseating only two members at a cost of over $30 million dollars. Those two seats may be the most expensive seats in state election history still not turning over a majority to the unions.

The union leaders became active after the Wall Street Bankers were bailed out under the TARP Program and many employees of brokerage houses were paid large bonuses. The media published the names and addresses of many of the recipients. The SEIU union leaders called out their members and organized bus trips to protest at the homes of those who received bonuses. This was clearly an organized activity to instill further hatred toward the Wall Street community. These Marxist tactics have become routine with protests in our states' capital cities against legislatures who are trying to reduce the influence of unions in state government.

People generally hold views consistent with their level of formal education. Therefore, controlling educational content is paramount to the ultimate success of the Socialist Movement. Obama's handlers knew if they could control health care, energy and education in our contemporary America, they could control the people. The key to influencing people to obey the dictates of government is to begin with our children. This begins with educating them early-on with teachings that are consistent with the long term agenda of the Socialist government. In most of our schools the true role of government is not being taught. Our school systems have eliminated lessons about the Declaration of Independence, our Constitution, and our long and historic struggles to become and remain a free nation. Our children are being indoctrinated with an incorrect understanding of the purpose of our form of government. Any education that does not include a solid understanding of the founding principles of this nation will misdirect our children. The failure to emphasize "American Exceptionalism" and this nation's accomplishments over the last 200 years denies our children an accurate portrayal of the greatness of our nation. When our educators demonize our country in our school systems, it furthers the agenda of a government whose primary goal is to take way our power and liberty. This reeducation process, one of the key Marxist tactics, is essential to progressively indoctrinate people into believing that we exist solely for the benefit of the state. This contradicts the true purpose of our American form of government which historically serves, at the pleasure of the people, to help preserve life, liberty and freedom for the people and to provide for our common defense.

Many parents and civic leaders decry a system that progressively costs more and produces less. We are watching children subverted to a cause while they fail to learn the basics of a good education. We are suffering from a decline in the quality of the education of our children. On the world stage, our American education system has dropped in ranking to 24th Place and continues to decline based on the Programme for International Assessment (PISA) test results for 15 years olds who are compared to 65 other countries around the world. These results were reported at the National Governor's Conference by Education Secretary Arne Duncan in February 2011. The major declines are in the key areas: math, science, and reading. The emphasis here in education has changed from promoting core requirements to a very broad generalized education program that fails to meet any goals to aid our children to become self-sufficient. Our average high school students lack basic reading and math skills and do not possess any job skills beyond the minimum wage requirement jobs needed for working in most fast food restaurants. When we compare ourselves to countries like China, Singapore, and Romania, our high school graduates are outperformed in mathematics by 3rd graders in those countries. For example, a second grader in China can multiply using the Times Tables up to 13 in their heads. It is the minimum requirement in many provinces in China for graduation to the 3rd grade. Our students have difficulty arriving at the answers without the benefit of a calculator, much less using the traditional long hand method of multiplication with pencil and paper. Our dropout rate in high schools around the country averages about 35% with rates of 60 to 70% in our inner cities. These failing children are our future. Our Federal Education Budget has ballooned to almost $100 billion yet we still fail at providing basic survival skills for our children.

An article in the USA Today, on March 28, 2010 reported wholesale irregularities on standardized tests used to evaluate student and teacher performance in Washington, D.C. Test answers on state aptitude tests were changed to improve test scores to help meet performance goals for pay bonuses for teachers and principals. Absurdly, bonuses were paid to teachers whose students could neither read nor write. Unions were the first to protest an investigation into the irregularities in test scores. No doubt with all this improper educational methodology, we are watching a generation being indoctrinated into Socialism. Clearly we are failing our children and our nation. Based on the Federal Budget figures for 2011, we are spending about $100 billion a year for the Department of Education and still getting inferior results.

The "dumbing-down" of society may not be intentional in all cases, but it is still disgraceful. Our second and third graders are often taught by people who went into teaching because they weren't good at math and science. This new touchy-feely education system continually lowers standards to meet the lowest level of performers. The misguided objective in our education system is to ensure that everyone obtains a satisfactory grade, one that doesn't humiliate the student, but it defeats the purpose of education. When we continually reduce performance standards to satisfy an archaic Bell Curve System, we lower the standards at both the top and the bottom. Those who meet the minimum level of proficiency and those below that standard under our declining standard system are the ones most prone to suffer low levels of self esteem. Personal self esteem is not improved by the denial of failure, but through the sense of improvement in a worthwhile effort. Those not motivated to embrace the importance of an education are the same pool of students who form the basis for lowering our national standards. Not at all surprising is the reality that our uneducated children grow up with poor self-images, hence perpetuating a low level of expectations as adults. The parents who say, "I can't do math", generally raise children who say, "I can't do math". These under-educated and under-challenged individuals become the sacrificial pawns used by our Socialistic leaders who are planning our future.

To correct this decline in our education system, we must provide the tools and types of education that provide a realistic approach to self reliance. Instead, our elected leaders rally to the cry, "You are a victim and the government will help you." Ironically, the government causing the problem purports to be able to fix the problem. When they combine our failing educational programs with a defined indoctrination curriculum, our children grow up with false opinions regarding the role of government. In essence, this system is developing a more pliable electorate through the reeducation process of revisionist history that will eventually erase our long and glorious history. When we consider the ballooning educational budget this reason alone could form a reasonable basis for minimizing the role of the Federal Department of Education. The Winter Conference of the National Association of Governors met in February 2011 in Washington and specifically addressed the role of the states in improving education. Large spending in Washington has not improved the quality of our education system. Dictating failing systems to our State and local school systems has resulted in declining assessment scores.

To preserve our founding spirit we must reverse this trend in the loss of our intellectualism. Reversing this trend is essential and can be achieved if we demand higher standards in our education systems at an earlier age similar to those competing nations whose children consistently outperform our children. If we examine the models of the most successful nations, and also compare the family unit structure of the various nations, we would undoubtedly discover that our declines in education and morals can be traced back to a significant increase in the number of unstable family units in our communities. The destruction of the family unit in America is at epidemic proportions and this must be reversed. It is no coincidence that our communities that have the highest incidence of fatherless homes have the lowest education levels. Our current social programs are perpetuating this problem. The on-going decline in traditional family units is a problem that must be corrected in order to regain our leadership position in the world and it cannot be achieved under our current social programs.

It is clear that developing support for Socialist programs does not rely on the most successful in our society, but rather on those who are cast into unsolvable social situations. For the Socialist, it is in their self interest to perpetuate and increase this underperforming segment of society to create a large category of people who are dependent upon the government. This requires long term strategies that absolutely do not breed the best into our society. The primary problem that we face as a nation with the mass implementation of more redistributive social programs is the overall drop in the level of education and intelligence of our people. If this is not true, then why have we seen the most significant declines in our educational results over the last 50 years while at the very same time we were experiencing our most prosperous period? We believe it is because during this same period we have witnessed the great expansion of politically motivated socialized programs that have failed to improve the quality of the very lives they were designed to help.

To continue to implement Socialist programs requires that Socialist leaders continue to reeducate our people to ensure they abandon classical ideas and learn to embrace "a more socially responsible" agenda. Social responsibility is defined to mean more allegiance to the government than to the people they serve. Today our schools are showing cartoons in the classrooms that impugn Capitalism and embrace Socialist beliefs. Al Gore's "An Inconvenient Truth" was taught as Gospel truth and our children are being indoctrinated with the belief that what is turning out to be false science is the truth. It is nevertheless promoting the "Cap and Trade" energy program with its charges for the excess use of carbon dioxide. In our new high-tech video world our children are being educated via cartoons rather than books. Indoctrination requires mass acceptance to be successful. Sadly enough, cartoons reach the widest possible audience to complete the indoctrination programs supported by special interest groups who are allowed into our school systems.

Implementation of Socialist goals requires that a variety of support groups be recruited and indoctrinated. The best support groups to enhance the accomplishment of more Socialized programs are what Hayek calls the "docile and gullible." These are the weakest in our society because they have not only been deprived of a good education, but also are deprived of an opportunity to become self supporting and independent. Through indoctrination they have become dependent upon government. Government control starts with creating dependency. A dog does not bite the hand that feeds him. The same theory applies to people. Today, we are seeing riots in Europe that bring back memories of the French Revolution. In Europe those who have been the most dependent upon the government for support are outraged and angry because the government system is broken. The primary proponents of Socialism appear to be the most violent. In America we are entering a period of increased government support to meet the needs of the people due to a long term economic downturn. The increase in Unemployment Benefits, sold on a humanitarian premise, may to just another attempt to create another constituency group at the taxpayer's expense. As Rahm Emanuel says, "Never let a good crisis go to waste." In fact, if you don't have one then it is recommended to create one, even if it is a false crisis. The Left assumes the ignorant electorate will not know the difference.

Dependence is being created through massive deficit spending programs developed to meet the purported needs of the people. The same government that created the chasm by destroying the free market system through irresponsible government programs will create mass dependency based on ever expanding, unsustainable social programs. If we study the riots in Greece, France, and Italy as well as the rioting and fighting in the Middle East, we will see a preview of what our children's lives will be like in the coming years. Hayek commented that dependency on government, "… is an instrument of political power, it creates a degree of dependence scarcely distinguishable from slavery." We are now witnessing in Europe the fruits of the Socialist system and its failures, that when governments can no longer live up to the unrealistic expectations they promised, the people will revolt.

Who are the docile and gullible? Many are people who have been living off the government for so many years that they have accepted the low level of support. Many have grown accustomed to a system which keeps them locked into a mode of what amounts to modern day slavery. The government does not appear to be committed to reducing the number of people on assistance. The government appears happy to perpetuate a system which breeds failure and lowers the self respect of our citizens. Any system that promotes failure and never offers a chance to improve the self respect of its people is not based on compassion. This is not caring for the poor but rather it is clearly government-sponsored servitude.

Many have learned to accept the status quo. Politicians who promote and expand government programs are chaining millions to a system of quiet servitude without any promise to improve their long term opportunities. President Reagan said it best when he said, "Government is not the solution to our problem. Government is the problem." There is no better example of our failed government solutions than when we drive through our inner cities. These are the areas with the highest dependency on government assistance. These neighborhoods have the highest unemployment rates and greatest threats of violence. If our governmental programs were working correctly, wouldn't we see some signs of success? Our so-called compassionate programs have not touched the surface of the real problem. The only conclusion that can be drawn from perpetuating these failed social programs is that they serve some greater purpose. If our social programs condemn our citizens to lives of poverty then we have already proved that our social programs do not work regardless of the source of funding. We are creating the worst in society not the best we have to offer. Is it unfair to conclude that this was deliberately done to produce a perpetual under class dependent upon government?

The third and final strategy that brings out the worst in people is to name a common enemy. To effectively organize and create unified support requires identifying the enemy. A government motivated enemies list provides the impetus to perpetuate the movement toward Socialism. Never before in our history have we seen such brutal attacks on our business community by our elected leaders. The government, to be successful in gaining support for massive changes, must create a perceived problem to then provide comprehensive transformative solutions. The solution never really intends to actually solve the root problem. It is really a part of a series of smoke screen issues to rile up the electorate in order to elevate government as the supreme protector of the people. Every issue must have an enemy. The revolutionaries of today have learned from history. In Germany during the early 20th century, the Jews were the targets because they were classically the store owners, business people and the bankers. They were the symbols of Capitalism. Rather than attack industry groups, which is the preferred method today, Nazis attacked and tried to exterminate an entire culture. Once the target was selected the indoctrination and hatred continued until the Second World War was started.

Who are the persecuted that make up the targets of hatred today? One clear target group is our largest industries. Many of our best companies are moving operations overseas, even those who have been the driving forces that have made our country great over the last century. Have there been mistakes? Of course, there have been. But today's Socialist government finds the answer is no to fix the problem, but instead we should destroy the entire system. Those who despise our way of life prefer to tear down the walls of the institutions that provide needed goods and services. We are confronted by groups who are actively trying to unhinge our economic culture using the same tactics of Nazi Germany. Today's enemies do not have faces. They are the buildings that house the corporate giants, the offices of doctors, hospitals, and insurance companies. They are banks, investment companies, and oil companies. The enemies list includes oil drillers, coal miners, manufacturers, and foresters. Any business based on the harvesting of natural resources is a villain. Any company that provides the conduit for the transfer of money is marked as a target. One perceived enemy is the insurance company that rejected a healthcare claim. Another is the logger harvesting trees in the forests of the Pacific Northwest. Any industry that uses natural resources or has any impact on the environment, whether real or imagined, is named an enemy of our society.

Our economy is being craftily dismantled. Where will it end? Our reliance on foreign natural resources has never been greater. A government that purports to despise the export of jobs overseas promotes the impetus through union support, high tax policy, and unworkable regulations which in turn encourages the exodus of American industry and the importation of natural resources from other countries. Iron ore is available from the shores of Minnesota, yet the ships rigged to haul the ore sit idle in harbors on Lake Michigan and Lake Superior. Instead, we import steel from Japan which uses their own ships to provide the raw materials to manufacture cars in Michigan. The net result of our governmental mismanagement is that our smoke stack industries are being dismantled and their workers sent to the unemployment lines. The demand for "clean energy" and higher union wages is the catalyst driving our unemployment. The clean energy solutions were supposed to provide clean jobs. They have not materialized yet we continue to live under harsh attacks. Our business leaders are fleeing America because untenable government regulations make it unprofitable to compete on the world stage. Yet, the government condemns those who are leaving while they fail to mention that they were the accomplices who forced them to leave.

Other common enemies include the coal companies that are accused of polluting our country when they provide power to our homes. The eight cylinder car is on the road to extinction because it uses too much fuel. The SUV is one of a whole series of well marked targets which are in the sights of the environmentalists. Slowly, the Socialist government garners support for a not so quiet revolution to eliminate the captains of industry and stifle our use of our own natural resources. Our whole system of life and survival is under attack as hated targets are gradually destroyed by those taught to hate America and what we stand for.

One more example and then we'll move on. Healthcare Reform was sold on the basis of reducing cost, improving service, and increasing the availability of access to healthcare to 30 million uninsured people. The hateful, greedy health insurance companies were the targeted faces used to unite support from the masses to satisfy the healthcare agenda. The goals of "reducing cost, providing greater access and better service" were the rallying cry to move this issue forward. Since then, facts are slowing being revealed that over the next 10 years we will have a shortage of 90,000 doctors requiring medical assistants and nurses to take greater roles in providing medical care. Our doctors and hospitals that were accused of price gouging and were the targets for healthcare abuse have been coerced into complacency. They have been lumped together with greedy drug companies and the medical equipment manufacturers who have been responsible for some of the greatest advancements in medical care, despite severe over regulation. In an attempt to punish these providers, the Healthcare Bill will levy heavy new taxes. This will further reduce the attempts to innovate in the future. There should be no wonder why our companies are relocating to other lands.

These people being demonized by the government are the ones who are responsible for extending our life expectancy rates by over 20 years in the last half century. Their very success in improving our life span is now blamed for the healthcare crisis. Early reports indicate that the numbers used to sell the "snake oil" solutions to the public are false. After six months of "finding out what is in the bill" as exclaimed by the Speaker of the House Nancy Pelosi who helped champion the government take over of one sixth of our economy, we are about to discover that the Healthcare Reform Bill was either a gigantic fraud to deceive the people or total ineptitude on the part of government. The healthcare reform bill was many years in the making by back room conspirators who released their programs to provide solutions based on false information and inaccurate cost and savings projections. There are estimates that claim that due to the rising costs of the healthcare reform legislation and its impact on the economy during a major recession could result in 50-80 million people losing healthcare coverage over the next ten years. When this is combined with the loss of medical professionals during a period of increasing demand, the result will be the complete freezing out of access to adequate healthcare. Those who will suffer first are the seniors and the lower income levels that will not be able to afford or get timely access to healthcare. If this is the true purpose of the plan then it is beginning to look like medical genocide.

It's not surprising that one year after the passage of Obamacare, opposition to the program has climbed to over 60%. There are 28 states that are using their legislative rights to attempt to nullify the healthcare bill joining together as plaintiffs against the United States Government. Using their power under the 10th Amendment of the Constitution, they are seeking to overrule the powers usurped by the Federal government. The methods employed to socialize our healthcare system, are the same tactics being employed in all our industry groups. In the name of social preservation, we are gradually destroying the foundation of our economic system through the persecution of the same entities that helped make this country great. As of August 12, 2011 the Eleventh Circuit Court of Appeals in Atlanta has ruled that the government mandate is unconstitutional. The court determined that Congress does not have the power to make citizens buy products, specifically insurance from private companies. This provides a serious blow to the entire healthcare bill because it removes the funding arm of the entire reform package. This court decision provides the Obama Administration a number of options which could possibly delay a final decision until after the 2012 elections. This decision was probably anticipated, but this decision combined with future pending court cases provides little security for the people in the interim. This is not only a temporary victory for the people but a victory for freedom.

Many of these scenarios that were predicted were ignored to over power a naïve public. An equally naïve body of legislators who have were accomplices to this pending disaster are slowly realizing the errors of their way. The enemies to our freedom, real or perceived, were required to move legislation forward against the will of the people. Polling indicated that Congress passed the Healthcare Reform Bill against a majority of about 52%. Six months following the passing of the bill those opposing it had risen to 67%. We might call this the organized "Duping of America."

There are many theories on group dynamics and the Socialists have been practicing the manipulation of people through the use of group dynamics for over 100 years. Using the Nazi Handbook, they have discovered that people will subscribe to various types of behavior and actions as a member of group when they would not participate in the same behavior as an individual. The creation of a variety of support groups to accomplish various agenda items is not new. There are groups that are designed to fight for issues and against issues. Those that are the most aggressive appear to be groups where anger is used to breed their passion. Anger and hostility are the best motivators to raise people to a level to accomplish activities as a group, where they would never conduct the same acts as single individuals. There is a sense of protection in a group. Individualism is lost and the feeling of responsibility is shifted to the group rather than assumed by the individual. During the peace riots of the 1960s we often saw peace turn into mayhem as soon as the first person threw a bottle. The first bottle was usually the instigating act that encouraged lawless behavior. Group organizers know that violence can be instigated after the group is elevated to a high pitched level of excitement. It only takes a few well disguised acts to incite a mob. These group leaders and planned agitators are representative of the worst kind of leaders. Group violence is becoming more common in Europe and some Latin American countries. It may be coming to America soon. Those that appear to be the most vocal and violent are those protesting against the government. Since over 50 percent of our economy is still dependent upon the free enterprise system we remain free from large scale violence. It is not unreasonable to assume that the organizers, the Marxist and Communist, will begin targeting our corporations since they have the ear, and maybe even the encouragement, of our White House. Big Government is walking a tight rope. As we shift to a more government controlled economy the threats of violence may increase as government is unprepared to meet the promises to the people. As Aristotle pointed out in his Book of Politics, circa 350BC, tyranny is the greatest enemy of the State. It is true over 2000 years later. He further believed that tyrants were fond of bad men because bad men could be motivated to bad things. There is no wickedness too great for the tyrant and the greatest tool of the tyrant is doing the unspeakable.

Tyrannical leadership under a totalitarian form of government in America requires abandoning our current form of government and denouncing the principles of the Declaration of Independence and the United States Constitution. Today we are at a crossroads where we as a people must decide if we will rule or the government will rule. To retain freedom requires that limits must be placed on government and these ideals must be enforced at every level. Our local governments control what happens in our backyards while the Federal government wants to control our water, air, natural resources, our education systems, our business climate, our salaries and our healthcare systems. Unless they are stopped we will be destined to a life of servitude to our government. The American way of life was founded a developing a government as a vehicle to promote our rights and liberties. The purpose of limited government is that it works for us. It was never intended as a power to destroy our rights to freedom. Unfortunately in America, the worst may be yet to come if we do not act to protect her.

Chapter 11 The End of Truth

"The prerequisite for an ideology is possession of a basic truth. For example, a Marxist begins with his prime truth that all evils are caused by the exploitation of the proletariat by the capitalist. From this he logically proceeds to the revolution to end capitalism, then into the third stage of reorganization into a new social order or the dictatorship of the proletariat, and finally the last stage --the political paradise of communism." Saul D. Alinsky, *Rules for Radicals, 1971*

The word "truth", at first glance, does not appear to be a difficult concept to understand. In one sense, the truth is the opposite of a lie. We know that 2 plus 2 equals 4. Many of us grew up with still another concept of the truth while watching the 1960s hit TV series, *Perry Mason*. "Do you swear to tell the truth, the whole truth, and nothing but the truth, so help you God?" The answer with hand on the Holy Bible by the witness was always an affirmative, "I do". We heard that George Washington could never tell a lie when he admitted to chopping down his father's precious cherry tree. A truth is something that is believed to be correct. The key word is "believed". However, making a statement based on a belief as to a fact or situation being true can actually be false if the basic premise is false. It is one's belief system that creates the context for evaluating whether something is true or false.

For instance, my wife gave me a lovely shirt. I liked it very much. I thought it was a red shirt, but she insisted it was orange. I compromised with the fact that it could be viewed as an orangey-colored red shirt. One day I was selected to participate in a group activity. The leader said pointing to me, "You, hey you in the orange shirt". My immediate thought was I was wrong. It is an orange shirt. Did I lie about it being red? No, of course not. My perception based on my belief led me to think that the shirt was red. My observation that the shirt was red was correct to me, but to others I was incorrect. Therefore, our belief systems, whether they are right or wrong, have a significant impact on "coloring" what we think is true.

Using the idea of truth based on beliefs systems, when we re-read Saul Alinsky's "basic truth" above we realize that a belief system constructed on the idea that all evils are caused by exploitation by Capitalists paves the way to a revolution to end Capitalism. Anyone who disagrees with the "basic truth" that Capitalism is the cause of social and economic evils will not support the conclusion that it should be destroyed. Unfortunately, we are hearing about more videos in the classroom and classes promoting the evils of Capitalism in schools starting as low as the second and third grades. If we took a survey of parents to determine if social economics was an appropriate topic to be taught to our elementary students, many of which can barely read or write, the answer would most likely be a resounding "No." The programs being taught in our schools is based on the theory of relative truth. There are dozens of other theories on the exact meaning of truth based on a variety of philosophies and the study of objective and subjective truth and the prevailing arguments go back to the time of ancient Greece and Rome. Theologians for instance state that one of the attributes of God is that He is Truth. Thus the meaning of "truth" can be the subject of intense study that would go far beyond the scope of this study. Let it suffice that teaching anti-capitalistic dogma to our children is wrong and it is no different than the German youth training by the Nazis. Brainwashing has no place in our schools and is an institutional system of developing a progressive belief system without the benefit of comparative analysis.

Belief itself can be based on scientific, mathematically provable observations, or based on a directed form of training, education or indoctrination. Those who teach Communism, who draw their belief systems from Karl Marx, believe that system to be true and promote propaganda to educate, reeducate, and indoctrinate new believers. There are those who hold opposing views. If they tend to view life based on Judeo-Christian value systems, then individuals will remain responsible for their actions rather than merely resolve to be go-along victims of a class warfare system carried out over hundreds of years

Today we are at a crossroads where the beliefs held by the signers of the Declaration of Independence and the Founding Fathers who confirmed the Constitution of the original thirteen colonies are colliding with the views held by Karl Marx and Friedrich Engels who wrote the *Communist Manifesto* in 1848. We can compare these two opposing philosophies simply by reviewing some of the highlights of the Declaration of Independence and the Communist Manifesto. These documents and their individual supporters are at war in an unsettled world. We can review the first two paragraphs of the Declaration of Independence and compare the "missions" of both documents and determine the belief systems that form the basis of our country versus the belief systems held by the Marxist and the numerous political factions operating openly in America today. While reading the *Communist Manifesto*, mentally note the number of actions that are currently being observed in our society today.

The Declaration of Independence

"When in the Course of human events it becomes necessary for one people to dissolve the political bands which have connected them with another and to assume among the powers of the earth, the separate and equal station to which the Laws of Nature and of Nature's God entitle them, a decent respect to the opinions of mankind requires that they should declare the causes which impel them to the separation."

"We hold these truths to be self-evident, that all men are created equal, that they are endowed by their Creator with certain unalienable Rights,that among these are Life, Liberty and the pursuit of Happiness. — That to secure these rights, Governments are instituted among Men, deriving their just powers from the consent of the governed, — That whenever any Form of Government becomes destructive of these ends, it is the Right of the People to alter or to abolish it, and to institute new Government, laying its foundation on such principles and organizing its powers in such form, as to them shall seem most likely to effect their Safety and Happiness. Prudence, indeed, will dictate that Governments long established should not be changed for light and transient causes; and accordingly all experience hath shewn that mankind are more disposed to suffer, while evils are sufferable than to right themselves by abolishing the forms to which they are accustomed. But when a long train of abuses and usurpations, pursuing invariably the same Object evinces a design to reduce them under absolute Despotism, it is their right, it is their duty, to throw off such Government, and to provide new Guards for their future security. — Such has been the patient sufferance of these Colonies; and such is now the necessity which constrains them to alter their former Systems of Government. The history of the present King of Great Britain is a history of repeated injuries and usurpations, all having in direct object the establishment of an absolute Tyranny over these States. To prove this, let Facts be submitted to a candid world."

The Communist Manifesto

The introduction or preamble to the Manifesto is claimed to have been one of the most powerful writings in the 19th Century to unify a group of unrelated people. Before examining the closing arguments of the Manifesto read the opening of the manifesto which contains the most famous words written by Karl Marx. These are the words that united a social revolution that still haunts us today.

"A specter is haunting Europe- the specter of Communism. All the Powers of old Europe have entered into a holy alliance to exorcise this specter: Pope and Tsar, Metternich and Guizot, French Radicals and German police spies.

Where is the party in opposition that has not been decried as Communistic by its opponents in power? Where is the Opposition that has not hurled back the branding reproach of Communism against the more advanced opposition parties, as well as against its reactionary adversaries?

Two things results from this fact:

1. Communism is already acknowledged by all European Powers to be itself a Power.
2. It is high time that Communists should openly, in the face of the whole world, publish their views, their aims, their tendencies, and meet this nursery tale of the Specter of Communism with a Manifesto of the party itself.

    To this end, Communist of various nationalities have assembled in London and sketched the following Manifesto, to be published in English, French, German, Italian, Flemish and Danish languages."

(Excerpts - closing argument)

"Undoubtedly, it will be said, religious, moral, philosophical and juridical (sic) ideas have been modified in the course of historical development, But, religion and all morality, philosophy, political science, and law, constantly survived this change.

There are besides, eternal truths, such as Freedom, Justice, etc., that are common to all states of society. But Communism abolishes eternal truths, it abolishes all religion and all morality, instead of constituting them on a new basis; it therefore acts in contrast to all past historical experience. What does this accusation reduce itself to? The history of all past society has consisted in the development of class antagonisms, antagonisms that assumed different forms at different epochs. But whatever form they may have taken, one fact is common to all past ages, viz., the exploitation of one part of society by the other. No wonder, then, that the social consciousness of past ages, despite all the multiplicity and variety it displays, moves within certain common forms, or general ideas, which cannot completely vanish except with the total disappearance of class antagonisms. The Communist revolution is the most radical rupture with traditional property relations; no wonder that its development involves the most radical rupture with traditional ideas.   But   let us have done with the bourgeois objections to Communism.

We have seen above that the first step in the revolution by the working class is to raise the proletariat to the position of ruling class to win the battle of democracy.   The proletariat will use its political supremacy to wrest, by degrees, all capital from the bourgeoisie, to centralize all instruments of production in the hands of the State, i.e. of the proletariat organized as the ruling class; and to increase the total of productive forces as rapidly as possible.

Of course, in the beginning this cannot be effected except by means of despotic inroads on the rights of property and on the conditions of bourgeois production; by means of measures, therefore, which appear economically insufficient and untenable but which, in the course of the movement, outstrip themselves, necessitate further inroads upon the old social order, and are unavoidable as a means of entirely revolutionizing the mode of production. These measures will of the course be different in different countries. Nevertheless in the most advance countries, the following will be pretty generally applicable.

1. Abolition of property in land and application of all rents of land to public purposes.
2. A heavy progressive or graduated income tax
3. Abolition of all rights of inheritance
4. Confiscation of the property of all emigrants and rebels
5. Centralization of credit in hands of the State, by means of a national bank with State capital and an exclusive monopoly.
6. Centralization of the means of communication and transport in the hands of the State.
7. Extension of factories and instrument of production owned by the State; the bringing into cultivation of wastelands, and the improvement of the soil generally in accordance with a common plan.
8. Equal liability of all to labor Establishment of industrial armies, especially for agriculture.
9. Combination of agriculture with manufacturing industries; gradual abolition of the distinction between town and country by a more equable distribution of population over the country.
10. Free education for all children in public schools, Abolition of children's factory labor in its present form. Combination of education with industrial production, etc.,etc.

When in the course of development class distinctions have disappeared and all production has been concentrated in the hands of a vast association of the whole nation, the public power will lose its political character. Political power, properly so called, is merely the organized power of one class for oppressing another. If the proletariat during its contest with the bourgeoisie is compelled, by the force of circumstances, to organize itself as a class, if by means of a revolution it makes itself the ruling class and, as such, sweeps away by force the old conditions of production, then it will, along with the conditions, have swept away the conditions for the existence of class antagonisms, and of classes generally, and will thereby have abolished its own supremacy as a class.

In place of the old bourgeois society, with its classes and class antagonism, we shall have an association in which the free development of each is the condition for the free development of all."

(This is the end of Chapter 2 of the Manifesto)

* * * * * * * * * * *

When we compare the Declaration of Independence to the Communist we immediately see that one is a document of hope and the other is a document of despair. The Declaration of Independence gives rights to the people and in a sharp, dark contrast the Communist Manifesto takes rights away from the people. "The truths that are self evident" annunciated in the second paragraph of the Declaration are openly denounced as "eternal truths" in the Communist Manifesto. The first step in moving toward a socialist agenda is to eliminate those truths. In reading the two most famous paragraphs in the Declaration we are reminded that the argument for separation from a tyrannical government is in the name for pursuing "unalienable rights." The closing summary of the Manifesto clearly indicts social classes and the restructuring of a distributional society based on ownership of property. All private property will revert to the state for the benefit of all people. It is their theory that elimination of property rights will remove class struggle. The social classes denounced in the Manifesto existed for centuries. Those classes were done away with in America and a new class of people were promised a right to opportunity. Where the Declaration sets a foundation for a future constitution of the people, the Manifesto establishes a foundation for total government control by a new ruling class. Our freedoms lost are clearly outlined in the *Communist Manifesto*. The similar steps outlined in the Manifesto were repeated in more depth and detail in a plan presented to President Franklin Roosevelt in 1933. It is more than coincidental that almost all of the points summarized in the *Communist Manifesto* reappeared in 1936. What is even scarier is that most of the plan has been accomplished in the United States in the last 80 years.

In addition to the ideas outlined in both documents, think about the tenor and tone in each of the stated goals of the Declaration of Independence and the *Communist Manifesto*. The Declaration is a document of hope, but not like the false hope promised by campaigning candidate for President Obama with his "Hope and Change". Like Obama, The Manifesto is a document of anger. Both of these historic documents should be required reading on a comparative basis in our school systems. Unfortunately, only the concept of one of them is highlighted in our education systems today. The Declaration of Independence is rarely studied in our schools anymore because the idea of hope and freedom is no longer paramount in our teachings of American history. The radicals have learned that despair is a better motivator of change than hope. This is the beginning of the eradication of the American way of life and its truth for our children. Unless things are corrected soon, there will be only one school of thought. Our children will no longer be offered the choice of hope in our country today because hope is rapidly being replaced by the message of despair. There are those of us who are holding dear to the principles of the Declaration of Independence, which is based on God and clearly and eloquently outlines the purpose of our separation from a despotic ruler and our pursuit of freedom for all men. The *Communist Manifesto* outlines the opposite point of view that religion and the will of the people are no longer supreme and that tyrannical rulers, with the aid of class warfare, will reorganize both the country and the world, with the intent to become the supreme rulers of the world.

These are two basic philosophical truths or belief systems that are directly opposed to each other. Collectively, the belief in one system or the other clearly defines and delineates the course of our system of government and ultimately our future way of life. We can chose to be free by restoring our system of government, which is being rapidly eroded, under the laws based on the Constitution of the United States which gives power to the people. Or, in turning our backs on the Constitution, we can throw away our belief system in the fundamental rights of liberty and freedom and cling to the methods and systems that replace individual control with dictatorial power that takes away not only our rights, but our property and, most importantly, our inalienable right to pursue happiness. Where do these opposing and contradictory views come from? Propaganda is the easy answer. But, what is propaganda?

Propaganda is the means for influencing political ideas through the presentation of information in any type of media. The purpose is to persuade one into believing a particular point of view. This is generally done by presenting a point of view and alternately avoiding, denying, or refuting a competing point of view. Most often, providing a one-sided argument and eliminating an alternate viewpoint avoids the possibility of choice. In propaganda, choice is never an option. In marketing this tactic is called advertising. In politics, it is called interpretation or persuasion or propaganda, which often like advertising, does not have to be based on truth.

The methods and tactics used to persuade viewpoints are becoming more important in politics. Politicians fight to gain power or remain in power and use excessive claims and often excessive threats based on individual differences and political posturing. The choice is between more government rule and intervention of our daily lives or less government interference. If you prefer the government moving farther to the left, then the word "interference" may be viewed as posturing for an anti-government position. If your belief system rests on the idea that more government control is better than less government control, than the word "interference" can be viewed as a positive aspect. It has been said in politics, "that beauty is in the eye of the beholder." The difference is your own point of view.

The history of the differences in political beliefs goes back over two millenniums to the time of Socrates, Plato and Aristotle who were the first to record the variations of political thought. These Greek philosophers were responsible for the classification of ancient thought, and unraveled the ideas that were used to develop the modern world. The evolution of thought created differing viewpoints overtime, but many of the philosophers in the past 200-300 years rooted their beliefs in the lineage of thought carried forward for two millenniums. The founding principles in a variety of government structures evolved based on Greek thought and were later influenced by religious beliefs. The intervening beliefs in religion led to the inclusion of freedom of religion in our Constitution in the principles outlined in the original Bill of Rights. Since 1787 when the Constitution was adopted, there have been proponents on both sides arguing over the level of government control and administration that should be injected into our daily lives. This fight continues with every election which postures one side against the other in deciding what method or level of government is best for our citizenry. When we review our particular beliefs and weigh those beliefs against the Constitutional Law, we often arrive at differing opinions. The truth, the absence of truth, or ultimately, the end of truth is dependent upon the course of action taken by each successive government through the political process. The interpretation of "what is government's role" is clearly a choice based on our belief systems. There are many who insist on more government control for the "common good". There are also those who also believe that less government control is in the best interest of "the common good." We cannot have it both ways. Therefore, we often vacillate due to political pressures and the party in power at the time.

Looking at our evolutionary process of government, it appears very certain that whatever ultimate role of government evolves, pursuit of happiness is not in the forefront today. As we move closer and closer to Socialism, we are not witnessing an overabundance of happiness. On the contrary, the government's self imposed responsibility to solve every imaginable problem has not provided for a happier society. Today, we see disruption, antagonism, and vitriol that separate the people of our United States. Through continued government interaction we have increasingly broken up into factions of discontent. As we move farther away from the principles of freedom we are witnessing a growth in our discontent. The *Communist Manifesto* uses word like "struggle," "misery," "grave digger," "destruction," "brutal," "exploitation," and "forcibly overthrow". A single word that never appears in the doctrine, neither the word nor the concept, is "happiness". As we gradually and progressively move closer to the principles outlined in the *Communist Manifesto*, that is void of happiness as a goal, we see greater equality in misery. It is most regrettable that the progressive socialization of our society will continue to broaden the disparity between the "haves" and the "have-nots" until a framework is created to totally destroy any semblance of American Exceptionalism. That is the stark truth facing us today if we do not meet the challenge to protect our American way of life by teaching the truth.

The Road to Socialism

Chapter 12   The Socialist Roots of Nazism

"It is thus necessary that the individual should finally come to realize that his own ego is of no importance in comparison with the existence of the nation, that the position of the individual is conditioned solely by the interests of the nation as a whole." Adolf Hitler

The rise and fall of Nazism covered only a short period of time between 1919 through 1945, yet its impact and long range effects continue to have significant overtones. The series of events that led to the development of the National Socialist Party (Nazi party) was as unifying to Germany as the Founding Fathers were in America. Germany, late to develop as a unified city-state, provided the environment for some of the world's greatest thinkers and the world's greatest atrocities. The philosophy of Nazism still causes chills to run up the spines of many people.

During the period after World War I, Germany slowly recovered from substantial losses resulting from imperialistic egotism. The landscape of Europe had been redrawn, major Empires eliminated, and the devastation of war gave way to a wholesale rebuilding of a national character and economies in almost every nation. The reparations imposed by the Treaty of Versailles choked the life out of post war Germany. Reactionary movements were instigated by a variety of new political parties, each with its own viewpoint and solutions. The competing ideologies provided many conflicts that were acted out in the streets. Socialistic ideas were prevalent at the time. Marxism and Communism were considered extremism. The tactics used by both were the step-children of roots of National Socialism. The National Socialist Party, or Nazism, began to evolve shortly after the end of World War I. It began when Professor *Johann Plenge*, a great authority on both Marx and Hegel, set the stage for a post war recovery plan based on Marxian philosophy. It was Plenge's initial belief that individualism could be preserved with the implementation of Marxism, but he soon learned that freedom had no place in a Socialist-Marxist agenda.

The hard working people and the youth were indoctrinated to love German Nationalism. The philosophers and educators at the time promoted the unity of the state. *Werner Sombart,* a noted German economist and social scientist was quoted by Hayek on page 183 of *The Road to Serfdom.* "The German idea of the state, as formulated by *Fichte, Lassalle*, and *Rodbertus*, is that the state is neither founded nor formed by individuals, nor an aggregate of individuals, nor is its purpose to serve any interest of individual. ...the individual has no rights but only duties. Claims of the individual are always an outcome of the commercial spirit. The ideals of 1789 - liberty, equality, fraternity are characteristically commercial ideals which have no other purpose but to secure certain advantages to individuals." Commercialism was the term used for Capitalism. It was clear that individualism found no home in German politics. The Germans held a view that war was sacred and a country's esteem was based in its militaristic superiority. That view provided a basis for the First World War, and later led to the Second World War.

The philosophers, educators, and intellectuals of Germany had the most influence over the social direction of the nation. During the 19th and 20th centuries scores of intellectuals rose to national fame as the thinkers of a nation and were held in high esteem. They shaped the political direction, the economy, the learning academies, and impacted almost every aspect of daily life. During the same time, Northern Germany clung to Lutheran Church values. The church remained supreme and for good reason. There was a mutual admiration among many of the intellectuals and the church which professed God's Will. Every controversial subject was justified in the light of God's Will.

The new expansion of "the scientific community" also was a justification for the revolutionary changes taking place in Europe, and with more zeal, specifically in Germany. Classical education of political thinkers advanced during the Marxian period and provided the social momentum required to influence the non-thinking public. The elevation of scientists gave credence to the ideas and theories of the educational community. The sciences were divided into two categories: social sciences and natural sciences. The social scientists included the studies of subjects that were not empirical, but often dependent upon social theories rather than quantitative, provable natural sciences like: biology, chemistry, physics, astronomy and the earth sciences. Social sciences were categorized as anthropology, archaeology, economics, history, law, political science and psychology. The social scientists became the social engineers for the rebuilding of Germany. Those raised in Germany were the most likely to entrust increased power to the State. People who academically disagreed with this political philosophy were exiled to other countries. There was no freedom of speech, thought or press. Therefore, the direction and influence of the national social scientists shaped the belief systems of the people, and when convenient, were reinforced through the church.

The growth of Nazism in 1919 was founded on the strong ideals and belief systems of the German people. Having been defeated in the First World War, the Germans returned with damaged egos and a need to rebuild both their nation and national character. The political parties were the central organizing force that held the people together. An Austrian war veteran, Adolf Hitler, then only 30 years old, swiftly emerged as the central figure to run the Nazi Party and rebuild Germany. He was charismatic, a forceful leader, and uncompromising.

Hitler called upon all citizens to sacrifice and compromise for the good of the State. Hitler was unyielding. He developed a nationalistic philosophy based on the "total state" concept of government partially adopted from Benito Mussolini, the Italian leader and head of the Fascist Party. Mussolini chose to implement a style of Socialism that was absent of class warfare. However, Hitler used race as his calling card for his totalitarian state. The Marxian approach attacked the capitalist as a target for class warfare; the Nazis chose the Jew and the non-Aryans. Future revolutions were based on any collective of people that could be made into a unifying target to motivate people to rally as a group. It was clear that to be successful a unifying enemy had to be created. The Jews were that unifier for the Nazis in Germany.

In February, 1920 the Nazi Party issued a manifesto that became the bedrock of the party and the nation. The "Twenty-Five Points" documented a list of items and ideals to be enforced for the further development of Germany. The Twenty Points covered policies and strategies for both domestic and international relations. The aim was to unite every faction in Germany under one unified nation and expel those who were not "true Germans". The doctrine addresses self determination of the individual, which is self determination toward the stated goals of the state, not the goals of any individual.

Note: The twenty five points are listed below. Using the internet several variations were discovered. Differences in the versions reviewed are based on various translators and some versions were summarized. The version below appears to be the most comprehensive one.

The Twenty Five Points of Hitler's Nazi Party

1. We demand the union of all Germans in a Great Germany on the basis of the principle of self-determination of all peoples.

2. We demand that the German people have rights equal to those of other nations, and that the Peace Treaties of Versailles and St. Germain shall be abrogated.

3. We demand land and territory (colonies) for the maintenance of our people and the settlement of our surplus population.

4. Only those who are our fellow countrymen can become citizens. Only those who have German blood, regardless of creed, can be our countrymen. Hence, no Jew can be a countryman.

5. Those who are not citizens must live in Germany as foreigners and must be subject to the law of aliens.

6. The right to choose the government and determine the laws of the State shall belong only to citizens. We therefore demand that no public office, of whatever nature, whether in the central government, the province, or the municipality, shall be held by anyone who is not a citizen.

We wage war against the corrupt parliamentary administration whereby men are appointed to posts by favor of the party without regard to character and fitness.

7. We demand that the State shall above all undertake to ensure that every citizen shall have the possibility of living decently and earning a livelihood. If it should not be possible to feed the whole population, then aliens (non-citizens) must be expelled from the Reich.

8. Any further immigration of non-Germans must be prevented. We demand that all non-Germans who have entered Germany since August 2, 1914, shall be compelled to leave the Reich immediately.

9. All citizens must possess equal rights and duties.

10. The first duty of every citizen must be to work mentally or physically. No individual shall do any work that offends against the interest of the community to the benefit of all.

Therefore we demand:

11. That all unearned income, and all income that does not arise from work, be abolished.

12. Since every war imposes on the people fearful sacrifices in blood and treasures, all personal profit arising from the war must be regarded as treason to the people. We therefore demand the total confiscation of all war profits.

13. We demand nationalization of all trusts.

14. We demand profit-sharing in large industries.

15. We demand a generous increase in old-age pensions.

16. We demand creation and maintenance of a healthy middle class, immediate

communalization of department stores which will be rented cheaply to small trades people, and the strongest consideration must be given to ensure that small traders shall deliver the supplies needed by the State, the provinces and municipalities.

17. We demand an agrarian reform in accordance with our national requirements, and the enactment of a program to expropriate the owners without compensation of any land needed for the common purpose, as well as the abolition of ground rents and the prohibition of all speculation in land.

18. We demand that ruthless war be waged against those who work to the injury of the common welfare. Traitors, usurers, profiteers, etc., are to be punished with death, regardless of creed or race.

19. We demand that Roman law, which saves a materialist ordering of the world, be replaced by German common law.

20. In order to make it possible for every capable and industrious German to obtain higher education, and thus the opportunity to reach into positions of leadership, the State must assume the responsibility of organizing thoroughly the entire cultural system of the people. The curricula of all educational establishments shall be adapted to practical life. The conception of the State Ideas (science of citizenry) must be taught in the schools from the very beginning. We demand that specifically talented children of poor parents, whatsoever their station or occupation, be educated at the expense of the State.

21. The state has the duty to help raise the standard of national health by providing maternity welfare centers, by prohibiting juvenile labor, by increasing physical fitness through the introduction of compulsory games and gymnastics, and by the greatest possible encouragement of associations concerned with the physical education of the young

22. We demand the abolition of the regular army and the creation of a national (folk) army.

23. We demand that there be a legal campaign against those who propagate deliberate political lies and disseminate them through the press. In order to make possible the creation of a German press, we demand:

(a) All editors and their assistance on newspapers published in the German language shall be German citizens.

(b) Non-German newspapers shall only be published with the express permission of the State. They must be published in the Germany language.

 Interests in or in any way affecting German newspapers shall be published in the German language.

(c) All financial interests in or in any way affecting German newspapers shall be forbidden to non-Germans by law, and we demand that the punishment for transgressing this law be the immediate suppression of the newspaper and the expulsion of the non-German from the Reich.

Newspapers transgressing against the common welfare shall be suppressed. We demand legal action against those tendencies in art and literature that have a disruptive influence upon the life of our folk, and the any organizations that offend against the foregoing demands shall be dissolved.

24. We demand freedom for all religious faiths in the state, insofar as they do not endanger its existence or offend the moral and ethical sense of the Germanic race. The party as such represents the point of view of the positive Christianity without binding itself to any one particular confession. It fights against the Jewish materialist spirit within and without, and is convinced that a lasting recovery of our folk can only come about from within on the principle:

COMMON GOOD BEFORE INDIVIDUAL GOOD

25. In order to carry out this program we demand: the creation of a strong central authority in the State, the unconditional authority by the political central parliament of the whole State and all its organizations.

The formation of professional committees and of committees representing the several estates of the realm, to ensure that the laws promulgated by the central authority shall be carried out by the federal states.

The leaders of the party undertake to promote the execution of the foregoing points at all costs, if necessary at the sacrifice of their own lives.
(End of Text)

        The twenty five points made it absolutely clear that the Nazis were determined to be in total control of the nation. Every facet of German life was to be governed for the good of the State. The first three points make it sound like there is concern for the individual, but that was never true. This manifesto provided the foundation and the justification for every government action for the next twenty five years. It provided the totalitarian basis for implementing

Socialism in Germany and some of the tenets remain true today. The concept of the individual was totally destroyed along with the right of ownership of private property.

Hitler's feelings regarding the people became law. "The system which Hitler established-- the social reality which so many Germans were so eager to embrace or so willing to endure--the politics which began in a theory and ended in Auschwitz was the "total state." ...The state must have absolute power over every man and over every sphere of human activity, the Nazis declared. 'The authority of the Fuhrer is not limited by checks and controls, by special autonomous bodies or individual rights, but it is free and independent, all-inclusive and unlimited,' said Ernst Huber, an official party spokesman, in 1933." "The concept of personal liberties of the individual as opposed to the authority of the state had to disappear since it is not to be reconciled with the principle of the nationalistic Reich. ... The constitution of the nationalistic Reich is therefore not based upon a system of inborn and inalienable rights of the individual." *Ominous Parallels, by Leonard Peikoff*, 1982 page 6.

The Code of Nazism was based on the idea of the total elimination of the individual requiring that all people surrender their personal rights and property to be a member of a group. There was only one form of allegiance and that was allegiance to the state. The people could be identified as members of a variety of groups, but none ever as sole individuals. The only legitimate purpose of the people was to sacrifice for the state.

Nazism brought with it a special brand of Socialism which varied from both the Marxian style and the Fascist Italian style. The Marxist beliefs were based on economic class warfare. Mussolini's version left the classes in tact. The Nazi philosophy was designed to create a master Aryan Race, using race as the issue rather than class warfare. Under Hitler there were two types of wars; the imperial expansionism war and the internal "cleansing war" to create the "master race" through mass annihilation. The goals created by Hitler required militaristic support to not only invade other nations and control the "inferior races", but also to insure compliance of the populous to ensure meeting the goals of Nazism. Due to organized indoctrination and propaganda, internal compliance was easily achieved through early indoctrination of the youth. The youth movement and the development of national loyalty provided a common feeling of "national pride" throughout Germany that led to unquestionable allegiance. The national spirit, in some ways, was similar to the founding spirit in America 150 years earlier.

Our Founding Fathers were not simply a rogue group of patriots who banded together to form a new nation. Like Germany, our founders were the historical philosophers and contemporary thinkers who were chosen to create the ideal society. After years of tyranny, administered by an English King, they refuted oppression and the absence of freedom that was rampant in the Colonies. In contrast, the German people were under the influence of a branch of philosophical thinkers who evolved to develop a new national character that chose the exact opposite direction, returning the people to more oppression and a tyrannical ruler emerged. The German philosophers and the intellectual class were opposed to individualism and focused on intellectual control. The original founding principles of Nazism were extrapolated from the original ideas of Plato, Kant, Hegel, and, Marx, who was previously expelled from Germany due to his revolutionary positions. Ironically, Marx whose ideas were the foundation of the Nazi Movement, never lived to see his ideas exported from Europe and applied in his homeland. A new brand of thinkers had evolved and the philosophy of reason was rejected because it led to independent thinking. Deductive reasoning, the enemy of the state, provided uncontrollable thought processes which may have tempted the citizens to challenge state controlled ideologies. This independent thinking had to be stopped.

Independent thinking was the mortal enemy of Statism. Hitler implored people to rely on their feelings and instincts, comparing them to animals that lacked the ability to reason. People were trained to rely purely upon instinct for their actions. Emotionalism took the place of reason. It was far easier to teach people what to believe and who to respect, along with providing them with an unwavering sense of national pride. The key was to remove any sense of independent thinking from the blend of beliefs. According to Peikoff, stressing an education of facts, dates, history, and any ideas contrary to the welfare of the nation, was not in the best interest of society. "Learning schools" were developed and encouraged by liberal progressives and national conservatives who offered education based on feelings and emotion rather than reasoning skills. This indoctrination and methodology was required to build an elevated level of emotionalism leading to what we would refer to today as "team building" in today's world. Adolf Hitler regarded himself as the supreme motivator inspiring unquestionable confidence and allegiance in the regime.

The liberal educational system was essential to develop a strong military complex, an essential part of managing the German people. It began with the emotionally charged youth movement instilling in them a special brand of patriotism. This was combined with the mandated ideals of the concept of selfless service to the State. Total control of every aspect of life was maintained based on the Platonian ideals that there was no room for individuals in a German society. This reinforced the idea that all people have one allegiance: to serve the State.

The Hitler Youth embraced the philosophy through continual

indoctrination hat there was no other purpose, and there was no nobler cause than to serve the State. While Germany developed into clusters of dedicated groups, there was one group that rose to ultimate power, and they controlled all individuals. That group was the military and particularly the SS. These groups had unlimited power to enforce compliance of all people. Military training started with the youth movement. The education system incorporated military training and discipline training. Full scale military duty was the next logical step for the youth movement. The techniques employed over centuries in various nations required strong militaries, who did not rely on thought. A strong military, by its nature, is trained to react to instructions and orders in a well defined hierarchy of command. The principles of military engagement have not changed over centuries and the never-to-be-challenged discipline employed then is still used today. A strong sense of military might promotes a strong sense of national character. The tools and techniques to create reactionary and ordered precision do not take years of indoctrination. The impressionable youth make the best candidates for a militia because they are the most pliable for developing a large scale system of enforcers. Independent thought has no place in military ground operations. Unquestionable allegiance is required to maintain order and compliance from the people to their leaders.

The German Philosophy developed in the 1920s which ended after World War II was characteristically flawed due to its bigotry, although it served to accomplish Hitler's domestic agenda. Germany's attempt to devour its neighbors and to expand its global reach required far more might than was available. When Germany lost territorial control of neighboring nations after World War I and the Treaty of Versailles, it had to begin rebuilding on an alternate theory of supremacy. The historic conquests were the imperialistic approach to expand the economic and cultural base was lost after World War I. Following the War, Germany chose to purify itself ethnically to regain world supremacy. It adopted ethnic cleansing as the method to develop the "master race." The simplest explanation was that developing a unified superior nation was a matter of science by removing the non-Aryans, and breeding, through eugenics, a superior culture. This idea was probably the closest any modern day society came to self-cloning. Today, less than 100 years later, we see the opposite trend with the expansion of multi-culturalism in most developing nations, with the exception of the Islamic Nations and Israel. Multi-culturalism has resulted in the mixing of various ethnicities in most developed nations. Those not participating or lagging behind are the under-developed African Nations which provide little or no opportunity, the Islamic Nations, who limit religious freedom and those nations with the severest forms of totalitarianism. These groups of nations epitomize the results of limiting capitalism, limiting religious freedom, and living under a dictatorial style of government. The nations restricting the most freedoms appear to be the countries suffering both economically and socially based on Western standards.

Nazism provides us with a preview of the impact of limited freedom of industry, the loss of religious choice, and the immoral implications of a strong totalitarian style of government to incorporate what was one of the worst portrayals of Socialism. Nazism was one of the most advanced forms of extremism for any developed nation. The parallels have not been repeated in developed nations, but some of the tactics and principles are used, in part, in a variety of nations, and are beginning to be seen in the United States and around the world. When we examine the brutality of war, in a variety of conflicts around the globe, we see the results of strict military actions. Germany used military action not only against other nations, but employed those principles within its own borders to manage the citizenry. The principles of annihilation whether used to control a culture or to demonize an economic faction ultimately utilize similar techniques. The Marxian principle that the end justifies the means erodes any sense of morality. Gradually, through indoctrination and at the dictates of expediency, immoral leaders automatically resort to immoral techniques.

It is clear that the socialization of a nation requires severe limits on freedom and individual choices to achieve compliance to a set of rules that are always reliant upon a dictatorial method of administration. The only difference we see today is the gradual increase of governmental control through the progressive elimination of rights that slowly limits our personal freedom. Individual self determination, which was the greatest threat to Nazism, must be preserved if we are to remain a free nation.

Chapter 13   The Totalitarians in Our Midst

"The great strength of the totalitarian state is that it forces those who fear it to imitate it." Adolph Hitler

The world we live in today is vastly different from the world we were familiar with fifty years ago. There are many who long for the "good old days" when life was simpler. Others enjoy living the "American Dream" based on the "progressiveness" we have made since the end of World War II. Our children have advantages today that many of us never dreamed of as children or even as young adults. Today our children "text" and "tweet," and play videos games like professionals. For most families, there is usually a car available in the driveway, and probably another one in the garage, and our kids become angry or upset when they are not available to take them to the Mall to hang out. The creature comforts that we enjoy and have grown to expect through the advancements in technology are the result of unfettered Capitalism and the human desire to innovate. The many things that we enjoy as Americans are also shared by people in most of the developed nations.

The countries that don't commonly have 46-inch televisions with 24 hour cable, garage door openers, microwave ovens and refrigerator/freezers with beverages dispensed through the door, I-pods and the other wizardry that evolves every six months also don't have clean water to drink or homes with electricity. They base their success in terms of incomes of a few dollars per month or year rather than dollars per hour. They lack the ability and do not possess the imagination to dream about the things that people in developed nations cannot seem to live without.

The human suffering in under-developed countries is brought on by disease, malnutrition, and man-made or even government instigated bloodshed which is common where there is excessive government control, corruption, and thwarted opportunities. Formal education is almost non-existent. The movement afoot to correct these imbalances or "injustices" between developed and under-developed nations is the philosophy of redistribution of wealth or Global Socialism.

America has tried to become the world's nation builder with little success. Today we are being attacked both internally and externally by forces who believe that our problem is our over consumptive lifestyles. On the reverse side, others claim we are harvesting the fruits of our freedom. Capitalism, the engine of development, has been diagnosed by its enemies as the culprit consuming the limited resources that deprive under-developed nations of the opportunity to develop. As stated earlier, more is never created by taking away from the producers and giving to the non-producers. Beginning in the 1960's with our liberal, socialized programs to provide subsidies to the poor, we have not improved the lot of the poor. We just seem to have made it easier to be poor and even then we are condemned for its perpetuation. Through the creation of "nationalized dependence" we have encouraged long term, government promoted poverty. We have virtually sponsored the life style of poverty without any regard for promoting self sufficiency. It is too facile to assert that America's "materialism" does not have any correlation with the nations that experience the most inhumane suffering. Those suffering thousands of miles away, or in the case of Cuba, only 90 miles away, are not the result of capitalism gone astray. This misery results from repressive governments that force poverty and deny individual accomplishments. The fact is that state run industrial complexes and fully subsidized government programs under totalitarian rule have not provided an ounce of progress in comparison to developed nations.

Many thinkers over the years have examined the imbalance between those nations that experience a higher standard of living to lesser developed nations. The underlying belief of the Marxist is that materialism is caused by exploitation of one class over another. It is further falsely believed and the myth is perpetuated that there is a finite amount of natural resources available in the world and the over accumulation in one area or nation deprives the availability of resources to lesser developed nations. This tune has been played for over 150 years using the Marxist agenda. The imbalances of wealth between nations are deemed to result from "social injustice." Social justice is claimed to be achieved by the redistribution of wealth making all societies equal. Marx and Engels argued for the redistribution between classes. Today's Marxists are seeking international redistribution between nations. America, the most prosperous nation in the history of the world, is being targeted from both within and from afar as the expected financier of Socialism throughout the world with the aid of the supporters of the United Nations. One of the justifications they point to is the wide disparity of income levels between the ultra-rich in America and those at the lowest levels: they argue that while the rich continue to get richer, the poor are lagging behind. They charge that corporations that provide the wealth of individuals, based on innovation and their capitalistic prowess, only reward those at the highest levels with the richest life styles. The others, those who remain and survive on government hand-outs, are claimed to be the victims of Capitalism.

Social Justice, a relatively new term, has no consistent definition. The progressive-left defines social justice as access to food, clothing, housing and medical care for all people. There is no mention of personal responsibility on the part of individuals to participate in acquiring the skills or display the effort to achieve what is being classified as "their basic rights". One could easily make the assumption that if all people elected to take advantage of their proclaimed "basic rights" eventually there would be no producers, no method of exchange, and civilization would eventually crumble. The true meaning of "basic rights" in the Marxist Doctrine comes down to the decree that each is entitled based upon need. Karl Marx popularized the Communist slogan, "From each according to his ability, to each according to his need." While this rallying slogan sounds very good on the surface, one must remember that the individual cannot seek work or endeavors based on their highest use or ability and their needs are determined by the State based on the utility of the person and their family. A person's value is not based on their overall contribution but on their future utility. There is very little difference between people and mules. Those on the right believe that the concept of "social justice" was contrived to create another propagandized tool to support class warfare, the justification for redistribution of wealth, and ultimately, the elimination of Capitalism.

As Hayek describes in *The Road to Serfdom*, the totalitarians are all around us. He uses examples from the 1930's to highlight the sentiments of the promoters and sympathizers after the First World War. The economic climate in Europe before and after the war was in turmoil with sporadic minor recoveries leading up to the Crash of 1929 which was the beginning of the First Great Depression. It was noted that most of the gifted legislators in the British Parliament tended to be "socialists at heart" which was the current mood of the day. They were struggling to resuscitate the economy while providing additional government support. Today the neighborhoods of Europe are on fire while the entitlement class more of what has been promised with little or no contribution. This indicates the inevitable degeneracy of society under a Socialist style of living..

During the same period, the situation in America paralleled the economic conditions in Europe. The recovery after World War I was both sporadic and listless. In America the war was funded by personal investment: through War Bonds bought by the people. The American people were patriotic. They suffered through a long period of rationing and price controls of basic consumer items which ultimately led to high inflation.

In England the shift to a war-time economy also was followed by severe inflation and brought England to its knees. This financial condition was blamed on failed capitalism and greedy individualism. This trend affected America until after World War II. There are two sets of dynamics at play that derailed the economic cycle and the free market system: building a war complex that diverts government funds to non-productive financial goals; and the subsequent clean-up resulting from the government's attempt to control an economy devoid of free-market capital required to sustain growth. Any gains realized from building the military complex are offset by the losses in the development of consumer goods and on-going long term capital expansion brought on by free market innovation. This is the classic economic argument between investing in "Guns or Butter". With limited resources the choices tend to restrict consumer goods through rationing of consumer goods and services resulting in price fixing. Price fixing whether in war time or dealing with limited resources has proved to be instrumental in leading to inequities or a lack of equilibrium in the markets ultimately resulting in rapidly rising inflation.

In economic terms "equilibrium" is a primary and necessary component of an efficient market under a free market system. Government intervention has provided fodder for those who espoused capitalism as the failing system when, in truth, government interference and imbalances in the macro-economic models by injecting artificial or non-free market influences into the system were probably the cause. As Hayek points out, this interference "does away with a freely adjusting price system for basic consumer goods. Bluntly put, during war the market system is more or less abandoned, as many parts of the economy are placed under central control." *The Road to Serfdom, pg 11.* Hayek feared that these policies would be further exploited by the Socialists during peace time. In most cases, the problems are further compounded by the creation of barriers to international trade imposed on many nations who were former enemies. In reaction to the results that were produced by governmental decisions, the governments then established a series of responses to re-stimulate the economy. History has proven that manipulating fiscal and monetary policy has not provided the positive results expected. Both in Europe and in America we see this scenario repeated over and over again from World War I through the Korean Conflict in 1952, Vietnam in the 1960s ending in early 1972, and up to and including our war efforts in the Middle East today.

Hayek completed *The Road to Serfdom* in the early 1940s. His narration of the "totalitarians amidst us" was based on samples of influential people who represented Socialist ideals prior to the conclusion of his work. He highlighted individuals and thoughts prevalent by Socialists at the time in the areas of economics, journalism and the sciences pointed out the proclaimed socialists in British Parliament who promoted the ideals of socialism in Europe, and specifically in England after the First World War. From 1937 through about 1942, prior to completing *The Road to Serfdom*, Hayek was teaching a summer program at the London Society of Economics (LSE). The series of lectures were most likely the basis for his book. The next year a counter class was offered to explain the benefits of Marxist theology and controlled economies in conflict with Hayek's teachings of the need for free market principles. Hayek's fear was that ultimately the process fostered by the intellectuals, "the impetus of the movement toward totalitarianisms comes mainly from two vested interests: organized capital and organized labor." *The Road to Serfdom, Page 204.* He cited the path taken by Germany during the two previous decades. Organized labor would provide the movement to destroy privately owned enterprises following the doctrine of the Communist Manifesto thereby setting the stage for Totalitarianism. Adding more fuel to the fire, there was also the continuing fear that industrial monopolies would be growing and would dictate prices internationally. The economic climate in America was far more active during the same period leading up to the 1940s. It seemed the worst enemies of Capitalism were not in the streets and the halls of higher learning. They were in the White House and continued to reside there during most of the 20th century.

Totalitarianism takes on many forms and is usually marked by the dictatorial style of leadership that controls it. The text book definition from *Wikipedia* describes it as "a political or state-run government system where the control of a single political group, person, faction, or class recognizes no limits to its authority and strives to regulate every aspect of public and private life. Totalitarianism is generally reinforced with authoritarianism, where ordinary citizens have little impact on national decision-making. Totalitarianism usually occurs with a predestined agenda requiring aggressive changes in the role of government and control over the people. The lines between public and private life become blurred as additional government control is administered through heavy handed regulations."

Ronald Reagan defined Totalitarianism with far greater specificity relating its effect on human life in his comments about Russia during the 1980s. In his memoires, *An American Life by Ronald Reagan, page 471* he states: "Soviet Communism was not just another competing economic system run by people who happened to disagree with us about the merits of capitalism and free enterprise: It was a predatory system of absolute, authoritarian rule that had an insatiable appetite for expansion; it was determined to impose tyranny wherever it went, rob people of fundamental human rights, destroy democratic governments, subvert churches and labor unions, turn the courts and the press into instruments of dictatorship, forbid free elections, imprison and execute critics without charge or trial, and reward the few at the top of the monolith with the spoils of corruptions and dictatorial rule. In short, it is against everything that America stood for, for more than 200 hundred years."

The election of Ronald Reagan in 1980 placed the first President in office who subscribed to modern conservative principles. Reagan, a former Democrat, was a disciple of Senator Barry Goldwater the noted Republican

Conservative who lost his presidential bid in a landslide to Lyndon Johnson in 1964. During most of the years in the 20th Century we were governed by big government spending, liberal presidents. The Republicans were far more moderate than the Democrats with the most progressive agendas who were what we call the "liberal tax and spend Democrats."

During the 20th century we struggled as a nation with two world wars, none of our making, a variety of interim recessions, and the Great Depression on the heels of the 1929 Stock Market Crash. The 50 years following World War II began with the election of a war hero, General Dwight D. Eisenhower, following the activist period of constant economic tinkering in response to the major events that consumed American life. One of our greatest periods of prosperity began in the early 1900s leading up to the 1929 Stock Market Crash. Our industrial complex was operating at full bore, with assembly lines racing. Those assembly lines were developed and improved by Henry Ford who made his first car in his garage. Andrew Carnegie championed the steel empire, railroad construction was booming, and the fanciful flight of Kitty Hawk led to an aero-evolution that took us from the Wright Brother's first flight of 110 feet to walking on the moon in only sixty years. We were mining our natural resources, drilling oil wells by the thousands, and taking advantage of new technology to harvest the natural resources that were the fountainhead of America. The factories were humming and America had become the producer to the world. American Capitalism provided the greatest progress the world had ever seen and the United States of America became the envy of developed world.

Looking back, Teddy Roosevelt assumed the presidency in 1901 after the assassination of President William McKinley and was the one of the most activist presidents and the premiere leader of the Progressive Movement. Along with major conservation projects, Roosevelt commenced the era of complex legislation and regulation. He took on labor and management problems and dealt with the growth of large corporations which were called "trusts" in those days. He tackled the monopolization of big business a threat in America as well as Europe. His fear was that these issues would lead to higher prices. Early progressivism was based on science and technology during the period of rapid industrialization, expansion, and modernization. Increased regulations came down for the securities industry and the oil industry which was dominated by the Rockefeller interests. Regulations were created for the railroads and all interstate commerce; roads, tolls, bridges, and trade, expanding the scope of the Interstate Commerce Commission. At the same time regulations were developed through the passage of the Pure Food and Drug Act and the Meat Inspection Act. This period of regulation increased government influence in every area of growth for both industry and commerce. This expansion provided the impetus for the Income Tax Amendment which was introduced to help pay for the expanded role of government. It was finally ratified in 1913 as the 13th Amendment. Increased government control and bigger government came with costs and those costs were borne by the corporations and the newly created tax payers.

President Teddy Roosevelt established controls for business and enterprise. Next in line was the social revolution brought forward by another activist with family connections. Franklin Delano Roosevelt (FDR) began a 16 year period as president that marked the social revolution in America while designing programs "to help the people". At the same time, more rules and regulations were developed to control monopolies that were feared both here and abroad. The FDR period was the greatest regulatory era in American history along and produced the further expansion of government control. The programs developed to stop out of control growth also led to the rise of organized labor. We were in a period that paralleled Hayek's greatest fears for Europe.

In 1932 FDR was elected based on his campaign for the New Deal. He was the popular Governor from New York who first created unemployment benefits for struggling workers. As President, he took office amid massive bank failures, significantly reduced levels of production which had dropped to 56% of our peak pre-1929 levels. Farmers, the backbone of the nation, were suffering severely and prices fell below production costs. FDR's promises included farm subsidies and created the Agricultural Adjustment Act (AAA) designed to increase prices during the Depression to help the farmers. Tragically to maintain prices, crops were destroyed while millions went hungry. The National Industrial Recovery Act (NIRA) was created to provide help for the 13 million unemployed and at the same time, balance the budget. The NIRA also had provisions to prohibit unfair labor practices, establish a minimum wage, set standard work hours and grant workers the right to collective bargaining establishing production and pricing levels. Parts of the National Recovery Act (NRA) were set aside by the Supreme Court as unworkable and overreaching. FDR's 16 year rein as President created massive social programs, including Social Security, work programs and public utility companies. The Tennessee Valley Authority (TVA) and his Public Works Administration (TWA) became hallmarks of his presidency. His promise to balance the budget was followed by aggressive increases in the progressive income tax system. Once again, government growth was financed through taxation and an alphabet full of government supplied work programs. The depression became The Great Depression lasting longer in the United States than any other nation. Current historians and economists blame the slow recovery on constant government mismanagement and interference in the free-economy. There are many economists and historians who believe that the massive explosion of government through stifling regulation and mismanaged government stimulus projects diverted badly needed funds for a timely recovery. Today, President Obama is following the failed policies of FDR attempting to restart our economy using growth in government as the prescription. Unfortunately, this medicine may financially kill the patient: the good people of America.

Today, during our toughest recession and impending decline in national prosperity economists are debating the FDR programs to stimulate the economy. If he wise sages compared the state of the nation in terms of its overall economic development they would realize that the programs that took over 10 years to restart the economy were very different than the economic environment we are dealing with today. Obama wants an infrastructure bank to "repair" our national infrastructure. FDR wanted a bank to build great dams, highways, and water systems to improve commerce. Obama's plans to fix pot holes and paint bridges and provide free internet service to the poor do not enhance commerce. These programs are necessary, they do increase the number of workers but they are not the formula for greatness. The quickest way to energize our economic base is to focus on the harvesting and exporting of our natural resources. Closing down access to our greatest natural resources and hoping that science and technology will come up with financially viable alternatives to global resource problems is like promising to win the lottery to bail our America. As our economy continues to erode we still have not found acceptable sources of alternative energy nor cars capable of meeting the needs of the American people using alternative sources of fuel. President Obama is looking for 20th century solutions in the midst of his failures in the 21st century. Our nation cannot wait while he tests is new world theories and our next generation is put on hold. As we will see, great Presidents must have great plans not great hopes.

Since the turn of the century up until the beginning of World War II under the direction of two distant Roosevelt cousins in the White House, with the help of Woodrow Wilson in between, we unwittingly watched the groundwork being laid to usher in the era of massive government regulation and control. During this period of progressive and liberal activism, under the guise of dealing with war and depression, the stage was set to control business and labor - the two keys to our future greatness. The war production of "the last great war to end all wars" injected billions into the economy through the production of airplanes, tanks, and munitions to support our troops abroad. At the end of the war the next generation of development was about to begin under the heavy handed regulations created in the first half of the century. Many of those programs set the groundwork for future government programs, the next being the Great Society under President Lyndon Baines Johnson who assumed the presidency after the assassination of John F. Kennedy, and who was elected for his own term in 1964. At the same time he gained control of both houses of Congress. Johnson swept all but 8 states obtaining 61% of the populous vote over Senator Barry Goldwater. Johnson became the most activist President of the 20th century after Franklin D. Roosevelt. With control of both Houses of Congress and the assurance of the people, the country was ripe for massive changes very similar to what we experienced when Barrack Obama was elected in 2008. Johnson did not seek a second term. It was reported that he felt the strain of his many years in Congress and the turmoil of the unsuccessful, undeclared war in Vietnam.

President Johnson's banner program was creating The Great Society which was a set of domestic programs built on the groundwork laid by FDR in his New Deal. Its two major goals were to provide social programs to eradicate poverty and eliminate racial injustice through a series of sweeping changes that were started with lofty ambition, the best of intentions, and ultimately opened a sieve of ever increasing government give-away programs that started out with about $3 billion dollars in the later half of 1960s which has grown into trillions of dollars today.

The Great Society's long term success depended upon a rapidly expanding economy. The world looked bright. Baby Boomers were entering the workforce, housing and construction were expanding at breakneck speed, and manufacturing was flourishing as the mainstay of our economy. Harvesting our abundant natural resources was essential to fuel and support our expansion. We mined iron ore in the north for smelting into steel, we drilled our own oil: gas was 25-30 cents a gallon in those days. A Volkswagen Beetle could drive over three hundred miles for less than $3.00. Our construction boomed with new housing built from materials supplied by US workers, and we exported excess lumber, cement, and autos around the world. Controlled immigration after World War II supplied more laborers, mostly from Europe. The richness of society highlighted the disparities in the neighborhoods of the poor which supplied increased social programs for support and education with the intent to create jobs programs for employing the "hardcore unemployed" and to bring about equality in the inner cities that were not benefiting like the rising middle class in the suburbs. Various support programs were developed and implemented by President Johnson's Congress and are still growing today. The 1960s brought us housing support programs through The Housing and Urban Development Office (HUD) in addition to government housing, food stamps, and the key to unlocking the door to unemployment: educational assistance with programs like Head Start and other neighborhood government funded coalitions. We witnessed sweeping changes in healthcare protection. This was not just for the poor. All people became eligible for Medicare under an expansion of the Social Security Act. Medicaid, a federally supervised program, was designed to meet the healthcare needs of the poor and was paid for with local state funding.

The Federal government began mandating programs required at the state level, without the funding allocations from Washington. With the growth in social programs came the expansion of government supervision and administration. The Health, Education, and Welfare Department (HEW) became the largest department in the Federal Government impacting cradle to grave programs for every tier of American society. The $14 trillion in Federal Debt we have today has its roots in the IOUs written to cure the social inequities and to promote social justice by the programs created by the Great Society. This burdensome debt is a drain on our future and has gradually led to our decline as a nation. President Obama in his January 2011 State of the Union Speech talked of investments in infrastructure and education to "restore America" back to its greatness which really is an indictment on the Great Society as the unnamed failure that it was in providing assistance for living with no real success in training and employing our youth, thus leading to decades of perpetual unemployment and welfare.

The War on Poverty (WOP) was a targeted program under The Great Society and the Economic Opportunity Act of 1964 which makes the WOP the longest running war in American history. The programs were based on education and training at all levels beginning with Head Start, including Volunteer Inner City Programs, Volunteers in Service to America (VISTA), work study programs, empowerment programs, and scholarship and grant programs spending billions of tax payer dollars to provide the opportunities for the poor in the inner cities with a concentrated focus on minorities and the hardcore unemployed. The government, in its compassionate wisdom, created programs to provide both education and services to meet the needs of the poor to integrate them into the workforce. At the same time, they began adopting legislation that restricted the workforce and set in motion the long term destructive cry to eliminate manufacturing through comprehensive changes in safety rules, government regulation for monitoring business activities through massive reporting of statistical reports to ensure that equality was beginning to take place in our businesses. Increased government regulation for those companies with the largest workforces required automation to meet reporting guidelines. We were beginning to experience the benefits of automation in clerical and office positions. Many of those affected first tended to be the ones in the largest communities at the lower pay scales. The War on Poverty with its massive subsidiary regulations, created an unfriendly business climate that began to systematically destroy the roots of its partners: the businesses that provided the jobs for the poor.

Fifty five years later we are witnessing the social impact of the declines in our most populated cities which have become chronic war zones due to out of control drug trafficking with almost total reliance on government programs. Ironically, The Great Society killed The Great Society with uncoordinated efforts that promoted job growth and training in one government department while they dismantled job growth in our manufacturing and mining industries and called for greater and greater governmental reporting leading to the automation of record keeping and reporting resulting in further losses of employment The increase in government regulations relating to protecting "society" lead to the economic destruction of those at the bottom of the economic ladder. This gradual and systematic decline has resulted in an increase in social support programs to take the place of the jobs that have been eliminated through excessive government regulation over the last 25 years. Capitalism has always been the economic solution to create a greater society, but the handcuffs placed on it by government bureaucrats who espouse job creation consistently create government programs, mandates, and environmental protections that defy the imagination of our entrepreneurial spirit. We have become too exhausted to create economically viable solutions to counteract the continuous interference of government.

Look at the impact of our increasing social programs in a period of increasing government regulation and control of manufacturing on one of our most prestigious cities in the last one hundred years. Detroit, Michigan, once the crown jewel of manufacturing in the world, formerly stood on the shoulders of the automobile industry from the early 1900s through the late 1960s. As a result of the manufacturing companies, Detroit boasted a population of over 1,850,000 which has declined to about 900,000 today according to City-Data.Com, a company that tracks population statistics. Today Detroit, ranks near the top of all major cities in the trio of statistics: Crime, Poverty, and Unemployment. The decline began in the mid-1960s in defiance of the Great Society Programs that were designed to reverse that trend: a trend that has continued for over 45 years. Poverty programs were implemented in the face of anti-business policies, followed by excessive mandates and reporting, increased regulatory interference and further impeded by continual labor union demands. The 1960s witnessed the beginning of the decline of the automobile industry which was the backbone of American Industrialization. By the 1970s over 70 percent of the manufactured automobile components were created outside the State of Michigan.

Today, forty years later, automobile and truck components are manufactured outside of the United States, with the deceptive call for creating a Greener America and the promise of higher paying jobs. The devil that destroyed the high paying jobs of the 20th Century accuses failed capitalism for the problems that are blighting our cities and communities around the country. Drug dealing in Detroit may be the major industry which accounts for the increase in violent crimes in a city that sees no hope of returning to splendor. In reality, government interference is the number one job killer and perpetuator of poverty in America today. Time Magazine featured Detroit as the cover story on September 24, 2009, *Detroit: The Death and Possible Life of a Great City*. The article chronicles the decline of Detroit and the hope that the Flex-Fuel Car will stimulate its revival. In February 2011 George Will, the noted syndicated columnist, stated at a lecture in Sarasota, Florida, "that by 2014 we hope to have 1 million energy efficient cars on the road. Today we have over 250 million cars on the road." The impact of 1 million cars over a four year period is less than one half of one percent over four years, a mere pittance of progress. The Greening of America will remain an amber-brown based even if we achieve those paltry result which is doubtful at this time. The sales results are dismal for "green cars" based on sales results through August 2011. An international study ranked the Chevy Volts 13th in the category of "green cars" due to its $41,000 price tag and 38 mile range on electricity. The Federal government is willing to give a $7500 tax credit for the purchase of a Green Car. This appears to be a massive amount of government spending for a car that ranks 13th in its class.

The CAFÉ standards that regulate minimum automobile standards by class have brought us two things, minimal improvements is gas savings and dramatically higher automobile costs, and the ancillary increase in traffic injuries through the development of the plastic cars that have replaced the metal tanks that used to protect us. The regulations requiring higher usage of costly ethanol fuel is depleting our food supply and adds to the cost of both gasoline and food. The by-product of this intensification of environmental protection has a direct impact on both economic and physical safety. The overall effect is reduced employment during a long term projected period of rising prices. The government is attempting to promote technology through legislation. There will never be enough legislation to replace the millions of jobs lost through misguided government regulation already in place. The lofty, single-focus goals of individual regulations never acknowledge the negative impact of the implementation of those regulations.

As we move away from individual economic independence to government sponsored collective financial salvation at a much reduced level than the life styles many were once accustomed, a larger percentage of our citizens are more and more reliant on the support from government program. On the surface this sounds like a humanitarian accomplishment. In truth it is the direct result of the failure on the part of our government to provide an atmosphere that promotes self reliance. This government provided reliance is compounded by the vastly increasing entitlement programs of Social Security and Medicare creating further unsustainable burdens on our ability to support society. Our long term government entitlement programs, coupled with the interim and temporary support programs required during times of economic downturn are crushing our ability to recover due to inadequate financial reserves. Recessions result in lower revenues or taxes at the time they are most needed. The design and development of our social programs have never been developed using true actuarial principles. This means that every major entitlement program is funded through an economically developed Ponzi scheme using tax payer dollars and foreign borrowing with no long term chance of evolutionary survival.

The well-intentioned elected officials, the "bleeding heart liberals" and those accommodating progressive Republicans are guilty of having created the inevitable collapse of our economic system. The underlying Socialist principles at work, whether recognized or not at the time, are the seeds planted decades ago that are growing the decay in our towns and cities across America. Excessive regulation combined with financial insolvency will ultimately cause the total collapse of our economic system until we develop realistic budget and deficit plans to ensure ability to meet the promises made by our politicians.

President Reagan feared the increase of Totalitarianism from abroad. The problem was much closer than he imagined in 1984. The Road to Socialism is paved with the transference of wealth from the Capitalist system followed by the destruction of the working class and the support for those who have been displaced. Our unwitting or possibly perverse elected officials whose decisions are leading to our national insolvency are the destructive "totalitarians in our midst."

Chapter 14   Material Conditions and Ideal Ends

"I predict future happiness for Americans if they can prevent the government from wasting the labors of the people under the pretense of taking care of them." Thomas Jefferson

The Socialist's greatest desire is to convince man that he should be more concerned for social well being than an emphasis on economic issues. Hayek opens his chapter with an opposing argument against this theme expressed by Peter Drucker, who stated that man was moving away from his focus on economic activities and more toward a social society in his *End of Economic Man: A Study of the New Totalitarianism,* as related by Bruce Caldwell, the editor of *The Road to Serfdom and footnoted on page 210.*. Drucker, an Austrian economist and educator, became a noted and well respected business consultant in America.   Searching for references about his early beliefs about Socialism did not reveal any references other than a remarkable review of his *End of Economic Man* written by the great Sir Winston Churchill which was posted on The Drucker Society website.   Drucker appears to have abandoned his earlier beliefs about Socialism to become a successful advisor to American capitalists.

Sir Winston may have been the influence that helped Drucker to see the light. Churchill was the outstanding politician and statesman who served as British Prime Minister twice; once before and during the Second World War and then again after the war between 1951 and 1955. As author, historian, and consummate orator, his opinions were highly respected in both Europe and America. His review of *The End of Economic Man* refutes Drucker's erroneous belief that Totalitarianism was the savior of society while Capitalism was crumbling under its failure to meet social goals. Hayek shared Churchill's view that Drucker's rationale was based on the false premise that social reconstruction would totally consume man.   Drucker claimed that we were moving away from economic matters since history revealed that the pursuit of liberty, equality and security are all economic concepts that would became passé.   Seventy years later these same goals remain in the forefront of our pursuits and are still debated by our legislatures at both the state and federal levels.   He further falsely put forth his thesis on "potential plenty"-- pseudo-theories about the inevitable trend toward monopolies that would deplete our natural resources, destroying stores of raw materials and suppressing innovation. This was not true. Government regulation would be our downfall. During the Franklin D. Roosevelt years many of these issues were debated. The real fears of this inevitability became a reality, but not at the hands of the capitalist. It was through the interfering hands of an ever-more Socialistic government with its excessive regulations that manipulated our monopolies.

Hayek contends that the people of Europe during the first half of the 20th century became less consumed with the discussion of economic matters. There were two critical reasons: the two global wars and subsequent high unemployment rate. Both were primary reasons for the people to rely heavily on the government to develop economic programs. This tended to leave people more ignorant and gradually separated from economic thinking even though pressing matters of financial well being were paramount at the time. This attitude was not limited to Europe, because the same ambivalence in America created a willingness to rely on the many social programs developed during the 20th century. The long term economic consequences were of no concern to the working man when the cost of acceptance initially appeared so small. No one seemed to care that these programs would grow over time to eventually consume half our Federal budget.

Churchill aptly warned us of Drucker's half baked theory: "The Marxian's offered the alternative of a classless society. But that has lost its attraction also, because it is clear that Socialism in practice creates a new and highly organized class structure of its own. The present social order having thus lost its theoretical justification, the average man is no longer prepared to tolerate its evil twins, war and unemployment. They have become demons which haunt him, and his last hope is that they will be exorcised through the miraculous intervention of a Demigod. That is the hope which the dictatorships satisfy. Men seek refuge in them not because they believe in them but because anything is better than present chaos." The Prime Minister went on to argue that "organization" is the key to Socialism even though it resulted in Totalitarianism because it would organize and control chaos. Creating and controlling chaos is the basic goal and vision of the Marxist to implement a Socialist system.

Sadly, our world today is immersed in economic chaos caused by governmental regulations, distractions and warring ideologies. While we are at war with our own political parties at home on budgets and deficit spending, the Middle East is aflame in their own chaos. During the winter of 2011, the Middle East ignited and erupted in civil wars between factions of the governments and their people. At the same time in America, the labor union leaders have become active in inflaming protestors to protect their supposed "rights" to collective bargaining, the sacred mission of the union movement. Union members were instigated by union leadership to march on State Capitals in the hopes of preserving their collective strength. Almost all state governors are forced to fight swollen budgets resulting from many years of out of control spending which is bankrupting their states. The fiscally conservative Tea Party groups are at odds with the coordinated protests in our State Capitals and stand against all those who do not want to rein in out of control state spending. The solution from the unions and their supporters can be heard in their chant, "Tax the Rich." Yet to many it is the union employees who are the privileged and the new rich with their lavish "Cadillac Benefit Plans." Government employees and Union members who make above average wages and benefits compared to private sector workers are demanding no curtailment of "their rights." They oppose any cuts during troubled economic times. Thankfully, the protests in hometown America are not as violent and destructive as the riots we have viewed in Europe started in the fall of 2010. Those protests erupted into fires and destruction of government and private property and were triggered by the governments attempts to change the retirement age and other work rules in Greece, a country with 20% unemployment and a total population just over 10.6 million, which is less people than the current number of unemployed in America. Other riots followed across Western Europe based on increased college tuition rates and the curtailing of many public services which the people continued to expect although their nations were broke.

The milder protests in American cities are in response to Republican controlled legislatures who are attempting to reduce the union's power and influence over public sector workers and the states they work for to help reduce their bloated budgets. The role of the Marxist is to continue to implant a sharp, pointed stick into the wounds of society. They always demand to take more from the rich to support others. In this case it is the taxpayers who are being sucked dry. Union workers are no longer the poor, the meek and the abused. They are the upper middle-class created through years of hard bargaining and weak governmental leadership across America. Those most guilty are the government officials who gave away tax payer money from what appeared to be the endless trough of tax money. The workers and their union leaders are demanding more and more from them. They are not protesting on behalf of the needy and the poor. They have become self-serving and time will tell how many will support their demanding protests during the next round of elections. A Rasmussen poll in March 2011 indicated that the majority of Americans are not sympathetic to the union cause and the lavish benefit plans adorned upon our government workers, which far exceeded the benefit plans of those taxpayers who paid their salaries and benefits.

The world we live in is becoming far more complex and we tend to elude the laws and regulations that stifle our ability to comprehend them. Many believe that these complex rules are created by politicians who expect us to follow them blindly without understanding them. This line of thinking will eventually lead to our destruction. Our citizens are caught in a dichotomy: "Knowledge is Power" versus "Ignorance is Bliss." For example: many refused to accept the massive, incomprehensible, two thousand pages of the Obama Healthcare Plan because of its perceived assumptions, contradictory arguments, and the absence of verifiable factual information. The majority opinion was: the people did not like the healthcare bill. It was so complicated and difficult to read, yet it was voted into law prior to being read by the very Congress who gave an oath to protect the people under the Constitution. A full year after its passage, it was discovered that over $100 billion of appropriations were hidden in the bill to begin the Federal implementation plan. It was obvious that this bill was designed to both the Republicans and the American people they were sworn to protect.

The authors of the bill are suspiciously unknown. The counter argument stated by then Speaker of the House, Nancy Pelosi, was, "Once the bill is passed we can learn what is in it." This classic comment by Pelosi should have been an embarrassment to the Speaker, but instead it displayed her basic arrogance to the people. Her attitude was, "We know what is best for you so just accept it and shut up." Imagine if a drug manufacturer said, "Here, take this pill. I am sure it is good for you. We haven't tested it yet, but we know that it is good for you." Would you swallow that pill? This may sound absurd, but that is exactly what Speaker Pelosi wanted you to swallow when they passed the Affordable Care Act. The backlash on the bill was tremendous due to the fear it created in the citizenry. It would force citizens to buy something, an act which two courts have already ruled is unconstitutional. As we continue to "learn more about the bill" more people dislike it. Two Federal Judges, Roger Vinson of Florida and Henry Hudson of Virginia, have ruled against the Constitutionality of the Affordable Health Care Act mainly because of violations of the Commerce Clause, the Proper and Necessary Clause, and the General Welfare Clause. The 11th Circuit Court of Appeals confirmed the unconstitutionality of the bill. The White House Department of Justice will be appealing these rulings, actually opposing the dozens of states bringing forth the argument. The cases will ultimately be consolidated and land in the Supreme Court and will become election folly in 2012.

Conversely, in 2010 Congress passed the Financial Reform Bill which was not as far reaching as the healthcare bill, because it was directed at financial institutions and did not openly threaten the security of individuals. The long term effects are not known. The financial reforms are the government's attempt to cure the ills they created while vilifying Wall Street Bankers. Congress surreptitiously castigated Wall Street for the problems caused by their poorly designed legislation which lacked the necessary oversight to protect investors and stockholders. The overall impact of financial reform will eventually affect individuals when the investment companies conduct more business overseas to escape the financial reporting required by the bill. The average person has limited understanding of the significance of the changes and does not seem to care. This is the "Perfect Storm" for government intervention and control. An uninformed electorate is a placid electorate. The healthcare bill and the financial reform bill will eventually result in the loss of individual and financial freedom. Both bills create massive oversight departments, committees and agencies that parallel the impact of advanced government planning, the primary tool of collectivism. These are the telltale signs of "Creeping Socialism."

The financial reform bill was another outgrowth of failed government policies and regulations. The focus of blame was purported to be on the "greedy Wall Street bankers" who adapted to the regulations created and allowed by Congress. The Wall Street investment community was then flogged for using the system created by the government. The Securities and Exchange Commission (SEC) ignored the problem until it blew up in their faces under George W. Bush when the Treasury Department became aware of massive institutional bank failures, including huge problems with the Federal Reserve. Similarly, the mismanagement of Medicare and Medicaid created inequities and inefficiencies in the total approach to healthcare by over managing services and creating unsustainable policy requirements resulting in failures in our healthcare administration. Without regard to the actual cost of providing healthcare services, the government has attempted to control cost-savings by regulating prices.

Price fixing failed to solve economic problems under Presidents Franklin D. Roosevelt, Nixon, and Carter who violated free market principles. When we examine Medicare, its very foundation is based on price regulation. The government determines reimbursement rates and arbitrarily sets prices for medical services. Never has price fixing improved the level of efficiency, quality of service or ultimate price of a product or service. Artificial pricing always denies the laws of supply and demand which means that prices are not equilibrium prices determined by cost and profit versus the price a willing buyer will pay. Pricing fixing always results in negative consequences: black market operations, corruption, suppression of innovation and investment by private industry. The market will not innovate hoping that they will be arbitrarily regulated on both quality and price. In theory price fixing at the government level is an inefficient market system.

The Internal Revenue Service has steadily grown since 1913 and has become the consummate tool of government. It is no longer simply the collector of income taxes. It has become the vehicle to modify and change economic behavior to support government's ideals. The IRS regulations are changed or updated more than any other agency in government. It responds to new taxes and updates based on new legislation each year. The changes to increase or decrease tax rates, to add tax credits to encourage certain types of behavior or investment, and other changes to programs effect the preparation of the hundreds of income tax forms and schedules each year. The IRS enforces the most complicated tax code in the world. IRS regulations have grown to over 70,000 pages which equates to approximately 130 reams of paper. That equates to one page for every word in this book. A small portion of our tax code is used to aid 200 million individual tax payers to prepare their annual tax returns and over half of them do not pay income taxes, but instead, normally receive a tax credit or refund from the government. The bulk of our cumbersome tax regulations are designed to provide incentives and disincentives for various activities that the government decides to encourage or discourage. The tax code is frequently used to stimulate certain behaviors and discourage others. Tax credits are used to encourage purchases as a reward or price reduction. Other taxes are used to penalize behavior, like cigarettes and gasoline. There are untold numbers of incentives for environmental activities that are paid directly to tax payers or through their utility companies. The tax code when used to modify individual behavior is a form of social engineering.

Unintended consequences are the normal result of government regulation. Fossil fuels are the major target of big government today. Ethanol, a product made from corn, is a controversial additive used to reduce the use of gasoline. The farmers of America receive special tax credits and subsidies for growing corn for ethanol production, an expensive process, which increases the cost of gasoline plus contains the hidden cost of government subsidies to divert corn production for gasoline production. As of 2011 it has been reported that corn production for ethanol now exceeds corn for consumption. The ethanol program diverts corn production used for food consumption thereby increasing supermarket prices. The increased use of ethanol in gasoline increases transportation costs for travel and the transportation costs for all products. The Ethanol Program is estimated to take billions of dollars out of American family's budgets plus the additional taxes required to pay tax credits and subsidies for the program. Another hidden cost of ethanol is when we use it in our lawn mowers and other 2 and 4 cycle engines. These engines require more repair and maintenance due to the destructive effects of ethanol. Our major attempt at using a natural renewable resource as a "green alternative" is another government boondoggle that is paid for by both the rich and the poor. Another negative attribute of subsidies is that it disguises the true costs of production adding another negative factor into the financial analysis equation thus hindering free market principles to work in the economy.

The government is the largest landlord in the country and Congress is not particularly good at managing real estate. Through a variety of government programs they provide government housing directly and through partnerships with private landlords to meet the social goals of providing housing assistance to the poor. The people who are aided with housing also usually qualify for food subsidies through the Food Stamp Program and Medicaid provided by their state government. There is a variety of overlapping safety net programs designed to assist the growing number of poor in this country. The housing programs are a significant portion of the subsidies provided to the poor and elderly. Government subsidized housing, what is commonly referred to as Section 8 housing, is designed to work in tandem with the local housing market through local offices. The government tends to pay higher rates for homes and apartments than the free market system. Private landlords are usually the big winners because rental reimbursement rates tend to be higher than free market rents. Rent schedules are designed for 2, 3, and 4 bedroom homes and the rate paid is not based on neighborhood or amenities. The landlord receives an automatic deposit into their checking account each month for the rent. In major metropolitan areas there are companies that specialize in only government subsidized housing due to the high level of profitability. Based on the income level of the tenant they may be required to pay a very small portion of the rent. In addition to rent subsidies there are also programs to assist with utility payments.

As a result of the housing bubble and the poor economy, rental rates have dropped in every sector of the rental market, with the exception of government subsidized housing. This is an ideal arrangement for the government sponsored tenant and the landlord. The only person who suffers is the taxpayer. The proposed 2012 Budget from the White House includes transferring more money to Section 8 housing while reducing the cost to maintain public housing projects, which have been a disaster for many decades.

We are seeing the elimination of our ideals through the destruction of the family unit and the minimizing of religious beliefs. The attacks on our religion and our family structure through the media, Hollywood, and in our school systems is common place. For instance, murder is immoral and illegal with the exception of action on the battlefield and under the rights of self defense. Murder is legal when performed by the government to punish criminals. Yet, while the values and ideals have long been known we have created a culture through poverty and the influx of the drug trade that often celebrates death and destruction as part of gangland rituals. Murder is seen almost on a daily basis in the so-called entertainment on TV and in the movies. It has lost its shock value.

The importance of the traditional family, composed of husband and wife and children, is being diminished through social changes and reorientation. The traditional family unit, the backbone of a civilized world may soon be an obsolete value in America. This reorientation is starting in the newly created households where living together without marriage saves money and complications. Single parent homes are becoming the norm which is approaching nearly fifty percent of the families with children. The destruction of the family unit has changed the role of educators who are being called upon to become surrogate parents in the classroom. It is far easier to implement societal changes through the education system than to rely on changes coming from traditional family values. Beginning with the Socialist movement, traditional family values have been a threat to Totalitarianism. Many of the views presented and sold in our classrooms promote government standards and points of views that are in contrast to the views held by most church going family members. These messages are destroying the beliefs of our children and our culture. The greatest injustices can be witnessed in our lower income communities. Perpetual poverty, especially in our inner cities, is a breeding ground for revolution in our poorest communities. They can be indoctrinated to become the tools of the uprising. If our elected leaders were sincere in their efforts to improve the quality of life of the poor, they would begin by improving their sense of self sufficiency and not by placating them with government housing and a flood of Food Stamps.

Our growing ghettos in the cities have been controlled for many decades by the liberal governments that have handed out welfare like candy. The cities with the greatest social problems are Oakland, New Orleans, Detroit, Baltimore, Trenton, and Washington D.C. to name only a few. They are the epitome of failed social programs that do not promote the ideals of family values. We have attempted to spare the feelings of children living in fatherless homes. Our "political correctness" denies both the problem and the behavioral changes required to change the thinking on a part of our culture which is in the greatest need of rescue. To make matters worse, we have increased our Aid to Dependent Children Program by ever higher payments to single mothers who have turned the government support programs of fatherless homes into a "cottage industry." There is the case of the never-married woman who called her HUD landlord with glee stating that she was pregnant again with her fourth child and finally would qualify for a four bedroom home after five years of having babies. This woman became a status symbol and a role model for her children. Sad as it is, she finally achieved her version of the American Dream, a four bedroom house at tax payer expense.

Capitalism did not cripple our inner cities or cause a torrent of failed economic policies. The undeniable cause is a progressively declining culture combined with poorly conceived, overly regulated, and mismanaged government programs that are blighting our inner cities, a trend that is gradually moving to suburbia. Our poor are the unwittingly pathetic victims of the social safety network programs that promote dependency and sloth. The government is creating a perpetual under class. Unfortunately, we have raised poverty to a higher level of acceptable behavior for those who need the most help. Our politicians pander to the poor and provide endless promises that are paid for with social programs using tax payer money better used to promote advancement and self pride to help our needy. The Socialists have consistently propagandized about the "social injustice"—another phrase they have adapted and changed to suit their agenda. We cannot end poverty by feeding people with no possibility of ever having a job. Those who have lived in second and third generations of government sponsored programs still lack the skill sets and the mindsets required to take care of themselves. Many in our largest cities, the low income or non-income earning inhabitants, rely on drugs, prostitution and other crimes to supplement their income. The permanent rehabilitation of inner city residents will take generations to change.

Unfortunately, solving these problems does not appear to be a high priority for our local and state governments. If the elimination or reduction of poverty was a priority we would not have perpetuated, nor increased the deplorable situation in the last sixty years. President Kennedy announced in 1963 that we would put a man on the moon. Five years later we saw it happen. Why can't we put an end to the misery of tens of millions of people in sixty years? If our elected officials would have addressed the real causes of poverty, the problem would be far smaller today. It is a far easier for our politicians to throw money at a problem, especially when it buys votes. Our government believes in social engineering yet it never engineers a society that is free of government subsistence or a society that is free to pursue individual happiness.

In reality we are at war on multiple fronts. We have the War on Poverty, the War on Drugs, and The War on Bad Education--another silent war. This war is a battle to keep our children from dropping to the bottom of the global achievement ladder based on comparative results with 30 other nations. But we have added another war; our newest war is the war against the people and industry under the guise of protecting the environment.

The environment is the latest battleground: our newest ideal is the Greening of America. The level of importance of this ideal seems to supersede job creation to fight our rising unemployment, managing our state and federal budgets, eliminating unnecessary regulations, and the real key, harvesting our national resources to improve the overall health of our nation. Eliminating our Balance of Payments problem and our reliance on foreign oil is the first step to reuniting America. Protection of the environment appears to overshadow every economic activity formerly cherished as the American way of life. The protection of air and water to promote the health and welfare of all other living creatures has taken priority over the liberties and rights of man. Our new singleness of purpose is dictated by the Environmental Protection Agency, who intercedes to stop any commercial activity that may impact the environment. Rather than help to clean up the factories that formerly polluted our communities, we have over regulated them into crumbling shells that closed and moved their production and our jobs to India, China and other more welcoming nations. This appears hypocritical. Contrary to our efforts to move toward globalism, we have transferred our environmental pollution to other nations. If we truly believed in global environmentalism we would have cleaned up our side of the street rather than to trash other countries. These nations, who have little no concern for environmental protection, are polluting their countries and impacting the globe while our unemployment rates continue to rise. Rather than seek to achieve a balance between industry and the environment our elected leaders chose to take actions to stifle our economy and transfer the pollution to other nations which is the very height of environmental hypocrisy.

Our long term dependence on resources and production from China, Japan, India, and the oil-rich nations in the Middle East is needlessly transferring our wealth to other countries—all in keeping with our goals to protect our environment. While we contribute to improving the economies of other nations, we increase our foreign debt and our higher interest costs, while we lose our own tax revenue, and experience radically declining employment. We are violating the basic economic principles of our sovereign country. We are instead pursuing a failing ideology. Capitalism is blamed for the failures, while the real problem is poor decision making on the part of our elected officials. The economic insecurity caused by "government risk" thwarts any immediate possibility of a sound economic recovery.

It has been estimated that over two trillion dollars of corporate investment funds are sitting idle offshore due to economic insecurity in American markets. Investors have fear during times of uncertainty, and prefer to sit on the sidelines rather than guess at what politicians will do. Clearly this is the main failure of the Obama Administration which has been unable to lead during a time of our greatest peril. President Obama stated on June 29, 2010, "For even as we celebrate tonight, we know the challenges that tomorrow will bring are the greatest of our lifetime -- two wars, a planet in peril, the worst financial crisis in a century." The economic peril referred to by the President is self inflicted, in the sense that he is failing to protect his own nation and people, a duty he was sworn to protect. A failed Stimulus Package of $780 billion that went to special interests and pet projects drained the national treasury yet has clearly not ignited the economic fire required for recovery. The steadfast adherence by his administration to behold a culture of environmental controls known as Global Warming, and now renamed "Climate Change" has destroyed the same economic culture that has built the greatest nation in the world. The Environmental Protection Agency, with a mere $10 billion budget out of more than one and a half trillion dollar government budget, holds the fate of our nation in its regulatory hands. It is as though we are witnessing the intentional strangulation of our economy and rapid decline of our once free nation. The EPA is the governmental agency that holds the value of a tree, a prairie varmint, and a purposeless aqueduct fish at a higher level than the fulfillment and basic needs of human beings. It is not being overly dramatic in saying that while most nations fear to be overthrown by other nations, our fear is now deeper than that—we are being destroyed from within. If this unreasonable control continues we will be overthrown by our own government, our enemy from within.

During the last century we have lost our primary purpose: our commitment "to promote Life, Liberty, and the pursuit of Happiness" and "to promote the General Welfare." The general welfare includes providing opportunities to be self sufficient, because not doing so affects the quality of life and general welfare of all our citizens. Sacrificing our economic well being also sacrifices our liberty and our standard of living. At the same time, as we decline in stature abroad we suffer more as a nation. Millions of jobs have been displaced and eliminated due to governmental policies that have robbed opportunities to improve the quality of life for millions of people in America. Hayek attributes the interim "salvation" or benefit to the economy to be a lowering of wages, which is a dreadful option for most people. This is the pathetic case of helping the few to the detriment of the many. He probably did not foresee the purposeful, self-defeating actions of the Socialists who force unemployment by chasing industries to other nations. In April of 2011, we are just beginning to see a slight rise in private employment after two years of a jobless recovery. Two years of fiscal and monetary programs have failed to provide the necessary stimulus to jump start a successful jobs program. In late December of 2011 the Bush Tax cuts which were due to expire were renewed providing some sense of stability in the economy. In contrast to Roosevelt's failed New Deal that dragged the depression out for over seven years. We appear to have been repeating the past by tearing apart the fabric of our economy, while the obvious economic solutions to this crisis were staring us right in the face. The Left still insists the $780 Billion Stimulus Package was too paltry should have been $2.3 trillion higher to meet the needs of counteracting the recession. Ironically, the $2.3 trillion number is the same number being thrown around for infra-structure repair programs. These programs are claimed to be essential to recovery and mimic the original jobs programs during the FDR New Deal Programs. Fixing pot holes and painting bridges is far different than creating all new transportation networks and water systems as was done in the 1930s. Where were these programs when tunnels were being dug under high-ways for turtle migration, and the San Francisco Bay Area water rat was getting a new habitat? Our shovel ready projects didn't exist and now we miraculously have $2.3 trillion in projects on the drawing board. Who are the beneficiaries of these jobs: it is mandated that union members must be used while those with minimum skills go unemployed.

The January 2011 Bureau of Labor and Statistics reported over 13.5 million people are jobless. Rather than send out armies of people with caulk guns it appears that someone who was serious about solving the largest unemployment problem in America history would be interested in unleashing millions of people with the stroke of a pen. Millions of people could be reemployed with the elimination of restrictions on oil exploration and the reopening the drilling for oil in the Gulf of Mexico from existing wells. We have oil in the Gulf, massive deposits of shale in the North West which are estimated to contain in the range of 200-300 billion barrels of oil, not to mention the proven reserves of oil in the Alaska Region where untold billions of barrels of oil may be recoverable. If we combined exploration with the temporary relaxation of automobile emission standards we would make the US immediately competitive again in the world market.

Many of our foreign trading partners do not share our interest in expensive alternative energy vehicles. It doesn't make sense to have the cleanest environment in a country that will ultimately devour itself, or better said, destroy itself through economic policies and regulations. Just wishing for technological advancements that far exceed the limits of science does not make economic sense in the short run. Energy Secretary Steven Chu said on one of the Sunday morning talk shows, "We may be five years away from producing vehicles that can go up to 200 miles on one battery charge." Further he said, "As people tend to replace cars they are electing vehicles that get better gas mileage." Those cars are not electric hybrid cars. The sales figures for the Chevy Volt, the $42,000 battery operated car that comes with a $7,500 tax credit reported total sales since late 2010 of 2029 according to The New American Newsletter dated August 4, 2011. These dismal results indicate that we are not ready to switch to inefficient electric cars that are priced two and half times a similar gas powered model that now provide our best gas mileage. Various reports from GM officials stated that sales were low due to the non-availability of the Chevy Volt. Later inquiries, Greg Martin, GMs Director of Communications indicated that 117 were available for sale plus each dealer probably had a "demo" available for sale which was not reported in the inventory figures. Contrary to Secretary Chu's assertion, the Chevy Tahoe, the largest production consumer vehicle remains one of the best GM sellers. While we struggle to meet environmental goals with generous tax payer funded tax credits we are seeing limited success in changing the buying patterns of our citizens.

The real villain is not Capitalism. It is a political plan that has hobbled our economy based on over control of our free market system destroying it with excessive government regulations. The words of Hayek during the period leading up to World War II, appearing on page 216 of *The Road to Serfdom,* ring especially true here: "Our world as it is, with everyone convinced that the material conditions here or there must be improved, our only chance of building a decent world is that we can continue to improve the general level of wealth. The one thing modern democracy will not bear without cracking is the necessity of a substantial lowering of the standards of living in peacetime or even prolonged stationariness of its economic conditions." This sounds like a warning. We must take heed of this warning from the past to preserve life as we know it.

Today's political climate finds us almost equally divided, among Republicans and Democrats, with a very large and growing segment of Independents. We tend to become weary of both parties and their time in office, and swing back and forth between Republicans and Democrats with the primary influence being the Independent voters. Since the end of World War II we have had six presidents from each party. The constant battling over ideologies, especially the warring between the extremes in each party, has brought us to this period of economic nightmares. The pendulum continues to swing back and forth while we search for solutions that work. At the same time our elected leaders continue to reward the special interest groups that back them each time they win the presidency. In their attempt to gain favor and to be re-elected, they steer away from the tough decisions refusing to address the entitlement programs that consume the largest portion of our nation's budget.

A free society should be based on individual liberty and freedom and be driven by what is Hayek called "multiple purposes". No society can exist with only one central theme or motivating principle. Hayek pointed out that the only dramatic exception to national single-mindedness was brought about by a time of war. During the two World Wars, nations united in purpose and dedicated millions of military men and women to war efforts. During these emergencies, each country was committed to maximum production for the war effort. Our factories were converted and dedicated to producing tens of thousands of tanks, millions of military support vehicles, and thousands of American airplanes which later blackened the skies over Europe and took on the vast Pacific battlefronts. Troops were moved in government-mandated Liberty Ships from our major ports along the Eastern and Western coasts. Our economy and our people joined forces in a common effort: To protect freedom.

During both the First and Second World Wars, men and women alike stood in line for days to enlist in the Armed Forces or to join the war effort in factories that worked around the clock to protect liberty and freedom here and abroad. But as one war followed another, from the Korean Conflict to our involvement in Vietnam in the 1960s, our united support for war waned. Soon the country was divided and there arose organized anti-war activists and protestors. College campuses were filled with protestors. Our country lost its singleness of purpose and was held in contempt by the youth of our nation. After the withdrawal of our forces in Viet Nam the nation settled back into a long era of resistance to the spread of Communism by both the Soviet Union and Communist China. But the Weatherman and other protestors were still out there, maturing and planning their next moves. The upheaval in the US in the 1990s was minimal compared to the total absorption of the wars of the first half of the century where millions made the ultimate sacrifice. Today our military presence around the world is felt through hundreds of military bases and operation centers maintained to keep the world stable. But this task of being the "world's policeman" has worn the country down both financially and militarily. Our role has shifted from warriors to "peace keepers." Many protest our self-appointed role as the world's protector from bully nations. In 2011 we find ourselves once more providing support against dictatorial leaders in the Middle East.

We are clearly divided on our use of the military to quell problems around the world. The wars being fought in Iraq and Afghanistan are extremely costly and are dividing our country and challenging our unified national purpose. Our commitment to provide hundreds of thousands of troops and government support personnel dwarfs all other nations combined. Many in America doubt and protest our involvement in world affairs and would prefer isolationism. During a global recession that began after the massive economic boom ending in 2005, it is believed by millions that our war effort against terrorism is draining the necessary funds needed to restart the economy.

At the same time there is also a call for more funding for domestic social programs. There are others who feel equally as strong that fighting against the increase in terrorist activism breeding in the Middle East is our only protection against further attacks at home. These arguments are proof that we have lost our unity of purpose: that consistent, nationalistic pride and commitment to being the harbingers of peace and liberty around the world. With the spread of nations who refute the creed of individual freedom we have lost much needed international support. As the globe becomes more oppressed by nations who sacrifice freedom for totalitarianism we are one of the few nations committed to the preservation of liberty and the ideals of a republic. We are rapidly becoming the global minority. Many believe that President Obama's actions of glad handing and bowing to foreign leaders, and criticizing our history around the world have not resulted in better international relations. As a partial result of his meek efforts and inexperience in foreign policy we are seeing an increase in unrest around the world. This may be a result of our perceived weaknesses based on our reliance on educators inexperienced in dealing with the real world in the White House rather than seasoned diplomats and experienced foreign advisors. We may be on a dangerous course. Our forces are split on many fronts under what appears to be a strategy of "divide and conquer." Many in our nation still believe in President Reagan's motto, "Peace through Strength." This appears to be a strategy we have abandoned.

The United States has not acquired, accumulated, or used hostile force to permanently take any land or govern any nation. We have the unique position of never having fought a foreign enemy on our own soil since the American Revolution with the sole exception of defending our country at Pearl Harbor. The anti-war rhetoric aimed at our national purpose is merely another internal anti-American attack used to inflame those members who are often more than pacifists, but rather haters of their own nation. The truth is that we have violated Hayek's warnings and have incited the Socialists who believe stronger domestic policies will cure an ailing nation.

Our position during the Obama Administration is fundamentally flawed. While we now defer, and some say cower, to the United Nations, those other nations who care more about jobs and their people than their environment are ultimately reaping the benefits of our former industries. When we were given those same choices, our elected leftist leaders would rather perish financially than arrive at common sense, cost effective solutions to address both our economic purpose and a Green Agenda. Under a Capitalist solution we could have selected the most cost effective way to prosper in a global economy: which would be the ultimate form of Globalism. Patriotism is not a corporate goal. Patriotism does not appear to be a goal of our government either when they alter the environmental regulations that weaken our economy and force the exporting of our manufacturing base and skilled workers to other nations. Their goal might be to improve social ideals at home. But unemployment is not a social ideal, yet it is one our President accepts when he says we must all sacrifice. With over thirteen and a half million people out of work, and millions more underemployed, it appears that we have sacrificed enough. In another act of hypocrisy, President Obama visited Brazil in March 2011 to provide $2 billion of our taxpayer support for their offshore oil exploration. He promised to be their "best customer" while 60,000 American oil workers remained unemployed from the government shutdown in the Gulf of Mexico following the BP oil spill. While he was on vacation in Brazil he gave away both our money and our jobs.

Hayek further warned that rebuilding a nation such as Great Britain after World War II should not be based on what he called "re-distributional means." Quite clearly he did not believe that to rebuild a nation it has to redistribute its citizens' wealth. To heal a nation in his mind, it would have to build an economic structure that produces long term sustainability. Ideally, a nation should remain self sufficient through the development of its own natural resources and take advantage of its unique talents and industries. For over fifty years, after the post war period, we have prospered by using our natural resources, creating jobs and expanding our industrial base. We have become the richest nation in the history of the world. Why would anyone or any social theory want to destroy a proven formula for success? A half century after our greatest victories and sacrifices, that change is underway. Our White House has been packed with educated academic liberals, left over from the 1960s who have been given an opportunity to implement their social theories to change this nation. Candidate Obama promised to "fundamental change this nation" to cheers of listeners who had no idea what he had in mind. The promise of hope and change has bred impatience and despair to an already worn electorate. The non-educated voters who applauded his call for "transformation" had no idea what was in store for them. The Obama Presidency has no mantel of success yet his rhetoric runs wild. He ran a campaign as a "unifier" yet our country has never been more divided. At every political juncture he attacks the Republicans who do not agree with his theory for social change which is the basis for his failed social and political reforms. When defeated in the political arena he resorts to Executive Orders to mandate policies that are defeated by the will of the people. His failure in unity results in a dictatorial style of governing.

On February 14, 2011 President Obama gave a speech to announce his proposed 2011-2012 budget. A key component of his economic expansion was "winterizing" homes of the poor to make them more economically efficient. His initial plan in the 2009 Stimulus Bill had been to retrain the unemployed in inner-cities to "environmentally" improve the homes of the poor. Obama's presidential hallmark may ultimately be the program called "Cash for Caulkers"—meaning superficial improvements. Many of us remember his plan to save gas by checking the air in our tires. Cash for Clunkers tried to remove old cars and make room for new ones at a huge per vehicle cost to the taxpayers. By destroying the government mandated trade-ins we reduced the supply of second hand vehicles and increased the cost of vehicles to the poor. It didn't take an economic genius to see that coming. One car dealer in Michigan said he made more money in the Cash for Clunkers Program then he made in five years. The program looked politically suspicious as a reward program for both union workers and democratic car dealers.

Our long term Unfunded Liabilities to support social programs is stated to be in excess of 27 trillion dollars. Our whopping National Debt has gone north of $14.3 trillion and the daily interest on that debt is $5 to 6 billion per day. This is a monstrous debt and if out of control spending is not halted it will be rising quickly to $20 trillion in less than five years due to continued deficit spending. We simply cannot settle this debt unless inflation roars out of control and the dollar becomes basically worthless. The reductions in unemployment will be paltry at best without a massive relaxation of job killing policies, yet we are continually asked to sacrifice by our President who truly believes he is aiding the economy by spending money we don't have. In all honesty, many of us have little left to give. The call from the "Left" attempts to deceive us into believing that material sacrifices will result in ideal gains.

There is irony in many of our greatest touted social programs. The War on Poverty is perpetuating our poverty, and the war on unemployment is proving to destroy more jobs. The printing of money is putting our children and their children in an impossible position of inheriting a heavy burden of debt. From the conservative's point of view, the lowering of tax rates is designed to stimulate business investment and place more money into the economy through private investment. The Democrats scoff at this proven strategy, and profess that the Food Stamp Program is an economic stimulus program. It is as though giving away money and weakening the resolve of the population will somehow create a healthy solution for the economy. What they don't take into account is that supermarket foods have a profit margin of only 2-4%.

Our economic decline will be debated for many years to come, but real progress will never be achieved by debate alone. We must make substantive changes. Our declines are a direct result of violating the underlying principle of the Constitution which forbids these expanding powers of government beyond its ability to govern. Many now believe that the United States is ungovernable due to its size. When we compare ourselves to the billions in China, the Middle East, and the hundreds of millions in Africa that suffer far more limitations in their style of living, it should give us hope that American ingenuity will be the saving grace for our country if we let it resume its previous path of economic freedom. The contrast between the original ideals of America that offers the opportunity for prosperity for all, a truly worthy goal, and the social reform goals of our long subtle and seductive progressive march to dependence on the government is stark in its contrasts. The pursuance of more and more social programs has interrupted national progress based on ill-conceived government manipulation of the economy for social purposes which has failed repeatedly, here and abroad, yet we continue to employ these costly, failing strategies. Instead, we should be building an Empire of Prosperity.

The justification for many of these social arguments claiming to produce the next Camelot, or better yet the Utopia which is supposed to be perfect for all, is that the government knows better than the individual how to manage the economy. It intends to pursue ideal ends by making the world a better place by appealing to our collective moral values. The collective salvation becomes the answer for everything in their minds. Yet, nowhere on earth has anyone ever created such a divine place or proved that it can be done. Of the over 168 countries in the world today no one can demonstrate a country that attracts more people than the United States of America. It would be a far strength of the imagination to say that they all came here to change us.

Our country was founded on Judeo-Christian principles, the moral values and ideals of individuals uniquely based on individual choice gifted to us by an Omnipotent God. The freedom to make decisions is rooted in particular value systems that are often cultural and most often based on religious beliefs by the majority of the citizens of our nation. These treasured ideals are nested in most individuals and they are the concepts and goals of individual freedom that are in direct conflict with the goals and touted principles of Socialism. Morals and individual liberties aggregate in total opposition to the world of conformity of complete government control. To effect the changes necessary to transform belief systems and values to coincide with increased government control requires a line of action that progressively moves us closer to the false hopes of Socialism. To facilitate these changes in our time-honored belief systems, the Socialists gradually restrict our behavior over long periods of time and employ long term rhetorical persuasion techniques to reorient both individual and cultural changes within a society. This is nothing less than long term, programmed social engineering. Using the tactics and strategies espoused in the Communist Manifesto and the 25 Rules of Nazism are the rules governing the Socialists today in this country. Using these rules it is possible to defy and to break down traditional belief systems that are founded in our most sacred principles.

Individuals that adopt the ideals of personal responsibility are the major threat to collective behavior. Personal responsibility is rooted in liberty. The thinking man is the enemy to those who believe we should be controlled because too much freedom makes man unmanageable. Man was not designed to be caged, yet when freedom is lost we are placed in invisible cages, imprisoned with bars made of government regulation and control.

The Socialist knows that as people's liberties are diminished we lose our collective abilities to solve human problems and become more reliant on government solutions. As the government gains in power we lose our innate abilities to initiate change, to create, to modernize, to improve, and to eliminate problems. When it becomes the role of government to innovate, it will be innovation by regulation--an oxymoron. Regulations are designed to control not innovate. We become innovative by using our talents that arise from the blending of education, spirit, circumstance, opportunity and yes, depending on the gifts provided by Divine Providence.

The Road to Socialism

Examining the government's success in the role as innovator, we must admit several failures. Government control has failed at education. It has destroyed the universal spirit of "can do" Americanism through its failure to unite the many cultures that refuse to integrate into American society. We are no longer a "melting pot," but instead, separated cultures resisting American integration. Government has eliminated circumstance and opportunity by not providing the appropriate climate or conditions that are made by interactive marketplaces. The government will ultimately rule against God himself or the divinity as an individual sees it, unless we see drastic changes in our freedom of religion, one of our founding principles. To use an analogy, when we progressively take the meat, potatoes and vegetables out of the stew there is little else left to eat. If we look at the Totalitarian nations with their high levels of technology, for instance China, Iran, Russia, and North Korea, we should realize we are not importing their technology. They are stealing ours. As we move one step closer to Socialism, during a period of decline in economic growth, our only hope will be those capitalistic companies that have the capital remaining to innovate and renew progress for the rest of the world. Our most valuable material goods are not stored in government vaults. They are located in our businesses and industries and the people who have not been taken over by government. These are the creators of wealth, the independent individuals who innovate and lead the march forward into the future.

Government control of the automobile industry will not create innovation in the car industry. The financial industry will not be able to help to expand the economy by operating with hundreds of thousands of pages of new regulations that heavily burden it after the passage of the newly enacted Financial Reform legislation. The quality of Healthcare will suffer at the hands of the bureaucrats and like energy prices, the prices will "necessarily skyrocket." The plight of the poor will not improve until we change from subsistence support to teaching self sufficiency. The government housing agencies, Freddie Mac and Fannie Mae, the culprits responsible for the global economic meltdown, still remain unregulated amidst the heavy handed regulations designed to make the system better. Both agencies are insolvent and will be in the next round of bailouts if we have any money left. The government's role in promoting home ownership has already destroyed the housing market and pulled trillions of dollars in investment funds out of the economy while robbing Americans and foreign investors alike. We have proven over and over again that a return to the original ideals of the American Constitution is the only way out of the abysmal mess created by the Socialists. We must re-instill our material conditions and seek our original founding ideals. Only through the resurrection of our inalienable rights, Life, Liberty and the Pursuit of Happiness, can we return our country to its golden splendor.

The Road to Socialism

Chapter 15   The Prospects of International Order

"That there is little hope of international order or lasting peace so long as every country is free to employ whatever measure it thinks desirable in its own immediate interest, however damaging they may be to others, need little emphasis now." F.A. Hayek, The Road to Serfdom

It is has been the dream of many world leaders to create a global alliance, a One World Government. This would be more than just a treaty organization, but rather a full fledged unification of dissimilar countries with the goals of world peace, smoother operations and equality of all peoples. In this ideal scenario, a new order would be created as a world without borders.

Hayek warned of the problems and obstacles facing the creation of an idealistic Global Society. In order for their dreams to become a reality, many odd bedfellows would have to come together to live in harmony. Yet, the real world is continually in strife with national struggles and cross border conflicts. To achieve world unification would require far more commonality in governments than exists today. To overlay a supreme world government on this present world with its divergent points of view would mean that some nations would have to sacrifice power and influence and many large powers may not be willing to make the necessary sacrifices. If this is done by subverting these powers and replacing their governments with tyrannical leaders, true freedom will be lost.

Today the world is in turbulence. As we survey the globe we see uprisings in every region of the world. The Middle East is afire with the unrest of its people against dictatorial regimes that enforce totalitarianism. The Sunnis and Shiites are fighting each other for supremacy in the Muslim faith. The European nations united through the European Union are gradually crumbling under the weight of unsustainable social programs. Too many promises have been made that cannot be paid for. As the people come to realize that their governments are financially over-extended and are essentially bankrupt, and worse yet, are continually falling ever more deeply into debt. They have become demoralized and have taken to the streets. They clamor for fulfillment of the promises made by their individual governments. Unions and government workers are organizing to take their anger to the streets and unite social unrest.

America itself is in a grave situation. It is stressed to the point of a national depression caused by the daunting reality that our economic balloon has burst under a series of missteps caused by government regulations and the greed of free market Wall Street Bankers. The wild, reckless approach to globalizing debt through home ownership for those who could least afford it, has collateralized our futures while destroying pensions funds here and abroad. Investor nations around the world gambled imprudently on risky investments to gain higher returns for their constituencies. In the midst of this global disarray, nations around the world are under attack by both the Socialist-Marxists who want to replace individualism with government control, and the Islamist radicals who act out their hatred with suicide attacks and acts of brutality against the innocent with the purpose of creating fear and insecurity. One scheme of the self-appointed intellectual elite is to cause top to bottom chaos in the world so they can install their New World Order, a system of internationalized Socialism. The sad irony of all this is that what they offer is going to ruin the social and economic progress of the entire world. The Islamists offer a Taliban like world of subjugation of women, the brutally harsh Shiria Law, and the destruction of the infidels. The Socialists push their reforms even in the face of the clear evidence that many countries are imploding under the weight of their own Socialist policies.

In this world of uncertainty, America, once the shining beacon of freedom, now sees her own light flickering. Many now realize that we have been weakened from within by groups who hate the America of Capitalism, the land of the free and home of the brave, that shining light on the hill.

There is no model in the world today that can provide a reasonable blueprint for unifying dissimilar nations. One such model is said to be the global peacekeeper called The United Nations, a 66- year- old organization first named by President Franklin D. Roosevelt in 1942, which has grown to 192 member nations. The UN lists their mission and purpose on their website which is copied below from their web:

The UN Mission

"The United Nations is an international organization founded in 1945 after the Second World War by 51 countries committed to maintaining international peace and security, developing friendly relations among nations and promoting social progress, better living standards and human rights."

The UN Has 4 Main Purposes

To keep peace throughout the world;

To develop friendly relations among nations;

To help nations work together to improve the lives of poor people, to conquer hunger

To be a center for harmonizing the actions of nations to achieve these goals.

The United Nations has expanded its role beyond their weakly stated mission and purpose to become the global watch dog for the environment by using a program they adopted in 1992 called *Agenda 21*. This program is designed to implement changes in governments from the heads of state all the way down to our local community leaders. The *American Thinker* published an article by Scott Strezelczyk and Richard Rothschild, dated October 28, 2009, called "UN Agenda 21 – *Coming to a Neighborhood Near You.*" *Agenda 21* appears to be the greatest threat to personal freedom under the guise of curing poverty throughout the world under the tenets of environmentalism. They have combined two issues that must be delivered together which call for improving the human condition without any negative impact on our renewable natural resources. Below is the opening paragraph of the article from the American Thinker regarding *Agenda 21*.

"Most Americans are unaware that one of the greatest threats to their freedom may be a United Nations program known as *Agenda 21*. The United Nations Department of Economic and Social Affairs, Division for Sustainable Development created *Agenda 21* as a sustainability agenda which is arguably an amalgamation of Socialism and extreme environmentalism brushed with anti-American, anti-capitalist overtones."

This agenda calls for nationalizing land to restrict living and personal use, thus forcing people to live in community settlements in densely populated areas. Public transportation and "high speed rail" would eliminate the ownership of private vehicles to reduce the need for fossil fuels, deemed one of the greatest threats to the world. All local municipalities that subscribe to follow the Agenda 21 protocol are pre-disposing their citizens to the ground rules of the agenda. The average person and those elected officials who serve them, who have adopted this protocol, are probably blissfully ignorant of the commitments they have made on behalf of their neighbors. *Agenda 21* is wrapped in a cloth of finely woven fabric that appears on the surface to be an admirable program. There is no other single document that limits freedom on a global basis more than *Agenda 21*. The plan of 40 chapters and over 1200 pages uses the word "environment" in its many variations in the majority of the paragraphs. The United Nations has united the global Socialism Movement and environmentalism in the name of eradicating poverty. As we have learned, the poor are never cured by artificial incentives that do not promote a work ethic. Chapter 29 of the plan, "Strengthening the Role of the Worker and their Trade Unions" dedicates only one page, I repeat one page, to workers who are assumed to be union members working in concert with the government. It doesn't take much of a leap to see that private industry will not be called upon to help solve poverty. This can only mean that in the eyes of the United Nations, governments will be the primary driver in eradicating poverty through re-distributional means. There are only a few countries that have assets to redistribute. The only means available will be to confiscate assets through global eminent domain.

In his book, *The New Road to Serfdom, A letter of Warning to America*, Daniel Hannan, a Member of the European Parliament representing the UK, highlights some of the major structural differences between the United States of America and the European Union (EU), which is composed of 27 formerly independent sovereign nations. The EU has evolved over time since 1957 from six core nations: Belgium, Netherlands, Germany, France, Luxembourg and Italy. The membership grew although 18 European countries abstained from joining the Union, most notably Switzerland and Norway from the West and 16 Eastern European nations, the largest being Russia.

Hannon points to America which was founded with a U.S. Constitution of 7,200 words preserving "the rights" of the people. The EU was founded with a constitutional doctrine of over 76,000 words mainly giving all power to the Union. Each member state retained power over their military, foreign policy, and international trade agreements. The EU created another layer of taxation to oversee the issues of human rights, protection of the environment, and the common currency, the Euro, based on the Euro Zone, composed of only 17 member nations. The EU maintains an open border policy with free movement between nations. It supervises a common justice system similar to a World Court and coordinates trade policies. The population of the EU nations is slightly over 500 million while the United States has a population of 309 million. Hannan fears that the United States may move closer to a European model of government by sacrificing freedom and prosperity for uniformity. In short, concise language, Hannan says the European Union model does not work.

In comparing the size of a nation to its Income per Capita, Hannan discovered that the larger the nation the lower the per capita income. The United States ranked 18th with an income per capita of $46,900 which is less than half of Liechtenstein, Qatar, Luxembourg, and Norway, and only two thirds of the per capita income of Ireland, Switzerland, and Denmark. The source of the data was the *CIA World Factbook* provided in *The New Road to Serfdom*, *page 55.* The nations that have higher incomes per capita are viewed as "tax havens" due to their particularly low tax rates. According to the *Heritage Foundation's Economic Freedom Index,* these nations share the phenomenon of having a low cost of government due to a higher level of prosperity while having a low cost of social programs. The evidence is clear that jobs improve society to a greater extent than social welfare does.

The Economic Freedom Index is published on-line annually based on ten primary components of freedom which are totaled into an index number. The components are: Business Freedom, Trade Freedom, Fiscal Freedom, Government Spending, Monetary Freedom, Investment Freedom, Financial Freedom, Property Rights, Freedom from Corruption, and Labor Freedom. These factors of freedom are calculated into an Index for 183 nations. The United States ranks 9th on the index of freedom for 2010, down one notch from 2009. Ranking 1 through 8 are: Hong Kong, Singapore, Australia, New Zealand, Switzerland, Canada, Ireland, and Denmark. It is interesting to note that the more restrictive and tyrannical a government, the lower the score on the index. Many of the countries in the lower half of the index share one common factor: they are primarily countries run by dictators. The last ten on the freedom list are somewhat predictable: Timor-Leste, Iran, Democratic Republic of Congo, Libya, Burma, Venezuela, Eritrea, Cuba, Zimbabwe and North Korea. Not included due to lack of available information are: Afghanistan, Iraq, Liechtenstein, and Sudan. We can assume that Liechtenstein's lack of information is the result of privacy laws.

What is interesting to note is that Mr. Hannan warns President Obama not to follow the EU model that has failed to achieve its stated goals. The goals of peace and human rights are the stated goals of the EU yet the funding is not available and must be paid for by the individual members which continue to fund their own militaries and social programs as well and are insolvent. The EU has adopted an open border policy for free movement between the member nations.

The failure of our own administration here in America to enforce our Immigration and Homeland Security laws on our borders is, in essence, an open border policy. Although the government fails to acknowledge the deliberate influx of immigrants to America, the numbers are growing and crime is rising along our borders to the South. Canada, on the other hand, maintains a shared border protection program with US and the flow is controlled. Oddly, as a matter of policy, we control the border to the North while ignoring and clearly downplay the human trafficking and drug smuggling from the South.

Is the prospect of an International Order imposed on the world looming in the not so distant future? Probably not. The complexities and divisions around the world today do not provide a solid basis for the unity of nations. Each region of the globe is suffering from not enough income and too many debts. As countries begin to unify within their own borders talk of international unity will temporarily subside. It is hard to rush to assist your neighbor when your own house is on fire. The devastating destruction in Japan, caused by parallel natural disasters, the massive earthquake and tsunami, did not bring the immediate aid that we saw when Haiti was struck by their earthquake only a year before. The world humanitarian outreach for Haiti, a failing dictatorship, drew over a billion dollars in aid. The money donated to earthquake victims has never been accounted for which may have discouraged future donors from offering support for another troubled nation. Perhaps the economic realities in the world today have set in.

Clearly, when nations are unable to meet the needs of their own people they are hard pressed to provide funds for humanitarian support. America seems to be the exception to the rule when it comes to humanitarian support. It is hard to believe that nations would be willing to sacrifice more freedom to create "a greater world order."

As Socialism fails in each country that has tried it, can it succeed on a global level? If not, then according to Karl Marx, the next step is Global Communism?

Chapter 16   Conclusion

The purpose of this book is to help educate people about some of the history, the background, and the goals of both Socialism and Capitalism. It is meant to be an illuminating aid regarding the choices we may be forced to make regarding the road to travel on our short journey to our ultimate destiny. This has been an Odyssey for many and a Star Trek adventure for others who may not have had the opportunity to explore our past or foresee our future in light of what we have said here.

The previous chapters were patterned after *The Road to Serfdom* but were expanded to include developments from the past century to specifically relate the effects of Socialism in America. The chapters are not yet complete nor were they intended to be. They are suggestive only. They are the stepping stones that can guide you to your own conclusions. The causes, the beginnings, and the current status of Capitalism and Socialism can consume vast volumes as indicated by the many sources referenced.

We have covered some of the horror stories of Totalitarian dictators who have been the cruelest in the history of the world, and have had no respect for the people they govern. Unfortunately, this cruelty continues today in some areas of the world. We have only alluded to other causes of societal unrest, such as the Muslin Brotherhood and Radical Islam. We realize, as well, that there are powerful men such as George Soros who have the financial means to push their causes while undermining our spirit of American Exceptionalism. Yet, we are equally troubled by excesses on the other side by the greedy capitalists who take advantage of their power to move the markets and have no regard for fairness and operate without an ounce of concern for the helpless people they affect. Obviously, in this world today we have powerful and destructive forces on both sides of the political and sociological spectrum.

Our goal going forward should be to preserve a nation that was founded on goodness conducting the greatest experiment in the history of governance. Living under the world's oldest Constitution, the odds are not great that we shall find a better way that survives the same test of time. While we bicker back and forth about the roles of peoples and individuals it is still in the best interest of others when we come together to share our differences and have wholesome dialog about ways to bridge the gap.

The United States of America is not a monarchy. We lived under one of those and living under tyranny did not meet our demands nor satisfy the rights of our diverse population. We have suffered through stern leaders and weak leaders who have not always made the best decisions as viewed by many. History has been kind to some and harsher on others. The 20th Century brought us the greatest expansion of government and entitlement programs that "progressive" thinkers designed by watering down the Constitution to meet the social goals of the nation. It also brought us face to face with the failures of some of our programs that did not lift up those who needed it the most. In some cases, it actually perpetuated their suffering and we have ignored their cries for help.

As we continue to move forward into the 21st Century we are a nation divided. Our political system, designed to operate taking into account differing points of view, has been contentious and divided, our Rule of Law is broken and our financial treasures have been ransacked. On both sides, banners of truth are hoisted into national prominence by passion from these true believers. Our dearest concern is that our elected leaders, our representatives, operate with the highest moral and ethical standards. Sacrificing our collective social souls on behalf of winning is not a true moral victory. Anytime we have a lapse of our national values everyone suffers. To maintain our global presence in the world we must continue to ignite Miss Liberty's lamp of freedom. A world in strife awaits a nation with compassion and vision. We can be that nation. We are that nation.

Chapter 17   Become a Patriot

Are You A Patriot?

The election of Barack Hussein Obama in 2008 created a renaissance in political activism that has not been seen on the Right in our lifetime. The call to action was caused by the immediate implementation of radical Leftist policies soon after the President's inauguration hence, threatening the peace and serenity of the American people. His intent was to expand Big Government far in excess of any immediate needs. What emerged, to his surprise only weeks after he took office, was a clamor never seen before in American politics: a direct attack on the transformational policies of the President of the United States. The American people spontaneously went into action based on the on-air rant of Rick Santelli of CNBC. The Tea Party Movement erupted overnight and cast millions of patriots into small neighborhood groups planning April 15th Rallies insisting that we are Taxed Enough Already. While the liberal press tried to downplay our numbers, millions of people took to the streets with homemade signs and American flags demanding their country back. These initial protestors were the modern day patriots that formed the basis for a peaceful American Revolution-The Tea Party Movement. In the 2010 elections the Tea Parties proved that they are a major player in the world of politics by sweeping Republican candidates in the House of Representatives and our local communities as well the candidates in many statewide elections. A new political revolution is underway.

The roles of these independent and autonomous Tea Party groups were expanded after the 2010 elections. Their focus became the out of control spending in Washington resulting in   deficit spending and an unsustainable national debt. In contrast to the issue of taxation in our call for Independence in 1776, the patriots of 2011 peacefully called for fiscal responsibility. Hopefully, the days of financial irresponsibility will finally be over.

As the patriots move forward their roles will probably evolve into challenging the budgetary allocations consistent with the missions stated by each of the Federal Secretary's who should be accountable for the billions they are awarded each year. A review should be conducted to aid our elected officials to determine the relevance of our Departmental Budgets consistent with their roles under the Constitution. For instance, does anyone actually know what the Department of Education does with $100 billion it receives each year? What about the Department of Defense contractors in Afghanistan who, through fraud and abuse, wasted 30% of the $70 billion they already received this year? Today's patriots abhor hearing this information as painfully as the patriots of yesteryear who were denigrated by the tyrannical British Empire that abused them through "taxes without representation."

One of the greatest strategies for the advancement of Big Government is the take-over of the people through designed ignorance. Our failing school systems, with their Far Left Agenda and indoctrination programs, are emblematic of the "Progressive Movement" that is poisoning our children. Whether it is unintentional or by the design of well-crafted indoctrination programs, we must counteract this "progressive movement" to reverse this trend of the dumbing down of our culture. The Nazi Movement relied on indoctrinating their children to overpower their parents. These same tactics are being openly expressed by the President of the United States when he addresses children and tells then to "go home and educate your parents." To counteract this trend requires reinstituting traditional education in our schools and the process begins with electing candidates in our local towns and cities and putting patriotic conservatives on our school boards who support traditional educational values.

The key to taking back our country begins in our neighborhoods and requires education, unity, and coordination. Our early patriots banded together and used muskets to gain freedom from their tyrannical leaders. Today, our patriots use the ballot box: the most powerful tool we have in our arsenal. As true patriots, we must warn our friends and neighbors to inform them of the enslaving policies which will destroy our sense of American Exceptionalism. To be of service to our friends and country we must be armed with information. Disseminating information about liberty and freedom is one of the greatest fears of the Left. Our freedom is violated when our over-reaching Big Government recklessly takes our money and gives it to causes it feels are more meaningful to society than creating the much needed jobs in our communities. They squander our hard earned money on their misguided projects and build massive government bodies who insulate them from the people they serve. We must combat these attacks on our freedom or we will be doomed to become a society surrounded by failure not exceptionalism. At the same time, under the rampant expansion of our social programs we slip closer and closer toward Socialism. When 50% of our people are dependent upon "entitlement programs" we are in trouble as surely as the US Postal Service. To ensure our success and defend ourselves against this progressive movement we must become active patriots. Thomas Jefferson so aptly wrote in the Declaration of Independence that in defense of changing governments, great care should be given. In turn, changing the role of government should equally demand the same protection.

What is a Patriot?

An American Patriot is someone who loves his country but, not necessarily his government. Our government should be a service center for the people not an ultimate authority. Our government has defined duties outlined in the Constitution but, over time our elected officials expanded the role of government far beyond their delegated authority. When we do not approve of the change in direction, the Declaration of Independence instructs us to take action. Patriots revere the idea that our country represents our values. Our government is a reflection of the values of the people we send to Washington. Our values should represent who we are as a nation. It begins with Life, Liberty and the Pursuit of Happiness and it is our patriotic duty to fight to protect those values for posterity.

When we think of patriots, what comes to mind? For many, it is Paul Revere on his midnight ride, or muskets blazing and billowing with smoke, and town square criers in three cornered hats screaming, "Give me liberty or give me death." In comparison, today's rather harmless patriots are called "extremists" for honoring the United States Constitution, labeled "far right winged whackos" for demanding lower taxes, and accused of being "terrorists" for wanting smaller government. When we demand to keep more of our earnings and give less to the government, we are called selfish and uncompassionate. But, when we hand over our money we discover our government is wasteful and irresponsible. In the process we create a larger and larger government with un-definable goals and objectives.

Many of today's elected officials and the government they support celebrate hand-outs to any group that can be assembled under the Democratic Banner. In fact, "We Love Government Waste" could be the motto of the Left: not a very patriotic theme. So who are the patriots who can protect us from this Big Government takeover?

Patriots come in all shapes and sizes. They are old and they are young. Some are looking for their first job while others are awaiting their first golden age Social Security check. Some are rich and some are poor. They come in all colors and nationalities. Some are older than dirt by their own admonition. A rare few own horses and the majority have never fired a gun. Most patriots do not live in the inner cities of poorest cities in America but, despise what Big Government has done to those who do through the failed social policies that perpetuate a deplorable "system of living." Those who call themselves Patriots tend to be non-violent and non-confrontational despite the reports to the contrary by the Big Media. Most true patriots tend to be more virtuous and believe in faith, the family, and personal responsibility. Today's patriots will fight to preserve our nation on the march down the road to Socialism and the evils of Big Government. They firmly believe that with enough public support we can take back their country. If you are willing to support this cause then you are a patriot.

Being a patriot is easier than most would think. Today, we no longer have to ride a horse, carry a musket, and never have to host a meeting in the Town Square. Our First Amendment Rights allow us to hold hands with our neighbors and rally in public places carrying signs and waving American Flags supporting causes that promote freedom. Our 21st century tools display our patriotism with far more vigor and impact than were available to our forefathers. We have tools at our disposal to forge freedom and we never have to leave the comfort of our own homes and we can be just as patriotic as Paul Revere on his midnight ride. Computer technology allows us to ride at midnight or in the bright sunlight. Today, we can accomplish far more than the patriots who were protecting the four million people who proudly called themselves Americans in 1776.

There are a variety of things we can do as Patriots to take back our country. In many cases, we find that our politicians are not representing our views but instead support their own self-interests. That is not why we elected them. It has always been the role of "we the people" to elect politicians who represent our views, but sadly, over time we have become separated from many of those who represent us. Our failure is partly our own. We have become complacent and too involved in our everyday lives to take our government and the act of governing seriously. It was important to the people in the 18th century who cherished their newborn freedom but, over time we as a people abandoned our personal responsibility and took freedom for granted. To a fault, we lost our vigilance and we became overly reliant upon our elected leaders to protect our interests. In the process, we lost control of the management of our communities, our states, and ultimately our country. We became overly reliant on our elected representatives. For many, the political process was considered boring while others felt they did not have sufficient information or knowledge to become involved in the politics of government. Gradually our voter rolls declined and, as a result, only a small majority make the decisions for the whole. But, today this trend is turning around. Some of our greatest Founders, Thomas Jefferson, Benjamin Franklin and the beloved George Washington, told us that protecting our freedom is a responsibility: our responsibility. It begins in our neighborhoods and goes all the way up to the people we send to our State Capitals, and ultimately, to those we elect to represent us in Washington D.C. To become more involved we must be educated and engaged.

Patriots are Educated

We don't have to go back to school to learn how to be a patriot. In fact, I learned far more about American history, government and politics in the last three years in my living room than the average person learns in 12 years of formal education today. There are many things we can do at home and in our communities. Many of us found history boring while we were in school. I was no exception. Traditionally, history is taught from the perspective of memorizing a series of names, dates, and places which has little fascination unless the instructor is exceptional. Most of us did not have the luxury of being inspired by great history teachers. History becomes relevant when it provides a vision of the future. The study of history provides us with two warning signs: One says "STOP" the other says, "Continue at Your Own Risk."

To be interesting history must be relevant. It was my attempt to express the significance of certain points of history in my book *The Road to Socialism..* When we understand the consequences upon our lives as a result from the various events in history, it then becomes meaningful. It's not necessary to know every battle in the Revolutionary War or the names of the Generals on the winning and losing sides. But it is significant to understand why we fought the wars and the long term consequences and opportunities that resulted from those wars. For most of us, the undeclared war in Vietnam is still a mystery with no purpose. All wars should be evaluated on both their opportunities and consequences to understand if they were meaningful or not. Our involvement today in the Middle East is questionable to many. Without a beneficial altruistic purpose, for the Common Defense, we should never enter a war.

History does not have to be boring. Pick a topic and become an above average student of some aspect of history. As your knowledge base grows so will your interest level. For example: reading the Constitution does not make anyone a Constitutional Expert. Reading the *Federalist Papers*, written by James Madison, Alexander Hamilton, and John Jay is an excellent way to learn more about the intention of the United States Constitution. It is also a very dry way to learn about the Constitution but, your level of knowledge about the importance of the Constitution and its intent can be used to counteract those who want to replace it. Learning about the Founder Fathers, one of my particular favorites, will provide a perspective of the individual characters that debated the Constitution and will help us realize the genius of those who signed the greatest governmental document in the history of the world. Without some additional knowledge about the Constitution, especially in our schools, it could soon be retired and replaced by another form of government. If you want to think about something scary think about this. Think about the people in Washington who would be writing the new Constitution. It could be longer and more confusing than the Healthcare Bill. Our Constitution is 7,000 words and has been amended a relatively few times in over 200 years. In contrast, the European Union's Constitution is 76,000 words and their union is falling apart in less than 30 years due to the failures designed into their governing document. Our country has remained solid for over 200 years. Whether one studies the making of the Constitution, or one studies the Presidents, or other historical events that framed our nation, it is all important in learning how to protect our freedom from those who are out to destroy our way of life. As a suggestion, pick an area in which you can become an expert. Becoming an expert in any particular facet provides one with a sense of confidence and can add a new dimension to your life. The choice is yours and I guarantee that it will enrich your life.

There is no secret formula of what makes a patriot. It is something that is in each person's heart. It is a belief system, a culture, and set of principles that guide us in our daily lives. There are also those who have opposing views but, they also call themselves patriots : they just seem to live by a different set of values. For many of us we see our values in the America Flag. We feel a sense of pride when we hear the National Anthem and we appreciate the greatness of our country when we see a person in a military uniform. Sometimes when we see children playing in a school yard it reminds us that we are the greatest nation in the world and it is our responsibility to protect our nation for our future, the future of our children, and the generations that are to come.

Today, everyone realizes that our nation is facing some real threats. But we can have hope today because we know in our hearts that there are millions of people today that have finally become energized with the Spirit of America. Many now realize that we could lose everything we believe in if we let the wrong people continue run our country. In order to protect our liberty and freedom we must be better educated and informed and come together with our neighbors to ensure that the United States of America, the Land of the Free and the Home of the Brave will once again become a symbol to our children as the greatest nation in the world and it can be if we all work together for that common goal.

APPENDIX

The Four Pillars to Become an Armchair Activist

Many people belong to many organizations and support a variety of activities and causes. There are others who are more subdued and prefer to avoid the limelight and participate with a lower level of intensity. Some of our early patriots had printing presses and others wrote pamphlets about King George. Others attended secret meetings in Ale Houses and in the back rooms of churches. No matter what your preference, opportunities exist for all to become patriots. Patriots take many forms but what is important is what is in their soul.

Today's modern world provides us with opportunities that did not exist thirty years ago. The advancements in technology provide us with tools that literally make it possible to never leave our homes. We can communicate, do our shopping, and all the information and entertainment in the world is available and we never have to leave our homes. For those who are so inclined, they can become a new breed of activist: The Armchair Activist.

It is both our right and our responsibility to be vigilant to protect our future. So where should we start to take back America? Below are some very simply things to consider to become a Neighborhood Patriot whether you are active in an organized group or prefer to remain active on a viral basis.

Some will start out slowing while other may charge in with plenty of enthusiasm with their muskets blazing. No matter how one starts, it is important that everyone participate at some level to preserve our country and in doing so develop the tools to help others become better citizens too. The four pillars of becoming an Armchair Patriot are Education, Tea Party Movement, Politics, and using the modern tools of activism, the Internet and Facebook.

What follows is a list of suggestions to provide a basic understanding to help in serving your patriotic role to promote and protect the ideals of life, liberty and the pursuit of happiness. Just as the early patriots, we must understand our tyrannical enemies. Today they are not on foreign shores: most of them are elected leaders. Congress is filled with dozens of declared Socialists and Communists who are committed to destroying your freedom. These should be the first to go.

1. Education

Education is the tool of life and is critical to our national survival.

Below are many suggestions to learn more about the challenges we face and the heritage we are committed to preserve. To be successful we must increase our knowledge to understand the threats that we face as a nation and the information we need to survive.

Know Thy Enemy

There are three primary textbooks of the enemy and everyone should read them. These are the handbooks that they use without any sense of morals to win at any expense. If you do not read any others books you should be aware of the influence of these books. If you have college age children these books may be in their bedrooms. These books are easy to read and informative. The *Art of War* is a historical classic. Many people read it once a year due to its simplistic approach to battles not only in politics but in life. *The Communist Manifesto* is the ultimate goal of the Marxists for the world and the United States is the last frontier to be conquered. *Rules for Radicals* discusses the ugly tactics suggested as the tools for defeating any political opponent and is the primary tool used to defeat American Exceptionalism. It has been said that Republicans are too nice to use this book, but your enemies will do "whatever it takes" to win. You must be able to identify what they are doing to us in order to deflect their impact.

The Art of War, Sun Tzu, this ancient classic is easy to read and provides strategies to defeat the enemy. You are the enemy of Socialism and someone is out there right now trying to conquer you. Increased awareness is increased protection from the enemy.

The Communist Manifesto, Karl Marx and Friedrich Engels, these are the thoughts that are being inbred into our children and college students today. This book and its Marxist theories are being used to generate hate in our country by our educators. There are many versions available. Pick the shortest one, usually 50-60 pages or search the internet for an on-line copy. If you have a college student at home look in their room.

Rules for Radicals, Saul D. Alinsky, this is the strategy and playbook written by this country's greatest Community Organizer, a radical 1960s instigator. It is important to understand the techniques that are being used against us every day by other Alinsky followers who are being trained in our colleges. This book is easy to read, very informative, and will open your eyes to the massive planned and coordinated disruption that is going on today around the country. You will discover that what appears random is not.

The Communist Takeover of America Go to:
http://www.rense.com/general32/americ.htm

Declared Socialists in Congress (there are 70 of them in the 111th Congress)
Go to: *http://www.tysknews.com/Depts/gov_philosophy/dsa_members.htm*

Know Your American Heritage

Many are not aware of the depth of knowledge possessed by our Founding Fathers. While many were college educated, more were self-taught and were well versed in classical studies learning ancient history and particularly studying governments going back to the days of ancient Rome and Greece. It is not essential to read Plato and Aristotle, but learning about the Founding Fathers provides one with an understanding of the richness of the character that went into developing our great nation. The Constitution they created was called "an experiment in self-government" and it is the longest running experiment in the history of the world.

The National Center for Constitutional Studies is a great place to start. Their website is www.nccs.net. They provide books, DVDs, and other instructional material at reasonable prices. A Must Read is *The 5000 Year Leap*, by Cleon Skousen. This book provides a very short history of the founding of our Nation and describes the 28 founding principles of our Constitution. Study the principles that make us the greatest nation in the world.

Carry a copy of the *United States Constitution*. There are a variety of books about the Constitution. You cannot protect what you do not understand. You will be one-up on your elected leaders just knowing their responsibilities in the Constitution. As a group, buy them in bulk from NCCS or the Heritage Foundation and give them to schools.

There are many books available about the making of the Constitution. It is a story you should know. As many want you to believe, we didn't just happen to stumble across the ideas that created the longest running continuous Constitution in the history of the world. This document was bred from classical genius by people who studied government back to its roots in Plato and Aristotle providing us with a republic not a democracy.

Read *Miracle at Philadelphia,* by Catherine Drinker Bowen, and *The Founding Brothers*, by Joseph J. Ellis. NCCS has a video, *The Making of America*, a 90 minute video about how James Madison orchestrated the principles of the Constitution and he was its primary author. Learn how we abandoned the Articles of Confederation against all odds to create a new nation.

The Declaration of Independence is the Birth Certificate of our nation. It is available on-line and in most Constitutional booklets. Along with the Constitution they are our most important documents. Read it and know it.

The National Center for Constitution Studies has an excellent series including George Washington, Thomas Jefferson, and Benjamin Franklin. Refer to The NCCS.org for excellent, easy to read books and DVDs and other great materials. Make sure you get a copy of The 5000 Year Leap.

How much do you know about the presidents? Many study them in numerical order other. *The Forgotten Man*, by Amity Shale's, is an eye opener about Franklin D. Roosevelt and provides a history of his presidency and many of the social programs we live with today. It also outlines his years of dealing with the Great Depression and reveals how his policies prolonged the Great Depression. Obama and his economic advisors are using FDRs failed policies as a roadmap to turnaround the recession.

Study Conservatism from the Best

There are a variety of tools to learn about conservatism. It is important to understand your belief system and why you have adopted the political philosophy that you embrace. The average person is unable to explain why they are a Democrat or a Republican. It is critical that each and every person know and understand their beliefs to guide them on their journey. Our schools do not teach the philosophy of the right. This information cannot be found in American History text books. In fact, the people in the progressive movement do not want this information available to our children because they do not want to have to compete with another philosophy when their purpose is to grow government at the tax payer's expense. Below are some of my favorites.

Ronald Reagan, An America Life, by Ronald Reagan, He is accused by the Left as being a dummy and nothing could be farther from the truth. He was brilliant and the greatest America orator in modern history. Learn his history and his transformation from liberalism to conser-vatism. It is a great book, and easy to read in his own style.

Liberty and Tyranny, A Conservative Manifesto. Mark R. Levin. Levin highlights the principles of Conservatism in this easy to read short book.

The Sermon on the Mount, The Key to Success in Life, by Emmet Fox, This is a short book about the teaching of Jesus in an easy to read, but powerful dialogue about the guiding principles to help you live your life.

George Will is a syndicated columnist in many newspapers. Look at your Editorial Section or find him on-line.

The Heritage Foundation: Become a member or at the minimum sign up for their free on-line newsletters. There are a variety of newsletters so start with something that interests you.

The Daily Rasmussen Report: Sign up for this free daily report. It provides surveys and polls to help you follow the mood of the nation on a variety of different issues and politics. It has a Daily Tracking Poll of the President's Approval Rating, with a brief synopsis each day.

Rush Limbaugh, the King of Conservative Radio. There are many who don't like Rush's brand of humor, but he will grow on you once learn to separate the person from the message. He is one of the greatest proponents of Conservatism and the Left hates him for it. With a foot print of over 20 million listeners, he is one of the greatest influencers and protectors of our freedom.

www.Fairtax.org. Look at this.   Eliminating the abusive Internal Revenue Service will go a long by taking politics out of our Tax Code. Understand this concept to help educate others.

2. Join the Tea Party Movement

Joining a Tea Party Group might sound radical, extremist, and downright scary but it is not anything like what the liberal press wants you to believe. We are not the far right winged whackos with subversive views. We are your neighbors and our goal is Less Taxes and Smaller Government: not exactly revolutionary new ideas.

Tea Party groups support candidates that share their views. They are republicans, democrats, and independents. Many have no party affiliation and prefer to stay in the background. One thing they have in common is that they are the true Patriots. They believe in the ideals of the Declaration of Independence and honor the United States Constitution as the law of the land. It is not a "living document" and its tenets are not "optional" as some would want you to believe. Tea Party members are educated and they believe in continuing education. One of the primary purposes of most Tea Party groups is help educate others. The greatest problem we face today is the controlled ignorance that has been implanted in our children. To overthrow any government using non-violent means requires that the existing government or its enemies must discredit the existing system of government. This is done through repeated attempts to denigrate the Constitution and its supporters. The Tea Party Movement, as the protector of the Constitution, is the greatest threat to the Left who are attempting to expand the role of government beyond the delegated powers in the Constitution.

Tea Party members, both young and old, are the people who want to help to return this country to its lost splendor using non-violent means. They don't shout and yell. They believe in the political process. They are the silent Paul Revere's of your community warning people of the attacks being assaulted on our personal freedom each day. They wear the American Flag on their T-shirts and we see them at patriotic events on the Fourth of July, Memorial Day and Veterans Day. They support the men and women of our military that provide for our common defense. They are not the racists condemned by the people who are stealing our freedom. They don't belong to hate groups. They believe and work for freedom and support candidates who share their values. They believe in helping people to become self-reliant rather than victims of the Big Government social system. I am proud to be a member of several Tea Party groups and have found a home and friends that share my same sense of patriotism.

To find a meeting near you search on-line for groups in your area. They may be listed under Tea Party, 912 Groups, or search under Meetups.com.

3. Get Involved with local politics

Why Should I Become Involved In Local Politics? To help to effect needed change.

Only about 35% of the eligible people vote in any election and the margin for the winners is usually 1-3%. That means that less than 20% of the people make the decisions for how your towns and cities are run, whether you have a Bond Offering for a new sewer system, and what happens in your children's classroom. The Left likes those numbers because they can control most elections using their special interest groups. We as Patriots only have one special interest group and it is "We the People," a much harder constituency group to organize than the Union Shop Organizer, our union Teachers, the head of the Parent Teacher Association, or those who have been labeled the oppressed and the greatest voting block of all: the 35% of the workforce including their families, who work local, state and the Federal government. Only a small percentage of them vote, but they are consistently being organized to make their numbers better. The largest constituency group on the Right is the Tea Party Movement. The first nightmare the Left has seen since Ronald Reagan.

The Road to Socialism

Your local City, County and School Board elections are the first line of defense to take back America. Attend their meetings to see what they are doing. Learn about your local elected officials. Get involved. Remember, local politicians often become State or National candidates. You do not want to sit back idly while politicians who don't share your views use your community for political grooming. Become involved. Contact your local political party and join their website for updates of activities and things where you may have an opportunity to meet other like-minded people. Attend Town Hall meetings- visit your local elected officials at their offices. Organize groups to meet with them to express your priorities. These elected officials are your neighbors. Get to know them.

Be an activist - Call you're your local politicians and give them a piece of your mind. They may not like your opinion but, phone calls have impact more than E-Mails and Faxes. Remember, they want to get re-elected and you can help them or hurt them. If you have 100 or 200 people in your database tell them that you represent 200 voters. This gives you political clout. Look up the numbers of your Local, State officials. Make it a point to meet you US Congressperson. Put their phone numbers in your cell phone and call them any time there is an issue that you are concerned about call them and talk to their staff. Also sign up for their websites and newsletters. Stay informed with what they are doing. It is easy, simple, and you can get actually get their attention. If they don't listen tell all your friends in your database. Activists keep people informed.

Write letters to the Editor to your local newspaper. If you have an opinion or disagree with an article in the paper then voice your opinion. Read your papers guidelines for letters to the editor. On average, only one out of every twenty letters gets printed in the local papers.

In the last couple of years several of our local Tea Party members have decided to run for public office. Some were successful and some were not. Those who did not get the vote count are already planning their next campaign. If you are active in a Tea Party group you have a built in campaign staff who want to see one of their own succeed.

Volunteer to work on a candidate's campaign: a great way to know your candidate and make new friends.

Run for a local office. In the last couple of years several of our local Tea Party members ran for public office. Some were successful and some were not. Those who did not get the vote count the first time are already planning their next campaign. If you are active in a Tea Party group you have a built in campaign staff who want to see one of their own succeed.

4. The Internet and Social Media are Your Most Powerful Tools

These are the most powerful tools you have available to facilitate change in America and you never have to leave your home. You can start out very slowly or you can jump right in if you are actively using your computer.

Social Media, like Facebook and Twitter and many others, are the communications vehicles of the future and will continue to be essential to the success of our political candidates. The candidates and parties that master the use of technology will dominate politics. Candidate Obama proved the power of Facebook and Twitter by going after the young people and capitalizing on donations under $25. There are strategies that everyone can use to have the same impact. You too can be a power house of valuable information and education by following a simple process and you may have the ability to be a political fund raiser using some very simple ideas.

Your E-Mail Database

Your e-mail data base can be the most valuable tool you have in your political arsenal. The real value becomes apparent when we understand what we can do with these tools. When we work for local candidates we also help to influence what happens on the national level because our involvement with our neighbors can carry over to the Presidential election. Depending upon your state and how long you have lived in the general area, your contacts may be mostly local, out of the area, or a combination of both. As the world gets smaller through technology we all have the capability to stay in touch with people around the world and it costs nothing if it is done on the computer. E-Mail is the most common tool most people have today, second is Facebook.

The two most important things about using e-mail is having content and someone to send it to. Many people in organizations have the same people in their database and they take turns passing around the same E-mails. I call this the E-Mail Merry Go Round. If 10 people have 50 names each and they are all the same names, everyone tends to send the same e-mails to each other and the group does not get any larger and "you are preaching to the choir" over and over and over again. The key to being an Armchair Activist is to develop your own unique database for special purposes outside of your organization: those people who are not directly involved in the political process. We need tens of millions of new contacts. If a community organizer from Chicago can do it then we can do it too.

Use Groups for your Contacts. Learn to use Groups of Contacts in your E-mail data-base. Your internet provider has the capability of placing people in Groups. They may be called something else, but you have the functionality to place people that share the same characteristics in a common group. I use several groups to isolate people with different interests and localities.

I have a Group called Tea Party which is all my local Tea Party contacts and another group is active Republicans, of which many are also Tea Party members. I have another group for friends who live in State House District 69 and another set of people who live in State House District 70. I include my Democrats until they ask to be removed. The people in my House District groups all have something in common: they are not working members of the Republican Party and are not members of a Tea Party Group and they live in District 69 or 70. During election periods I forward information to them about our State candidates. These are people who are my personal friends who are not politically active but I want them to vote.

Another very important group is people who live Out of State, These are my conservative/republican friends who do not live in Florida. Some are politically active and some are not. I forward articles I write or other information to keep them abreast of what is going on. During non-election periods I share very little with them. Almost all of them are Friends on Facebook. I do try to keep them informed about politics in their state and forward articles to individuals if I think they are informative. In total, I have over three hundred people in my various Groups. I started this a couple of years ago and discovered that Dick Morris, the noted political strategist, calls this an "Electronic Precinct." It has no boundaries. I encourage everyone to forward information that I send to them. Since I write articles on a couple of blog sites, I send all my articles to everyone. Based on Statistical Tracking Systems I know that when I send out an article that I write to 250 people as many as 1,000 people read the article. That means that when I forward something it has a multiple of 4. This means for each E-mail I send, 4 people may read it. When you send something you have no idea of the impact of your message. Therefore, do not kill your golden geese by flooding them with every joke you get. Some will get tired and eventually delete you upon arrival. I try not to overdo it. Also when forwarding be courteous and Trim off the E-mail addresses of things you receive to avoid having your friends Spammed.

Your goal, like Paul Revere's is to alert as many people as possible of the potential threats to our freedom. You can do this by adding more people to your database. If you make a conscious effort to add people to you Contact List you can wind up with a very powerful database. This database will come in handy in the coming 2012 election cycle. Now is the time to start building your team for the next election.

I ask people to have a goal of setting up a database of people in various groups that include at least 100 friends. I then ask them to ask their 100 people to do the same thing. I call this The Amway Approach. I do this locally and with my Out of Area and Out of State people. The idea is to create a viral network of like-minded people. Look at the impact. If each person creates Groups that include 100 people, who forward information to 100 people, and those do the same, then it only takes four generations to reach 1 million people and one more generation to reach 100 million people. This is theoretically possible but in reality the cycle will breakdown before it reaches those levels. Start small and add to your list of friends. If you have 10 or 15 people today you have a good base. As you become more involved you will surely add more people to your database.

Using Facebook

I have to admit that I am a dolt when it comes to using all of the social sites with the exception of Facebook. I took a class on how to use Social Media and I selected Facebook because it made more sense to me than things like Tweeter. I don't tweet and I rarely Text, but someday, maybe sooner or later, I may be tweeting like a bird. It can be a powerful tool if used properly. I learned not to overload myself with too many contact programs, therefore Facebook is my program of choice because it provides the greatest amount of flexibility for staying in touch with my database which are my Friends.

Facebook takes a little bit of time to get used to. It is an excellent tool to both provide and get information, and to start a dialogue with like-minded people and those you may not share your views. I have run into many free and low cost seminars that teach the basics for using Facebook. What I find difficult is that Facebook is constantly updating features but, they are slow to add the instructions to the on-line Help Section. A year ago I bought the latest book on how to get the most out of Facebook and it was obsolete in only a few months.

Sign up for Facebook at Facebook.com. In addition to completing a Profile, you will be asked to post a Profile Picture. Many people, in the beginning, are afraid to post a picture. You don't have to use a current picture. You may use a picture of anything. Be creative. The purpose of a picture or some consistent symbol is to be recognized by people who are interested in you. Facebook provides a blank shadow picture if you do not post a picture. This standard silhouette gives people the impression that you are not engaged in the forum and they will not take you seriously. They may think you are hiding something. If you prefer, you can use a picture of your cat or dog or any other picture. Just make sure it is consistent and do not change your Profile Picture constantly. Consistency breeds familiarity. You are using Facebook to enhance your presence in the political arena. You will quickly find that everyone has an opinion. You will also find that if you are a regular you will actually make friends on Facebook with people you may never meet in person.

To start, begin by adding your friends from your current e-mail list. When you sign up you will be asked if you want Facebook to access your contact list to search for people you have in your E-mail database and they will locate them if they are on Facebook. You have the option of adding each person. The next thing you will do is complete a "Personal Profile" which is a series of questions about your likes and interests. I recommend that you do not list every band you have liked since high school because your Profile is the key to recommending Friends for you to consider adding to your list. The more information you put in your profile, the more people that will be suggested to you to "Friend". On Facebook you have Friends which is a noun and "Friending" is a verb requesting people to add. If people do not respond to your requests do not be offended. Many people sign up for Facebook and then abandon it, but Facebook appears to have an eternal life of its own.

Once you are set up start by contacting your real friends and let them know that you are on Facebook and no very little about it. You will immediately begin receiving posts from your friends. Start posting information about yourself. I suggest you do not tell them what you ate for lunch. Try to stick to topics and activities. You may find local articles in you on-line newspaper that you like. Post them and ask people for comments. You are also looking for people who do not share your point of view. These are the most important people on Facebook. Why are people who do not share your view point important? Because they have many similar friends that share their point of view and you can influence those people by posting on the pages of those you know.

When a friend on Facebook posts a comment or starts a discussion, it goes to not only you, but all their friends. Depending upon your Privacy Settings, if you respond to a particular item it goes to all your friends and their Friends. You can literally influence hundreds of people with your point of view without ever meeting them.

There are some unwritten rules that many people do not follow and it is to their detriment. Conservatives and others on the Right tend to be more reserved. Those on the Left, and especially the Far Left, tend to be angry. Those on the Right most often base their beliefs on Principles. Those on the

Left tend to express their views using emotion. The Right seems to view things based on the principles that support their concept of right and wrong. The Left tends to base their beliefs on Feelings, and then tend to be more emotional, and that often leads to anger. Anger can lead to violence. Never insult anyone on Facebook. You can disagree with an idea or belief system but never make it personal. Also be careful with your language, or you may be reported to the Facebook Police.

When responding or posting things do not get angry: be factual. Never criticize the person, or express your doubt in their belief. Instead you can artfully engage them in a conversation. Ask them to explain their belief or idea. You never have to challenge the idea you simply "ask a question." For example, if someone were to challenge the status quo and use the term, "social justice" you have a perfect opening to ask a question. In your Facebook Comment, ask, "I am not familiar with the term "social justice" what does it mean and why is it relevant?" This way the other person has to present a reason, to not only you, but to their whole Facebook Community. When you do this you may create a firestorm within their Friend Community. If you continue to ask questions of the various people in the debate you will find people who share your point of view. When you do "Friend them" and send them a message in your Friend Request and tell them that you are a friend of John or Mary or you like their comment about the President and that you like their point of view. If they have responded to one debate they will continue to respond to others. Your sincere question, without ever appearing confrontational, can start a debate that may impact thousands of people. I try to post 4 or 5 items per day. I have almost 1,000 friends on Facebook and the majority I have never met in person. Some of my distant friends, who I do actually know, have become Facebook friends with some of my local friends and they never knew that we had a common connection until they mutually "Friended" each other on Facebook.

You have many tools before you and it is time to get started.

Other Writings By the Author

Phil Frommholz, RedCounty.com

My writing career started with writing a variety of different types of articles as the mood moved me. Often I would wake up at two or three in the morning with an idea in my head and I would run to the computer and start writing. I have included some of the 32 articles I have written over the last two years. I have provided some comments under a few of the articles which I am particularly proud of for very personal reasons.

The articles are posted on **Colony Rabble**, part of the **RedCounty.com** family of writers. Below are the names of the articles. It may be faster to locate an article by

Typing: "Phil Frommholz, Red County, and the first couple of words in the title."

Once you locate a story simple click on "Phil Frommholz" under the name of the article and you will locate a listing of all articles. Again, it may be quicker to locate specific articles by doing a search. I hope you enjoy them.

9/11 The Day I Almost Met the President – I was 10 feet away from President George W. Bush when he announced we were attacked by terrorists. This is my personal story leading up to 9/11.

Falling Star Resurrected for a Day – This is a personal account of what it was like growing up in a small town in the 1950s and about a young boy, who was my neighbor and friend and was unusual in everyway. His life ended as a war hero in Vietnam.

Is Your Granny a Far Right Wing Radical – inspired by Jo An Schmidt an 82 year old Tea Party Patriot

Are You a Tea Party Extremist? Take the Test and Find Out

Senator Kerry Sucks at Tax Evasion

How to Kill the Healthcare Bill "Am I a Racist?"

You Have to Buy a Ticket- getting involved in the political process

Budget for Freedom – making a difference

Do You Know Where Your Patriotism Comes From?

The Power of One – You Can Make a Difference

The "Smoke and Mirrors" of Obamacare and the Witches of Washington

Can We Make a Difference? Yes We Can, One Step at a Time – what to do leading up to the 2010 elections. Note: It is still viable today

Obama's Hypothetical Energy Policy

The Reading of the Constitution by Congress

Am I a Nerd or What? Where are Your Tax Dollars Going?

BIBLIOGRAPHY

Alinsky, Saul D. *Rules for Radicals: A Practical Primer for Realistic Radicals.* New York: Vintage   Books,   1989.

Allison, Andrew M; Richard M. Maxfield; DeLynn K. Cook and Cleon W. Skousen. *The Real Thomas Jefferson.* National Center for Constitutional Studies, 2009.

Bastiat, Frederic. Translated and edited by Raoul Audouin. *Providence and Liberty.* Grand Rapids, Michigan: Action Institute, 2003.

Berlin, Isaiah, Karl *Marx, His Life and Environment, Time Reading Program, 1963*

Bowen, Catherine Drinker. *Miracle at Philadelphia: The Story of the Constitutional Convention May to   September 1787.* New York: Back Bay Books/ Little, Brown and Company, 1986.

Buchholz, Todd G. *New Ideas From Dead Economists: An Introduction to Modern Economic Thought.*   New York: Penguin Group, 2007.

Coulter, Ann. *Liberal Lies About the American Right.* New York: Three Rivers Press, 2002.

Davis, Kenneth C. Don't Know Much About History, Perenial, 2004

Douglass, Frederick. *Narrative of the Life of Frederick Douglass.* Clayton, Delaware: Prestwick House,   2006.

Ellis, Joseph J. *American Creation: Triumphs and Tragedies at the Founding of the Republic.* New York: Alfred A. Knoph, 2007.

Ellis, Joseph J. *Founding Brothers: The Revolutionary Generation.* New York: Alfred A. Knoph, 2002.

Friedman, Milton. *Capitalism and Freedom.* Chicago: The University of Chicago Press, 2002.

Hayek, Friedrich A. *The Constitution of Liberty.* Chicago: The University of Chicago Press, 1960.

Hayek, Friedrich A. *The Fatal Conceit, The Errors of Socialism.* Chicago: The Chicago Press, 1991.

Hayek, Friedrich A. *The Road to Serfdom, Text and Document.* Chicago: The Chicago Press, 2007.

Hamilton, Alexander; James Madison and John Jay. *The Federalist Papers.* New York: Penguin Group, 1999.

Hannan, Daniel. *The New Road to Serfdom: A letter of Warning to America.* New York: HarperCollins Publishers, 2010.

Harper, Timothy. *The Complete Idiot's Guide to the U.S. Constitution.* New York: Penguin Group, 2007.

Hill, Napoleon. *Law of Success.* Los Angeles, CA: Highroads Media Inc., 2004.

Hill, Napoleon. *The Think and Grow Rich Action Pack.* New York: Penguin

Group, 1990.

Jeffery, Douglas A. *The American Civil Liberties Union V. The Constitution.*
Claremont, California: The Claremont Institute, 1998.

Levin, Mark R. *Liberty and Tyranny: A Conservative Manifesto.* New York:
Simon & Schuster, Inc., 2009.

Marx, Karl and Friedrich Engels. *The Communist Manifesto and Other
Writings.* New York: Barnes & Noble, 2005.

McConnell, Patrick D. *Government of Deceit: A Sobering Analysis of
America's Finances, Governance and Society-and how we got here.*
Indianapolis, IN: Dog Ear Publishing, 2010.

Meyer, Stephen. *Getting to Purple: Uniting an Ever More Polarized Red and
Blue America.* Argyle, TX: Stewver Publishing, 2008.

McClanahan. *The Politically Incorrect Guide to The Founding Fathers.*
Washington, DC: Regnery Publishing, 2009.

Mises, Ludwig von. *Socialism: An Economic and Sociological Analysis.*
Indianapolis: Liberty Fund, 1981.

Moore, Marc A. General. *The Art of War.* United States: Sweet Water Press,
2004.

Morris, Dick and Eileen McGann. *2010 Take Back America: A Battle Plan.*
New York: HarperCollins, 2010.

Peikoff, Leonard. *The Ominous Parallels.* New York: Stein and Day, 1982.

Pitney, David Howard. *Martin Luther King Jr., Malcolm X, and the Civil Rights
Struggle of the 1950's and 1960s: A Brief History with Documents.* Boston:
Bedford/St. Martin's, 2004.

Reagan, Ronald. *An American Life.* New York: Simon and Schuster, 1990.

Roberts, Jim. *History of the World.* New York: Oxford University Press, 1992.

Schwarz, Dr. Fred, *What is Communism,* Christian Anti-Communism Crusade,
Manitou Springs, CO

Schweikart, Larry, and Allen, Michael, *A Patriot's History of the United States,*
Sentinel, 2004

Shlaes, Amity ,*The Forgotten Man, A New History Of The Great Depression,*
Harper Perennial, 2008

Skousen, W. Cleon. *The 5000 Year Leap: The 28 Great Ideas that Changed the
World.* United States: National Center for Constitutional Studies, 2006.

Sirico, Robert A. *A Moral Basis for Liberty.* New York: The Foundation for
Economic Education, Inc., 1994.

Sirico, Robert A. *Toward a Free and Virtuous Society.* Grand Rapids,
Michigan: Action Institute, 1997.

Sinclair, Upton. *The Jungle.* Tucson, AZ: See Sharp Press, 2003.

Smith, Adam. *Wealth of Nations.* New York: Prometheus Books, 1991.

Spalding, Matthew. *The Enduring Principles of the American Founding.*
Washington, DC: The Heritage Foundation, 2001.

Swank, Greg, The Communist takeover of America – 45 Declared Goals,

www.rense.com
Williams, Walter E, *Race & Economics*, Hoover Institution Press, 2011
Woods, Thomas E. *Nullification: How to Resist Federal Tyranny in the 21ˢᵗ Century*. Washington, DC: Regnery Publishing, Inc., 2010.

Wikipedia References

William Blackstone
Capitalism
Cloward-Piven Strategy
The Communist Manifesto
The Condition of the Working Class in England in 1844
French Revolution
Friedrich Engels
Epistemology
Feudalism
Germany
The Great Society
Georg Wilhelm Friedrich Hegel
David Hume
Friedrich List
John Locke
Industrial Revolution
Karl Mannheim
Abraham Maslow
Karl Marx
Carl Menger
Nazism
Plenary Power
Revolutions of 1847
Claude Henri de Rouvroy, compte de Saint-Simon
Oswald Spengler
Adam Smith
Gustav von Schmoller
Serfdom
Socialism
Social Sciences
Werner Sombart
Tariffs in United States History
Alexis de Tocqueville
Totalitarianism
Truth
Utopia

Miscellaneous Articles

Anti-Socialism, www.last.fm.group/Anti-Socialism
Collectivism vs individualism, FreedomKeys.com
Fidel latest to say Cuba's communism doesn't work, Associated Press, September 9,2010
Detroit: The Death – Possible Life – of a Great City, Time Magazine, Daniel Okrent,September 24,2009
Economic Opportunity & Prosperity, Index of Freedom (2010), www.heritage.org/index/
Dwight D Eisenhower Quotes, Brainy Quote.com
Richard M. Nixon – Domestic polices, www.presidentprofiles.com
Obama Administration Tap Patricia Geoghegan Acting Pay Czar, September 10, 2010, www.online.wsj.com/article/BT-CO-20100910-711831.html
Rise of Hitler: The 25 Points of Hitler's Nazi Party, www.historyplace.com/wordwar2/riseof hitler/25points.htm
Alexis de Tocqueville Quotes, Brainyquote.com
Where Does Productivity Come From?, Bojidar Marinov, September 2, 2009, www.americanvision.org
Utopia from Routledge Dictionary of Economics, Second Edition, BookRags.com
11% Say Communism is better than U.S. System of Politics and Economics, Rasmussen Reports, March 17, 2011
2011 Index of Economic Freedom, Heritage Foundation, http://www.heritage.org/index/

ABOUT THE AUTHOR

The Road to Socialism

I started this adventure on *The Road to Socialism* in June 2010. It has required extensive research and non-stop reading. It is based on the economic classic work of Fredrich A. Hayek, a noted Austrian economist and professor, who moved to London in the 1930s and later to America in the late 1940s. His classic work, *The Road to Serfdom*, is a very difficult book to read and was probably composed of a series of lectures for economists and economic students at the London School of Economics. It is my premise that his message, dating back to 1944, was critical and that Americans should be aware of the concepts presented by Hayek since the average person does not study economics in school today. I have Americanized the book, interjecting history, basic economics and bringing Hayeks ideas up to date to help educate people today, especially our students, using current events and key hallmarks in American history as examples of the expanding role of our government.

Writing Experience

My initial writing experience began writing proposals and project studies for the various programs we developed as the bank was going through its initial automation phases in the 1970s. I was personally assigned many high level special studies addressing issues specifically for Senior Management and the Board of Directors. In a consulting capacity, I frequently addressed Senior Management Groups verbally and with written reports tailored to the specific needs of each management group.

My 9/11 Experience with President Bush.

It wasn't until a few years ago that I started writing again. I was the contract mover hired by the White House Special Events Office in Washington, and was called upon to set up the Emma Booker Elementary School in Sarasota, Florida for a visit from President George W. Bush. The President was going to announce the "No Child Left

Behind Program". The date was September 11th, 2001. In a blog called, *"The Day I Almost Met the President,"* I chronicled my experiences leading up to the President's announcement that we had been attacked. Last summer I met Karl Rove, the White House Chief of Staff for President Bush, who was with the President on 9/11 and he forwarded my article to the President. In our follow-up correspondence Mr. Rove has agreed to review this book.

I have written over 30 articles in the last two years with a loyal following on RedCounty.com, a national blog site. My articles average over 700 reads without any promotion. I recently began posting my articles on Facebook which has increased readership from the low levels in the beginning. Refer to the Other Writings by the Author at the end of this book.

Family Life

I have two grown children who both live near Las Vegas, Ethan Frommholz and Kalian Kesick. Kalian and husband Ken have provided me with three beautiful grandchildren: Kyler, and the twins Kaden and Kole. I also have a second family. My wife Judy Weber and I raised her daughter Jackie since she was 7 years old. Jackie and her husband Batista have a little girl named Elsa who arrived on August 2, 2011. We have a dog named Hudson and a cat named Buster, after Buster Crabbe. Jackie, who works for Phil the Mover, brings her dog Jackson to work each day along with our Grand Daughter Elsa. We are one big happy family.

Other Interests

Flying High

September 11, 2001 was to be a momentous day for me. I was scheduled to take my first flying lesson that day. Based on the opportunity to help the White House, I rescheduled my long awaited first lesson. In May of 2002 I received my Private Pilot's License and fly frequently in a Beechcraft Musketeer which I jointly own with several other pilots.

Running Far

Previous to developing complications from an active lifestyle, I ran over 30 Marathons including New York City, Chicago, the first two Disney Marathons, Twin Cities, and Grandma's Marathon in Duluth, MN, all multiple times. My greatest running achievement was finishing the 50 Mile Voyager Run in Northern Minnesota. That wilderness run was the beginning of the end of my running career.

There are parallels between running and writing. Both require the discipline to complete tasks every day, often under solitary conditions and for long periods of time. Both also give one the opportunity to examine the road to their soul.

Formal Education

BA- Business Administration, Golden Gate University, San Francisco, 1972
MBA- Business Management, Golden Gate University, San Francisco, 1974
Doctoral Candidate, Banking & Finance, Golden Gate University

Additional Education

Completed an untold number of college level courses in a variety of subjects, but most specifically: real estate, appraisal, and real estate lending courses. I obtained a real estate license in Florida, a Mortgage Broker's License, and followed those with Insurance and Investment Licenses and other related certificates.

Work Experience

Currently owner and operator of a small local moving company, Phil the Mover, Inc and involved in the real estate business with my wife, Judy Weber. We have been active in real estate through brokerage representing buyers and sellers and as investors. I previously owned an Interstate moving company for about 10 years hauling and delivery antiques and household goods throughout the 26 Eastern States, travelling extensively.

1990-1993 Established and operated a small chain of Old Fashioned Candy Shops located in malls in Minnesota, Iowa and Florida.

1985-1993 Worked as a Business Analyst for Warrington Associates, now known as Sunguard Financial Systems, Hopkins, MN, developing customized financial reporting systems and fixed income securities processing for many of the top 200 banks in the country.

1972-1985 Bank of America NT&SA, San Francisco. Worked in a variety of positions, starting with all aspects of retail banking, consulting and advisory positions. I specialized in all aspects of real estate loan origination, local and centralized processing, and ultimately the pooling, packaging, and distribution of mortgaged-backed securities. I was the Project Manager for developing and implementing an automated Cost Accounting System for International Branch Operations, and was the Project Manager responsible for converting to an automated on-line Bond Trading System for the bank's Broker-Dealer Investment Division.

Beginning of the Entrepreneurial Spirit

In 1990 I started a retail chain of Old Fashioned Candy Shoppes in Minnesota, Iowa, Branson, Missouri and Sarasota, Florida. It was the most fun I ever had in business. Unfortunately, it was not nearly as profitable as it was fun. It took everything I had ever learned to make a go of an unusual approach of combining selling candy with entertainment.

The Road to Socialism

www.ingramcontent.com/pod-product-compliance
Lightning Source LLC
Chambersburg PA
CBHW060844280326
41934CB00007B/910